INTENTIONAL ATTENTION

INTENTIONAL ATTENTION

The Science and

Practice of

FOCUS

Under

Pressure

JUSTIN ANDERSON

WILEY

For general information on our other products and services or for technical support, please contact our Customer Care Department within the United States at (800) 762-2974, outside the United States at (317) 572-3993 or fax (317) 572-4002.

Wiley also publishes its books in a variety of electronic formats. Some content that appears in print may not be available in electronic formats. For more information about Wiley products, visit our website at www.wiley.com.

Library of Congress Cataloging-in-Publication Data is Available:

ISBN 9781394373796 (Cloth)
ISBN 9781394373819 (ePDF)
ISBN 9781394373802 (ePub)

Cover Design: Wiley
Cover Image: © Wenda / stock.adobe.com
Printed and bound by CPI Group (UK) Ltd, Croydon, CR0 4YY

C9781394373796_270426

For Ailey, Kiera, and the family who shaped this journey—
who bring me back to what matters most and
remind me that being intentionally present is
the greatest gift one can give.

Contents

Contents

Foreword

"What is he thinking?" If I had a dollar for every time I heard a coach say that on a headset on gameday, I would be a much richer man. During my NFL career as a coach, it was easy to see that the best teams, the best players, and even the best coaches had a little edge to them that seemed hard to describe or put into words. It seemed like during a game, a practice, or even a film session, the highest performers were operating in a superior way. It has become evident to me in recent years that what I was witnessing or feeling from those elite performers was their ability to put their attention where it was needed. Whether it be focus, confidence, resilience, or even their emotional regulation, they had the ability to "lock in" during critical moments.

I met Dr. Justin Anderson in Indianapolis at the NFL Scouting Combine in 2021. We had some mutual friendships that put us in contact. That one-hour meeting left me astounded. It was evident after talking with Doc that I wanted to find better answers about where I was putting my attention. He gave me a simplified blueprint of concepts to work on to improve my attention as it related to my performance. It worked. I found myself searching for more. How much better could I get if I could master some of the performance psychology that has been studied and understood for years? Doc has the knowledge—I just had to keep learning.

I knew it could be a competitive advantage for a team to adopt a process of maximizing themselves daily to be psychologically trained in the critical moments that impact winning and losing games. It was a no-brainer to hire Doc to not only educate and apply these concepts but to fully integrate them into our team. I have seen incredible improvements with players, coaches, and staff who work with Doc because they more deeply understand the concept of Intentional Attention. The exciting thing about this concept is that no matter how far along you are, there is always room for improvement.

Reading has always been a way for me to expand my mind about whatever topic I was interested in or wanted to learn more about. Buckle up, because what you are about to dive into will force thought on how the brain plays a gigantic role in performance. Doc will explain how you can achieve greater performance simply by understanding how to train your attention, and how to be intentional about it at the same time.

—By Jonathan Gannon, NFL Coach

Introduction: The Myth of the Naturally Clutch Performer

"Under pressure, we don't rise to the occasion—we sink to the level of our training."

—Adapted from Archilochus

"I think I'm going to quit the game."

That's how he started. No hello. No small talk. Just a few words that hit the air like a confession.

He was an NBA All-Star. A former first-round pick. Eight years in the league. A player known for his grit, leadership, and consistency in big moments. But now, sitting across from me, he looked like a man unraveling. His body was beat up from the wear and tear of the season. His shot had abandoned him. And his confidence had quietly followed.

He was in the second-to-last year of his contract—the kind of year where every possession matters. Front offices start talking. Extension negotiations begin. Trade conversations heat up. For a player at his level, this wasn't just about playing well—it was about proving value. Cementing trust. Securing a deal that could be worth tens of millions of dollars.

And right now? He felt broken.

His slump was brutal. Over the last 22 games, he was shooting just 18% from three. His contract had a performance bonus clause that paid out if he cleared 33% from deep. Every miss wasn't just a hit to his ego—it was a hit to his wallet. Hundreds of thousands of dollars were vanishing with every miss.

He'd tried everything. More film. More shots. High-priced specialist shooting coaches. Extra reps after games. Practice during off days. In empty gyms. On the road. At home. Nothing helped. In fact, the harder he chased it, the further it seemed to slip away.

But what really broke him—the moment he knew he was spiraling—wasn't the slump. It was the defense. Or rather, the absence of it.

"They're leaving me open," he said. "That's the biggest insult. They're stepping back and daring me to shoot. Like I don't even belong out there."

It wasn't just about missed shots anymore. It was about identity. This was someone who had built a reputation on being clutch—trusted when the game was tight, the clock was low, and everything was on the line. Now, he didn't just feel like he was letting others down. He felt like he was disappearing.

What he was experiencing wasn't a lack of talent. It wasn't laziness. It wasn't even just a crisis of confidence.

It was attention: misplaced, overextended, and hijacked by pressure.

What he was experiencing wasn't rare. In fact, it's something we've seen hundreds of times. When we founded Premier, we saw the same pattern in youth and high school athletes—bright, driven competitors whose attention was consumed by outcomes instead of execution. As our work expanded into college programs, sales teams, and mid-level managers, the story repeated itself: talented people pulled off course by untrained attention. And when we began consulting with professional and Olympic athletes, Fortune 500 executives, and other elite performers, the pattern didn't disappear—it

Introduction: The Myth of the Naturally Clutch Performer

simply became more expensive. Whether the stakes were financial, reputational, or emotional, the underlying challenge was the same. Mismanaged attention doesn't discriminate by skill level or salary; it's a universal performance constraint. We've seen it across every level of competition and every arena of work. Attention, it turns out, shapes nearly every aspect of performance—it determines whether our best preparation ever gets expressed.

When we talked, it became clear that his mind wasn't just on his mechanics. It was ricocheting between contract incentives, media narratives, teammate expectations, and the rising fear of what failure might cost him. Every time he stepped onto the court, he wasn't playing the game in front of him—he was navigating a minefield of what the future might hold.

And here's what's interesting and most important to understand about this situation: His brain was doing exactly what it was designed to do.

In high-pressure environments, the human brain naturally shifts into protection mode. It starts scanning for threats, calculating risk, and tightening control—not to help us perform, but to protect us. Whether it's a collapsing shooting percentage or a charging bear, the brain's protective systems don't always differentiate between types of threat—they assess physical and existential threats in largely the same manner.

This isn't a character flaw or mental weakness. It's how we're wired.

The challenge is that while this threat-scanning response serves us well for survival, it can become a hindrance to performance. Clutch execution doesn't emerge from protection; it flows from clarity, presence, and assertive action. And while these responses might feel instinctive in the moment, they're actually skills that can be developed and refined.

Under Pressure, Performance Dips

The idea that some people are just "built differently"—wired to thrive in pressure moments with supernatural calm and precision—makes for compelling highlight reels, discussions with scouts at the Combine, and perhaps even better sports documentaries. But when we examine the evidence, this notion is largely mythical.

Michael Jordan is often cited as the embodiment of clutch greatness. And yes, he delivered in iconic moments. But what's most revealing is that even Jordan didn't consistently outperform his remarkable averages under pressure; he just essentially *maintained* them.

As Weisinger and Pawliw-Fry (2015) note in *Performing Under Pressure*, the highest performers do not perform better when the stakes rise; they perform closer to their baseline while others deteriorate.

Like other greats, Jordan didn't ascend into superhuman territory in clutch moments—he remained consistent. And in high-stress environments, that consistency *is* elite performance.

Decades of research across performance domains show that under intense stress, people rarely "rise to the occasion." Instead, they default to the level of their preparation. As Grossman (2008) observed in military and high-stakes performance contexts, pressure doesn't create new abilities—it exposes and amplifies existing training. Team-based decision-making studies echo this pattern: When arousal spikes and the stakes are high, even seasoned professionals fall back on the cognitive scripts they've rehearsed most often (Driskell et al., 1999).

This is also supported by what we are learning from studies on the brain. Neuroscience shows that in moments of uncertainty, the brain doesn't generate novel solutions—it retrieves and reconstructs patterns from previous experience (Schacter and Addis, 2007). Our default mode is familiarity, not innovation. Bargh and Chartrand (1999) found that much of this retrieval process operates below conscious awareness, pulling on whatever neural pathways have been most consistently reinforced.

When pressure spikes, your brain doesn't search for magic—it searches for established patterns. And those patterns, whether helpful or harmful, are built through repeated experience. The top performers under pressure aren't relying purely on instinct or raw grit. They're drawing on trained attentional systems—internal frameworks that help them filter out noise, interpret emotion constructively, and return to their strategic approach.

Neuroscientific research (Miller & Cohen, 2001) has shown that these systems are governed by the prefrontal cortex. These systems allow performers to override reactive impulses and sustain goal-directed focus. Similarly, Posner and Rothbart (2007) demonstrated that attentional networks—when trained deliberately—can regulate emotion, inhibit distraction, and support higher-order performance even under pressure.

Top performers learned to keep their attention anchored on the variables that drive performance. Not because they were born with something special, but because they've developed something specific.

Some discover this ability through experience and natural development, but increasingly, far more elite performers are training it with deliberate intention. We wanted to understand whether that ability could be trained—and if so, how consistently it could transform performance across domains.

Training the Mind's Most Valuable Resource

For nearly two decades, I've worked in some of the most competitive arenas in the world—serving as Director of High Performance Psychology for multiple teams in the NFL, NBA, MLB, and NHL, and as founder of Premier Sport Psychology and Premier Performance Advising. These roles have given me a front-row seat to thousands of teachable moments with some of the world's greatest athletes, coaches, and executives.

Across all of those touchpoints, one pattern has stood out with remarkable clarity: The performers who consistently deliver under pressure aren't fundamentally different from their peers in talent or drive. What sets them apart is how intentional they are in managing their mental resources.

Specifically, they have learned how to direct and sustain their attention with precision—especially when it matters most. As we studied this phenomenon, one truth rose to the top again and again: Attention is the single most important driver of performance in high-stakes moments.

Even more encouraging was the realization that attention is not a fixed trait. It is a skill—one that can be trained, strengthened, and refined just like strength, speed, or strategy. That insight quickly became the gateway into all of our mental training. At first, our efforts centered on building simple tools: focus cues and reset routines that helped athletes reengage in the moment. But as we dug deeper, it became clear these tools pointed to something larger: the need for a structured framework that could capture both the depth and breadth of attentional training.

That framework is what we now call **Intentional Attention**—a deliberate approach to harnessing the mind's most valuable resource in order to perform with clarity, consistency, and conviction when it matters most.

What's more, we found this skill extends far beyond competitive arenas; it helps all of us navigate the day-to-day pressures of modern life. Performance is performance, whether it takes place on a field, in a boardroom, in a classroom, or at home. Each of us is asked to show up and deliver in ways that matter. And the more we refined and applied these methods across contexts, the more convinced we became: Intentional Attention is a central performance skill that allows people to sustain their best when it matters most.

This book lays out how to train it. Built on scientific research, tested in real-world practice, and sharpened through thousands of hours alongside elite performers, it introduces a structured, three-part system for developing attention as a skill—something we can all practice, strengthen, and carry with us into every high-stakes moment.

- Part I explores how the brain operates and why attention sits at the center of nearly everything it does. Many readers are surprised to learn how much their thoughts, emotions, and decision-making are driven not just by willpower or motivation, but by the underlying attentional architecture of the brain itself. Attention is not just another mental skill; it's the gateway to learning, memory, emotion regulation, and execution. When we can't manage our attention, we struggle to manage our minds. This section reveals why that is, grounding the discussion in evolutionary psychology and modern neuroscience.

- Part II introduces the attentional architecture we use to train elite performers—athletes, coaches, and leaders across every major arena of competition. These methods have been refined through work with players and staff from the NFL, NBA, WNBA, MLB, NHL, MLS, and NWSL, as well as USA National Teams, collegiate athletic departments, special forces operatives, executives, doctors, lawyers, and educators. The principles are universal, and we'll provide practical examples to help you integrate them into your own routines.

Introduction: The Myth of the Naturally Clutch Performer

- Part III explores how training attention translates into execution under pressure. Through case studies and practical insights drawn from elite performers, we'll illuminate how Intentional Attention can transform both performance and well-being. This part highlights what many high performers do to optimize their craft—and how the same framework can be taught and applied to help others lead, perform, and live with greater clarity and control.

That's the core of this book: not simply to inform, but to equip. To provide practical, tested strategies designed to help readers better understand, train, and direct their attention, especially in moments when pressure is high and distractions persistent.

Intentional Attention is intended to be a new perspective on how to train and develop our mental game—a controllable one that, when practiced consistently, can build greater resilience, confidence, performance, and overall well-being. Beyond merely chasing outcomes, this approach shapes how individuals engage with the world: with a steadier presence, and deeper alignment between who they are and who they truly wish to become. Regardless of the arena, training Intentional Attention represents a meaningful shift—one capable of profoundly transforming how we navigate today's fragmented and competitive landscape.

We can't stop pressure from coming. But we can train where our attention goes when it does. That's the real art of performance—and the heart of Intentional Attention.

A Note on a Broader Conversation

In today's world, attention may well be our most valuable resource. Individuals and teams that learn to manage it with intention tend to build stronger relationships, protect their mental health, navigate complexity more effectively, and—yes—perform at higher levels.

As Chris Hayes writes in *The Sirens' Call*:

"Information is abundant; attention is scarce. Information is theoretically infinite, while attention is constrained. This is why information is cheap and attention is expensive."

In a world of infinite data, attention is becoming the currency that gives information its value. Our attentional architecture shapes what we notice next, what we believe, how we behave, and ultimately, what matters most in our lives.

Much has been written about this shift—particularly in the context of politics, media, and culture. Authors like Hayes have offered compelling insights into how attention is shaped, captured, and even weaponized. These conversations are important. They spotlight the societal stakes of where attention flows, and who or what influences it.

While this book doesn't attempt to tackle those topics directly, it sits adjacent to them. Like many who have written on this topic, we believe attentional management isn't just important—it's *critical*. In an era where billions of dollars and entire industries are engineered to capture it, the ability to own our attention has become one of the most essential life skills of our time.

Yet understanding alone isn't enough. Knowing our attention is being pulled doesn't give us the ability to redirect it. That's why our work focuses not on diagnosing the problem, but on training a solution. We ask different—but deeply related—questions:

- *What happens when we train attention deliberately?*

- *How can we develop a more effective attentional operating system—one that gives people personal agency rather than taking it away?*

- *What shifts when individuals and teams learn to manage their attention as precisely as they manage their bodies?*

Introduction: The Myth of the Naturally Clutch Performer

- *And how might that change not just performance under pressure, but the quality of everyday life?*

These questions matter because attention shapes everything else—our focus in competition, our clarity in leadership, our empathy in relationships, and even our sense of purpose. It determines whether we react to life or respond with more intention.

Performance isn't reserved for athletes, coaches, or executives. Each of us performs every day: in conversations, decisions, meetings, creative pursuits, parenting, caregiving, and countless other roles. And while distractions may differ, they are everywhere, but the internal challenge is the same: staying focused on what matters when it matters most.

That's why the ideas in this book aren't limited to elite performers. While our casework is rooted in high-stakes environments—NFL sidelines, MLB clubhouses, Olympic training centers, and boardrooms—the principles we've learned apply far beyond them. Our goal wasn't to further highlight attention as a cultural force; we're presenting it as a *trainable skill* that can be developed. One that separates those who merely survive pressure from those who thrive in it.

We've studied, observed, and developed these concepts and applied training for nearly two decades in environments where performance is visible and pressure is relentless. Those settings have allowed us to test the framework and witness its impact in real time—where every move, decision, and outcome is scrutinized from every angle. If it can stand up there, we believe it can stand up most anywhere.

We also recognize the limits of our expertise. We're not political theorists or cultural critics. We don't pretend to have all the answers about attention's role in the broader information economy. But if this book contributes to that larger conversation—and perhaps helps others think differently about how they develop and manage their attention—we're honored to play a part. Because when attention is managed with intention, it doesn't just change performance. It changes how we live.

Part I

The Cognitive Foundations of Intentional Attention: Understanding the System That Drives Performance

Chapter 1

The Skill That Holds Everything Together

"The successful warrior is the average man, with laser-like focus."

—Bruce Lee

When we can't manage our attention—on demand under pressure, when fatigued, and when it counts—performance becomes vulnerable.

It doesn't matter how talented, prepared, or experienced we are. When attention unravels, everything else can follow: decision-making, confidence, composure, and execution.

Step onto a field during a playoff game, or into a boardroom before a high-stakes presentation, and you might think you're looking at two different worlds.

One where a quarterback stands on the sidelines, helmet in hand, as the stadium pulses around him. The roar is deafening, but what's louder is the replay looping in his mind. Two missed throws. One turnover. His jaw tightens. He scrolls through the tablet in front of him, pretending to absorb the play breakdown, but his focus has already turned inward. The field is cloudy. His vision is tunneling as adrenaline floods his system. He's not thinking about footwork, progressions, or coverage—he's fighting the noise inside his own head.

Across the country, a CEO stands in front of her investors. Her slide deck is flawless, her metrics strong, but her pulse spikes as she begins. Her breath shortens. A small stumble in her opening line sends her spiraling into self-monitoring. She starts hearing her own voice instead of her message. Her attention—like the quarterback's—has turned inward, away from execution and toward evaluation.

The environments couldn't be more different—one filled with helmets, pads, and adrenaline; the other with suits, slides, and strategy documents.

But if you tune in to the psychology, you'll notice something remarkable.

The emotions? Nearly identical.

The mind? Racing.

The stakes? Just as real.

Different arenas, same fundamental challenge. Both performers have trained their bodies and refined their plans to the highest level. But in this moment, neither needs more skill—they need more command of where their attention goes.

What's happening beneath these moments of unraveling isn't weakness—it's wiring.

Living in the Attention Economy

In a world engineered to hijack attention—from algorithmic platforms to overstimulating workplaces—the ability to manage attention isn't just advantageous, it may be a necessity (Gazzaley & Rosen, 2016; Rosen et al., 2020).

Every day, attention faces structural challenges. Smartphones ping. Notifications break flow. Social media algorithms exploit our brain's attentional reward circuitry, delivering unpredictable hits of validation and emotionally charged content that keep us coming back for more (Montag et al., 2019; Turel et al., 2014). These environments are not neutral; they are architected to keep us hooked.

Behavioral economists and neuroscientists have demonstrated that these micro-interruptions impair working memory, slow decision-making, and erode cognitive endurance (Ophir et al., 2009; Wilmer et al., 2017). Even brief glances at a phone—what researchers refer to as *attention residue*—can reduce mental clarity and task performance for several minutes (Leroy, 2009; Mark et al., 2008).

Our physical environments don't help much either. Open office designs, constant alerts, and cultural glorification of multitasking further fragment attention. Once celebrated as a sign of efficiency, multitasking is now widely understood as a cognitive liability and often associated with poorer accuracy, slower performance, and weaker retention (Ophir et al., 2009; Rubinstein et al., 2001).

Unfortunately, this new state of being doesn't appear to be a passing inconvenience—it's a systemic shift. We now live in what many refer to as the attention economy—a system where human attention is mined, packaged, and sold (Davenport & Beck, 2001; Williams, 2018; Wu, 2016). Platforms are optimized to capture and commodify focus, turning distraction into a global marketplace of attention.

In the sporting arenas it's no different; athletes are bombarded with data, analytics, more complex schemes, and media and social media requests, on top of the physical and technical training. Consequently, attentional control becomes more than a performance asset; it can also become a form of psychological preservation. It can help maintain mental clarity, emotional stability, and alignment with long-term goals in a world built to pull focus in every direction.

Why Training Attention Matters in Sport and Life

Yet despite its importance, most people have never been taught how to train attention deliberately. For all the investment in physical, tactical, and even cognitive training across industries, the foundational

The Skill That Holds Everything Together

system that governs how individuals engage with all other skills remains largely misunderstood and significantly underdeveloped.

In fact, in our work across high-performance domains, attention consistently emerges as one of the most overlooked and under-trained capacities in human performance. It's often assumed that people instinctively know how to manage their focus. But in reality, most don't—and fewer have ever been given the insight, tools, or opportunities to learn and train it.

Yet the science is clear: Attention plays a foundational role on which every other skill rests (Mrazek et al., 2013; Posner & Rothbart, 2007; Tang et al., 2015).

Without it, performance becomes unstable. With it, we gain leverage over pressure, decision-making, emotion, and execution itself.

That's why Intentional Attention is more than a cognitive process—it can be a performance multiplier. In a world where distractions are constant and pressure is unrelenting, the ability to manage attention is both a competitive advantage and a critical life skill. And perhaps most importantly, it's a skill that can be strengthened through awareness, repetition, reflection, and renewal. Because when we train attention, we don't just improve performance—we reshape who we become under pressure.

How the Brain Manages Focus

To understand how attention becomes the linchpin of performance, we need to look at what's happening inside the brain when focus holds—or breaks.

Most of us seem to understand that what often sets the "good" apart from the "great" isn't always talent or effort—we've found that it's the ability to stay composed when conditions get hard. High performers learn to recognize where their attention goes under stress and to redirect it toward data that brings them closer to their goals.

As prominent neuroscientists Posner and Rothbart (2007) and Tang et al. (2015) have shown, deliberate attention training can rewire the very systems responsible for executive control and emotional regulation—the difference between panic and poise. Put simply, attention can be trained—systematically, practically, and with measurable impact on how we perform under pressure.

Top-Down Versus Bottom-Up: The Push-Pull of Attentional Control

In neuroscience and psychology, there is a process known as top-down attentional control—a system regulated by the prefrontal cortex that allows individuals to guide focus deliberately, inhibit distractions, regulate emotions, and align attention with goals (Banich et al., 2009; Gratton et al., 2018; Miller & Cohen, 2001).

It's how a quarterback reads his progressions as the pocket collapses around him, and how a leader holds composure when tension fills the room.

Top-down control can function as an antidote to the brain's natural attentional reactivity.

By contrast, *bottom-up attention*—the brain's default attentional mode—is often driven by survival mechanisms, novelty, or emotional salience. It's reflexive and pulls focus toward whatever stimulus feels most urgent or intense in the moment. Top-down control is what allows us to override that impulse and choose what truly matters.

While top-down attention is controllable, it's also fragile and taxing. It naturally degrades quickly under conditions of fatigue, stress, or chronic distraction (Banich et al., 2009; Gratton et al., 2018). The good news is that it is trainable. Like other performance systems, it can be strengthened and restored through deliberate, repeated practice—a foundation that some high-performing organizations are beginning to prioritize.

Of course, this challenge isn't confined to game days or board-rooms. The same attentional fragility plays out across our daily lives—because the everyday environments we inhabit are now engineered to compete for our focus.

Because at the highest levels of performance, success rarely comes down to knowledge, strength, or even experience. It comes down to presence and attention toward variables that we can control when everything around us—and inside us—starts to move.

This is the heart of Intentional Attention: the ability to guide our focus where it matters most, under the conditions that matter most. It's the discipline of returning—again and again—to what's essential, even when emotion, fatigue, or fear demand otherwise. In that return lies the difference between reaction and response, between being pulled by circumstance and choosing with intention.

And it's a trainable discipline—one that can be strengthened, renewed, and carried across every performance domain of life. We build it through awareness, repetitive practice, and deliberate recovery. And while it doesn't promise to eliminate agitation, doubt, or chaos, it offers something far more useful: a reliable way to move through them with poise and control.

Because when we pursue anything challenging and worthwhile, pressure will be present, fatigue will be likely, and distraction will always tempt. But when attention is trained with intention, those conditions no longer dictate behavior—they become information we can work with.

To understand why attention falters—and how it can be trained—we need to look more deeply at the mechanisms that govern focus. And that's where this journey begins.

Chapter 2

Hijacked: Our Minds Under Fire

"We suffer more in imagination than in reality."

—Seneca

It was the first drive of his NFL debut.

Playoff implications. National stage. First offensive series.

The punt team had just set them up with great field position—starting his offense on the opponent's 18-yard line. Red zone. Momentum.

This was everything he'd worked for.

Then the play call came in.

The one he didn't want.

The original script that he and the coaches had reviewed several times over the past few days was thrown out because they found themselves starting in the red zone. Something they hadn't accounted for.

Gun Trips Right F Short 83 Z Counter Y Shallow—Alert X Sluggo.

He never liked the way it set up. The primary read—Z on the counter-shallow—had him firing back across his body at an inside-breaking angle with compressed space near the hash. Timing had to be perfect. And likely against a defensive look that would rotate late, he *knew* the safety would be driving hard on anything underneath.

The alert—X on the Sluggo—offered a shot outside, but it demanded he hold the safety with his eyes, pump action, then reset and rip a second-window throw on rhythm. Not just to a spot, but to a lane—between the trailing corner and the apex of the sinking safety. He wasn't just aiming for a completion. He was trying to hit a moving dime 18 yards downfield, against a bait-heavy secondary trained to punish hesitation. One misstep, one tick late, and the ball's going the other way.

"This isn't going to work," he thought. "I hate this play."

Underneath his composed exterior and high draft status also lived significant doubt. An athlete as talented and coveted as he was still questioned himself.

Before the game even started, his mind had wandered to thoughts about failing and wondering when his success might run out.

He would try to remind himself and others around him that he was fully confident and capable. It was this type of internal back-and-forth that was exhausting for him.

To combat it, he would often reach for the familiar advice commonly provided by coaches in college, which he understood as a mental override for this type of unconfident thinking.

"Think positive," the voice of his former college mental performance coach echoed. With that thought, he knew he had to refocus on the current situation.

"Damn, I'm walking up to the line . . . get this together," he thought, attempting to snap back into the moment.

"You've got this. You like this play."

Yet, unfortunately for him, that line of thinking didn't last long in his intelligent mind. Another internal voice quickly challenged it: *"No you don't. This thing could get picked."*

Conflicting voices. Mind wandering in multiple directions, no anchor, no clear direction.

He began his cadence, "White 80, White 80"—dummy calls that could be used to change the play, but this was a go.

"Hut, HUT, Hut." He gave a hard count on the second "hut" but quickly moved to the third. The ball fired back to him in the shotgun position on the first sound of the "H."

He snared the ball out of the air and looked toward his primary receiver, but with his mind still racing, he didn't lock onto his first key. He simply scanned the field in that direction, already believing it wouldn't be there.

"Couldn't be"—not with the pre-snap look he got or thought he was going to get. In reality, he realized now that his pre-snap read wasn't as detailed as he would have liked, because his attention was fragmented and in the middle of a full internal debate about whether he liked the play or could actually execute it.

"Okay, let that go." He skipped by his first receiver, turned his head toward his second option outside.

"No good, timing's wrong." He quickly moved off him.

"Get to your outlet receiver." Running back sliding out to the flat. Safety valve.

These thoughts raced through his head in rapid succession.

By this time, he had already held onto the ball a fraction of a second too long—he could feel it. According to 2024 data, NFL quarterbacks have an average of 2.63 seconds to throw the ball. Not much time to process a significant amount of information, let alone make accurate decisions.

He cocked his arm. Pressure was coming off the edge. His internal clock told him he had only fractions of seconds before he was going to get hit from the left side.

He let it go just as he took the hit.

As he hit the turf, he watched the ball float toward his running back—just in time to see a linebacker jump in front of the ball.

Interception.

His worst fear, realized. His doubts were confirmed. His confidence shattered. His clarity on what to do next—muddied. In less than three seconds, his attention had traveled from the field, to the fear, to the fallout.

Without realizing it, he had entered a mental spiral.

What hurt more was when he watched the replay on his iPad on the sideline. He noticed that the primary receiver on the play was open.

"I can make that throw 10 out of 10 times in practice. Why wasn't it there when I needed it most?" he thought to himself.

Our quarterback continued thinking that if he had just "trusted" the read and maintained a confident mindset, he could have delivered a touchdown—just as the offensive coordinator told him he would, given the defense and formation they had been playing in the red zone.

"Why didn't I?" he wondered.

"I just need to trust myself out there."

Unfortunately, when the mind starts to accelerate—racing like water over rapids and that river is full of doubt, fear, or indecision—telling ourselves to "just trust" often isn't enough. It's vague. It lacks structure. And in high-pressure moments, vagueness is where execution can break down. The mind starts searching for certainty, and if we don't provide it with something concrete, what it focuses on can truly be unpredictable.

The Problem with Trusting Yourself

The truth is, mental performance coaching has often missed the mark for years. In an effort to help athletes overcome mental disruptions and perform at their best, we've sometimes inadvertently added more noise to the system. We've relied on vague blanket phrases like *"trust yourself"* or *"stay positive"*—without ever defining what it actually means to *trust a throw*, or how to implement an *optimal mindset* in real time. These phrases have become empty catchalls, recycled by elite coaches and media personalities alike, often used to gloss over a deeper lack of understanding about what's truly happening inside a performer's brain.

Unfortunately, our quarterback was becoming another victim of this well-intentioned but misguided advice. To compound matters, he was becoming highly self-critical. He was going to revert to methods that had helped him in the past: being hard on himself and working harder. This approach had served him before, and hopefully it would help here. The challenge was that being highly self-critical wouldn't be difficult because he genuinely believed something was wrong with him. This experience seemed to confirm it in his mind.

Others in the league seemed to do it so easily; they always looked supremely confident. Why couldn't he? He couldn't "think positive enough" or didn't have the "mental toughness" to play in this league, he thought.

His mind was now, unfortunately, slipping deeper into a negative cycle of complexity. In this case, his intelligent human brain wasn't helping him perform better—it was interfering, now using negative self-talk that was creating strong beliefs that only muddied potential solutions further. He was slipping into a negative pattern that many great athletes struggle to recover from without help. Yet he didn't want to seek help, because that would signal to everyone that something was wrong.

Stranded. Alone. Lost.

The Internal Distractor: When the Mind Turns on Itself

One of the most powerful—and overlooked—distractors isn't external at all. It's us. When attention turns inward without direction or guardrails, it often lands on discomfort, doubt, or perceived deficit. Self-conscious attention becomes self-critical attention.

Under pressure, that inward pull can be the difference between flow and freeze. Many intelligent athletes and leaders over-index on internal analysis—they think deeply, anticipate outcomes, and imagine contingencies. But when that same strength turns inward during performance, it can overwhelm the system and can become paralysis by analysis, creating hesitations in performance states frequently known as choking (Baumeister & Showers, 1986). The mind that's built for pattern recognition and prediction suddenly becomes its own interference pattern.

In this state, even the best-trained performers can lock up, not because they don't care or aren't capable, but because their attention collapses inward. They begin monitoring themselves instead of executing. Movements tighten. Reactions slow. Awareness fragments. As Masters (1992) demonstrated, when performers begin to consciously monitor mechanics that are normally automatic, performance efficiency collapses. In other words, what was once fluid becomes forced—the brain's effort to "help" actually interferes with execution.

Ironically, from our experience, intelligence can make this worse. The same mental horsepower that helps an athlete or executive prepare with precision can also generate more "what ifs" under pressure. Less analytical performers sometimes appear more clutch—not because they're tougher or more confident, but because they simply don't entertain as many internal possibilities.

However, when high-intelligence performers learn to train and direct their attention, that analytical power becomes their greatest asset. Once they understand how to aim their cognition toward performance-relevant cues, processes, and execution—their intelligence compounds rather than constricts. They don't lose their edge; they sharpen it.

The biggest distractor isn't failure, the crowd, or even pressure—it's our own untrained attention turning against us. But when awareness meets structure, the same mind that once interfered becomes the mind that leads. What we once labeled as mental weakness is often nothing more than a biological misfire—a finely tuned brain operating without clear direction. To understand why, we need to look beneath the surface and explore what's actually happening inside the brain under pressure.

What We Missed About the Brain

Part of the challenge for mental training was that, for a long time, we simply didn't understand how the brain worked. We especially didn't fully comprehend how the brain functioned under pressure—especially in environments where movement was required, that were fast-paced, high-stakes, or cognitively demanding. So, coaches defaulted to what had worked for them. Advice was passed down generationally, rooted more in personal experience than in actual cognitive mechanics. But much of that guidance was built on misidentified sources—attributing success or failure to surface-level traits rather than the underlying mental processes driving performance.

That's changing. In recent years, performance psychologists have begun to unpack how the brain actually operates under acute stress and distraction. With advances in neurocognitive science and applied biotechnology, we now have access to deeper, more precise insights into how attention, perception, and decision-making are impacted in high-stress moments. And perhaps equally important—we have now designed and tested interventions that aren't based on clichés, but on actual mental processes.

We're moving from *"be confident"* to: here's how you build cognitive stability under pressure. From *"trust yourself"* to: here's how to train the attentional systems that allow "trust" to emerge from controllable actions.

Intentional Attention represents a step in that direction—a performance framework rooted not in motivational language, but in the deliberate training of where, how, and when we direct our mental energy. It's not about trying harder. It's about training more intelligently, with improved awareness and tools that align with how the brain actually performs under pressure.

Chapter 3

The Old Brain in a Modern Arena

"Our brain's shortcuts are ancient maps drawn for another world."

—Unknown

It wasn't about mechanics, arm strength, or preparation; it was about attention.

Both our NBA and NFL players' attention had been hijacked—not by laziness, failure of willpower, or lack of toughness—but by something far more primitive. They didn't feel distracted—they felt tense, tight, and suddenly uncertain. Their brains weren't failing; they were protecting.

From an evolutionary standpoint, the human brain is wired to prioritize threat detection—not the refined motor control or nuanced decision-making that modern performance demands. Our ancestors didn't need to stay calm under scrutiny; they needed to react fast under threat. Thousands of years later, the same circuitry still drives our attention. When stress rises, the brain doesn't instinctively lock on to performance-relevant cues. It scans for danger—anything uncertain, novel, or uncomfortable.

So when stress rises, our neural resources that influence our attention don't instinctively stay locked on performance-relevant cues. The brain defaults to a survival pattern and begins scanning for anything novel, uncertain, or uncomfortable—because those things might signal danger. It does this largely beneath our conscious awareness. That quiet shift—an internal pull on the attentional steering wheel—can redirect focus in ways even the most skilled athletes can't always recognize in real time.

And at the highest level of sport, where the margins are razor thin, that shift is often enough to derail performance.

We've seen this pattern unfold time and again—perhaps nowhere more visibly than in golf, where the mental game is laid bare for all to see. The pull on attention under pressure is not just theoretical; it's observable, even among the most accomplished players in the sport. One event where this stands out is the Masters Tournament—arguably one of the most mentally demanding stages in all of sport.

In 2016, Jordan Spieth—already a Masters champion—carried a five-shot lead into the back nine on Sunday. Then a few errant shots, combined with the rising emotional weight of the moment, began to pull his focus. His tempo quickened. His pre-shot mental routine jumbled. His focus narrowed—not on the target, but on the mistake he feared repeating. Which ironically led to a stretch that included a quadruple bogey on the 12th hole and in just under 30 minutes, the lead was gone. Spieth finished tied for fourth.

Rory McIlroy, too, has felt that invisible pull on the steering wheel. In 2011, he entered Sunday at the Masters with a four-shot lead and finished with a final-round 80—a collapse that knocked him completely out of contention. It wasn't a failure of physical talent or preparation. It was a reflection of how difficult it is—even for the best in the world—to keep control of their mental game when pressure spikes. In moments athletes spend their entire lives chasing, the brain's survival system can quietly take the attentional wheel without the performer knowing. And when that internal attention shifts without warning, performance can unravel in moments.

Yet McIlroy's story also shows what's possible when that internal system is trained. In 2025, after several years of intentional mental work, he returned to Augusta with a quieter mind and a steadier process. He entered the final round with a two-stroke lead, faced down a double bogey and a missed short putt on 18, and still managed to collect himself, execute under playoff pressure, and win his first green jacket—completing the career Grand Slam.

What changed? The swing wasn't dramatically different. But the steering wheel was more stable. That shift came from the inside.

McIlroy's turnaround wasn't about discovering new talent. It was about learning to navigate what had always been there: his own internal attentional architecture. The threat he'd learned to manage wasn't a charging animal or a sudden physical risk. It was emotional. Psychological. It was the fear of failure. The possibility of letting himself or others down. The quiet weight of falling short on the very stage he'd worked so long to reach.

This is why, in moments that matter most, our attention often drifts—not toward our training, but naturally toward our doubts or fears.

We see this all the time in the work we do with high performers. One of the most common examples comes from executives who are also amateur golfers.

"I step up to the first tee with a clear plan. I've rehearsed the mechanics. I've visualized the shot. But right before I swing, all I can think about is the group behind me watching. I find myself worrying about what they're thinking, or what happens if I mess up."

And just like that, much like our quarterback or elite basketball player, the attention shifts. The human brain is no longer executing. It's avoiding. Not focused on the target, but pulled toward and distracted by a perceived threat. The threat of failure or embarrassment.

Attention Is Weighted Toward Threats

To fully understand why our attention gets hijacked in pressure moments—times when we most want to perform our best, when everything we've worked for is on the line—we need to understand our biology. And to do that, we need to look backward. Way backward.

Tens of thousands of years ago, our ancestors weren't scanning for feedback after presentations or worrying about failing in front of a crowd during a game. They were scanning the brush line for signs of danger. Life-or-death danger. The kind that makes you wonder: Was that a shadow . . . or a predator?

In that environment, over thousands of years, our survival didn't depend on clarity or calm. It depended on sensitivity to threat. The people who mis-assessed, paused, or didn't react strongly and decisively to potential threats often didn't pass on their genes. The ones who reacted quickly—who assumed the worst and prepared for danger—lived to reproduce.

That wiring still exists today. It evolved into the modern brain's tendency to give more weight to potential threats than to neutral or positive information. In psychology, this tendency is known as negativity bias.

Even if nine things go right, the one thing that goes wrong often becomes the spotlight of our attention. Baumeister et al. (2001a) found that negative events impact our cognition and behavior more strongly than positive ones of equal intensity. This bias affects how we interpret feedback, outcomes, and even our own thoughts.

It's why we remember the one missed shot more than the five we made. Why we can't shake off a critical comment even after receiving praise. And why doubt often sticks faster and stronger than confidence.

What's particularly interesting is that this response becomes even more oppressive when others are watching.

Social Judgment

Dickerson and Kemeny (2004) found that social-evaluative threats—situations where we fear being judged or negatively evaluated—trigger significant cortisol release and emotional dysregulation. In other words, our bodies respond to psychological visibility as if it were physical danger.

Just like the predator many generations ago, social exposure and threats to our reputation or standing—especially when it risks our social status or belonging—also activate our survival systems.

From an evolutionary standpoint, one of the biggest threats to survival, historically, was social exclusion.

As humans evolved in small, interdependent groups, being accepted by the tribe wasn't optional—it was essential for survival. Social rejection meant losing access to shared resources, protection, and opportunities for reproduction. It meant being alone. And in ancestral environments, being alone was often a death sentence.

This explains why modern social stressors—being benched, criticized, rejected, ghosted, humiliated—still trigger the same physiological and emotional responses as physical threats. The brain doesn't distinguish between the two. It recognizes and prioritizes the risk.

Eisenberger et al. (2003) demonstrated that social pain—such as exclusion or rejection—activates the same neural pathways in the brain (specifically the dorsal anterior cingulate cortex) as physical pain. Our brains are wired to treat "being left out" or rejected like being wounded.

So when a performer senses the judgment of others—when the stakes are visible and the impact on social status is possible—their biology is responding exactly the way it was designed to: urgently, protectively, but often in ways that don't serve performance in today's world, where the consequences of failure in most performance environments no longer equate to social isolation or death.

Of course, in domains like the military, emergency response, or extreme sports, the stakes can still be life-or-death. Yet, even in these environments, the perceived judgment of others often induces stress responses that are as significant as those triggered by actual physical danger.

This is the biology we all inherited.

Our default brain is protective, not primarily focused on peak performance.

That's why, in high-pressure moments, under stress, or when fatigued, we often start playing "not to mess up" instead of playing to win. Our brains don't want us to be hurt. Our attention quickly and subtly shifts from execution to evaluation, from presence to protection.

This isn't a flaw, it's a feature in our design; a well-built survival operating system that has served humans for generations. It's hard-wired into us. But if we hope to perform at our best in today's world, we need to better understand that design. Because once we do, we can develop more effective strategies to work with it—rather than wishing we had inherited a different biology, or blaming ourselves and believing there's something fundamentally wrong with us for how we show up under pressure. Once we learn and train this attentional system—to recognize, direct, and reset our attention—our mental game won't be our enemy, it will be our edge.

Chapter 4

The Performance Control Tower: How Your Brain Manages Focus Under Fire

"The greatest weapon against stress is our ability to choose one thought over another."

—William James

Understanding attention in high-stakes environments requires more than a look at our evolutionary history. We have to step inside the control tower: the brain. Here, we address the systems that govern attention when the stakes rise: the subconscious that drives rapid interpretation, the habits that build unconscious bias, the amygdala that hijacks attention under threat, and the prefrontal cortex that can steady, analyze, or abandon us in critical moments. By the end, we'll see how this architecture shapes performance "under pressure"— and why knowing our hardware is central to training attention more efficiently.

The Subconscious: Fast, Familiar, and Focused on Survival

It's widely understood that roughly 95% of brain activity occurs below conscious awareness (Bargh & Chartrand, 1999). This means that most of what drives our perception, behavior, and attention unfolds without deliberate choice. It operates more like an autopilot system—quiet, fast, and constantly adjusting based on prior experience, pattern recognition, and perceived risk. Most of the time, we're not steering our responses. We're being guided by them.

When a quarterback hears the play call, sees the defensive alignment, and thinks *this won't work*, that thought didn't appear from nowhere. It was shaped by subconscious pattern recognition—a compilation of past experiences, stored repetitions, and environmental associations processed without his conscious permission.

The subconscious is remarkably fast, with a primary concern for safety. But like any fast-moving system, it sacrifices accuracy for speed. It's not a surgeon making precise, deliberate cuts—it's a butcher: efficient, decisive, and "close enough." It gets the job done quickly, even if it occasionally takes off a little more than necessary. And when it makes errors, it tends to err on the side of survival.

That's the subconscious in pressure moments. It notices a pattern that feels vaguely dangerous—whether it's a confusing coverage look, a reminder of a past mistake, or just the fear of falling short and it makes a rapid judgment call:

Get ready. Something problematic could happen.

From a survival standpoint, close enough is good enough. Accuracy is optional; speed is required. Once that "close enough" threat is tagged, the system flips the alarm.

Habits: The Builders of Bias

If the subconscious is the butcher, then habits and prior experiences are the blueprint it cuts from.

What we repeatedly do—how we eat, scroll, speak up, avoid conflict, lean in, or pull back—carves grooves in the brain's neural pathways. Repetition creates familiarity. Familiarity becomes preference—even when that preference doesn't align with truth, performance, goals, or growth.

Neuroscience calls this experience-dependent plasticity: the brain's wiring adapts based on repeated input (Buonomano & Merzenich, 1998). Our habits aren't just behaviors; they're training for how we interpret the world.

This matters because the subconscious doesn't pull from neutral ground. It pulls from what's been rehearsed. If daily routines reinforce certain narratives—"I only play well under warm conditions," "conflict is dangerous," "I can't trust my teammates in crucial moments"—those narratives become filters—not by choice, but by practice.

As one Harvard Business Review piece notes, "unconscious bias is not a reflection of our beliefs so much as it is a reflection of what our brains have been most exposed to and what they've had the most practice reacting to" (Harvard Business Review, 2017). The brain isn't making a moral decision; it's making a familiar one.

And reinforcement doesn't require deliberate intention; it just requires repetition. A study in *Nature Communications* showed that as habits form, neural efficiency increases in the basal ganglia (associated with automatic behavior), while activation decreases in prefrontal regions linked to conscious control (Liu et al., 2022). In other words, the more a pattern repeats, the more control is handed off—especially under stress.

That's how quiet, routine defaults end up guiding our most critical decisions.

When those defaults are rehearsed through self-criticism and the constant mental replay of our lowest moments, they do more than shape perception—they can trap attention in loops that resurface when the stress spikes.

A Player's Rumination Loop: Practicing the Problem

Consider a WNBA player we worked with who was referred by an assistant coach because "she can be too hard on herself." The coach shared that after difficult games, she seemed to ruminate on every missed shot and tough possession.

The coach was right. She confirmed that her inner dialogue was sharp and relentlessly self-critical. In the past, however, those perfectionistic tendencies had served her well. They fueled her motivation, accelerated her growth, and sharpened her skill development.

Earlier in her career, even when her inner voice was harsh, she could still dominate—not because her mindset was optimal or her attention well-directed, but because her talent outpaced the demands of her environment. If her outside shot wasn't falling, she could drive to the rim or find another way to produce. She won. She was praised. And that loop—effort, criticism, reward—was reinforced.

But now, at the professional level, the margin is thinner. Everyone is fast. Everyone is skilled. Open looks are harder to come by, and converting those few opportunities often determines playing time—and contracts. She's no longer in full control of the game. And in this unfamiliar space—where she's fighting for minutes, every possession is scrutinized, and every outcome carries weight—her attention shifts.

She hasn't stopped working. But what used to be aggressive, assertive reps have become careful. She isn't practicing execution anymore; she's rehearsing hesitation.

Her awareness narrows. Her body tightens and fatigues faster. Her decisions slow as she overanalyzes each move. She's not falling apart, but her system is quietly constricting under the weight of heightened expectations.

After games, she turns to the only post-performance strategy she knows: self-criticism. The tool that once fueled her improvement now compounds the problem. On the bus, in the hotel, lying awake at night, she grooves that pattern—replaying every mistake, every miss, every subtle cue of disappointment from coaches or teammates. Not once, but hundreds of times. Without realizing it, she's practicing the emotion of failure. And what's practiced becomes familiar.

In her mental replay, these cues take center stage. She notices them far more than performance-relevant cues and behaviors—instructional self-talk like "attack the rim," or controllables like sprinting in transition and encouraging her teammates. She isn't drifting toward negativity; she's training her focus to live there.

Without a structured reset or recovery process, her brain begins tagging those emotional and sensory signals as "known." And what's familiar becomes efficient—automatic. Over time, those pathways become well-worn neural highways.

So the next time she's open in the corner with under a minute to play, her body may be ready, but her attention isn't. It defaults to what's been rehearsed: threat, not freedom. Hesitation, not aggression.

This is how performance bias gets built—not consciously, but subconsciously.

And this is what we see over and over again in elite environments: athletes with real talent and proven success, caught in loops they can't fully explain. They're not underperforming because they forgot how to play. They're underperforming because they've unintentionally trained their attention on the wrong loops—performance-irrelevant cues that now run on autopilot in competition.

These loops don't just reflect mindset; they reflect physiology. Once the subconscious tags a moment as a threat, another system takes over—the brain's internal alarm: the amygdala.

The Amygdala and the Threat Response Cycle

When the subconscious detects threat, it signals an alert—largely generated from the amygdala, the brain's smoke detector. Deep in the limbic system, it's our internal first responder. It doesn't fact-check; it quickly reacts. Its job is to initiate a survival response the moment something might go wrong (Dickerson & Kemeny, 2004; LeDoux, 1996).

It evolved when the cost of delay was death—not a missed shot.

Today, it still treats performance threats like life-or-death scenarios: public speaking, critical errors, social rejection, or the fear of letting a teammate down. When triggered, the amygdala initiates a cascade of neurochemical and physiological reactions we call the Threat Response Cycle. See Figure 4.1.

Once a threat is perceived, the amygdala contributes to the release of cortisol and adrenaline (Dickerson and Kemeny, 2004), directly impacting the autonomic nervous system (ANS).

The ANS is the body's operating system that regulates automatic functions like heart rate, breathing, digestion, and pupil dilation. And when threat is detected, one specific branch of the ANS takes over: the sympathetic nervous system (SNS).

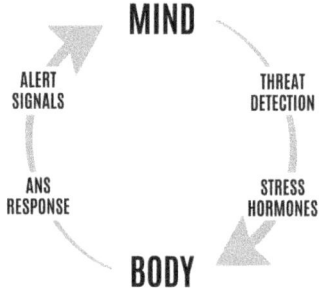

Figure 4.1 The Threat Response Cycle.
Source: Justin Anderson.

The SNS is responsible for the classic *fight, flight, or freeze* response. It speeds up heart rate, restricts digestion, heightens alertness, and prepares the body to defend, escape, or stall in a panic.

What's interesting is that the moment the body enters this mobilized state, it sends that data back to the brain—a bottom-up signal reinforcing the idea that something's wrong.

In short:

- The **mind detects a threat**, activating the body.
- The **body responds**, escalating stress signals back to the brain.
- The **brain ramps up its scanning**, narrowing, analyzing, and fixating its attention further.

This recursive loop doesn't just prepare us for danger—it can lock us into it. It narrows focus, hijacks emotion, and reduces the cognitive bandwidth needed for problem-solving, fluid execution, and strategic thinking.

Of course, this loop is highly effective if we're facing a bear. It's less helpful when we're standing over a putt on the 18th green.

This was the quarterback's reality in Chapter 2. His brain wasn't failing him—it was doing its job. But in protecting him, it suppressed the very region he needed most: the prefrontal cortex, the command center for conscious focus and execution.

The Prefrontal Cortex: When Strength Feels Like Weakness

The prefrontal cortex (PFC) is the CEO of the brain. It governs the high-order functions that define elite performance: planning, focus, inhibition, and adaptation. In the language of performance, it allows us to pause, prioritize, and execute under pressure. This region sits at the heart of Intentional Attention—the ability to choose where and how to direct our focus in real time.

Neuroscience refers to this as executive control—and it's distributed across a network of PFC subregions:

- Dorsolateral PFC (dlPFC): Holds task rules in working memory and manages sustained focus (Miller & Cohen, 2001).

- Anterior cingulate cortex (ACC): Detects conflict, tracks errors, and helps reallocate attention (Botvinick et al., 2001).

- Ventromedial PFC (vmPFC): Evaluates risk, reward, and moral or social implications of decisions (Bechara et al., 2000; Roy et al., 2012).

Under calm, focused conditions, this network performs beautifully. It allows us to weigh options, resist reactive impulses, and initiate behavior aligned with goals—not emotions. But under pressure, the PFC becomes vulnerable. Its processing is slower, cognitively demanding, and metabolically expensive—requiring a steady supply of glucose and oxygen to function optimally. It's also highly sensitive to stress hormones like cortisol and norepinephrine, which can rapidly disrupt its activity and hand control to more reactive brain regions (Arnsten, 2009).

When threat is perceived—physical, social, reputational—the brain reallocates resources toward speed and survival. The amygdala activates, attention narrows, and blood flow is reduced to the PFC (Arnsten et al., 2012; Hermans et al., 2014). Arnsten (2014) states that the very part of the brain we rely on to exert control is the first to be compromised by stress. This process, called neural reallocation, is adaptive in a war zone but can be costly to our best performers when fatigue or pressure mount.

Performance in Real Time: The Quarterback Revisited

This was the quarterback's reality in Chapter 2. The pressure of the moment—his NFL debut, the disrupted plan, and the play he didn't like—was registered as potential threats. His brain executed its built-in survival protocol: shift control away from deliberate processing and toward faster, reactive systems.

The game didn't just feel faster. It was faster for him. His prefrontal cortex didn't fail; it was sidelined by our brain's natural design.

Film later showed the route was open, but he hesitated. His working memory—the play call, the timing window, the safety rotation—was no longer fully online. His eyes saw the opportunity, but his brain couldn't act on it. The result wasn't a bad decision. It was *no decision*.

His strengths—pattern recognition, calm execution, clutch awareness—had been suppressed by a system built to protect him.

After the game, he said it "felt like the game sped up a bit." What actually happened was simpler—and far more universal: His attentional control system was overridden by a faster, older operating system.

This is the paradox of high performance: The very systems we train to lead us during big opportunities are also the most fragile under stress. The PFC is where rhythm, presence, and leadership live—but it's the first to go offline when we feel unsettled, unprepared, or overwhelmed.

How the Brain Shows Up in Other Domains

This isn't just a quarterback problem. The same override happens on Wall Street, classrooms, hospitals, and negotiation tables—anywhere pressure and evaluation collide.

- **An Executive Manager**, preparing to give feedback to an under-performing employee known to react defensively, freezes mid-sentence in the middle of the performance review. Later, he admits he knew what he wanted to say but "couldn't find the words." Post-session review showed increased heart rate, clenched posture, and narrowed gaze—classic signs of PFC suppression. Once he practiced pausing, regulating breath, and orienting toward his core message, he regained executive control in those important settings.

- **An NBA Player** we profiled in the Introduction slipped into a slump when his shooting percentage dropped and opponents began disrespecting his range. His instinct was to "get that confident feeling back." But the harder he chased emotion, the more he lost focus. When he reviewed his game tape, the issue wasn't form or mechanics—it was his attention. His PFC had disengaged, leaving his focus stuck on the threat to his identity. Performance improved only when he practiced *redirecting attention back to controllable actions*: behaviors like his floor spacing, sprinting in transition, and connecting with teammates.

These are subtle but significant neurological shifts that reshape how our attentional system functions. The encouraging truth? We now know it can be trained.

When the PFC Is Engaged with Performance-Relevant Cues

When we ask high performers what it feels like to be in the zone, one phrase comes up again and again:

"I wasn't thinking. I was just doing."

They don't mean there was an absence of thought. They mean their minds were clear—free from over-analysis and judgment.

Upon closer examination, they weren't just avoiding judgment; they were doing something even more important: directing their attention toward performance-relevant data—information that enhances execution because it's controllable, present-moment, target-driven, and tied to behavior.

Neurologically, this reflects highly selective PFC activity: performance-relevant cues are processed; distractions—both internal and external distractions—are filtered out (Christoff et al., 2009; Hölzel et al., 2011). It's not a passive state. It's the byproduct of **optimized attentional management**—and precisely where our mental training should be focused.

From Thought to Attention

Models like **nonjudgmental thinking** (Kabat-Zinn, 1990) and **neutral thinking** (Moawad & Staples, 2020) have helped many performers reduce interference. But neuroscience has shown that changing thoughts under pressure is difficult. Stress amplifies default cognitive loops (Arnsten, 2009; Lieberman et al., 2007).

Training attention, however, appears to be more accessible.

In fact, more recent research shows that attentional training can reduce default mode network (DMN) activity—activity linked to self-evaluation and rumination—and can more efficiently increase focus on performance-relevant cues (Fox et al., 2016; Tang et al., 2015). And when attention becomes stable and well-directed, it can reshape the quality of cognition.

In applied terms, this doesn't mean *thinking less*. It means targeting attention more surgically, with greater precision—so that cognitive resources align with task demands.

The Other Side of the Sympathetic System: Parasympathetic Recovery

Once the threat passes, the parasympathetic system re-engages to restore internal balance. Yet under chronic or repeated stress—especially social-evaluative stress, like performance scrutiny—many of us will stay locked in an elevated sympathetic state longer than necessary.

Again, this isn't a sign of mental weakness; it's a system that hasn't been trained to shift gears effectively. That transition is critical for replenishing the attentional energy required for focus and composure.

The irony is that, when trained properly, those same attentional systems can help drive the shift—from sympathetic activation to parasympathetic recovery. In doing so, we can direct our focus toward the signals and environments that most efficiently restore our attentional energy.

Built to Survive, Trained to Perform

The patterns described throughout this chapter highlight what many mistake as flaws—the proverbial choke in sport. But they're not flaws at all. They are simply features of a cognitive system designed to protect us.

Here's what we know:

- Stress impairs prefrontal cortex function and enhances amygdala dominance (Arnsten, 2009; Hermans et al., 2014).

- Chronic stress reduces PFC gray matter and increases amygdala (limbic) reactivity (Goldfarb et al., 2020).

- Emotionally ambiguous threats—like social rejection or professional uncertainty—can rapidly shift control between the amygdala (limbic) and the prefrontal cortex (executive) systems (Haller et al., 2023).
- Under pressure, leaders and performers often default to tunnel vision, defensiveness, and micromanagement—not from weakness, but from protective wiring (Harvard Business Review, 2022).

This chapter explored how and why the brain allocates attention under fire, and how our internal systems naturally protect, and sometimes override our best intentions.

In Part II, we'll begin to move from understanding to training: learning how to optimize this internal operating system for the demands of modern performance. We'll build the capacity to notice where attention drifts and how to take back the controls when it does.

But before we go there, we need to examine our natural developmental gaps—and how traditional cognitive training has often failed to accelerate our mental development.

Chapter 5

The Developmental Gap: Why Physical Peak Outpaces Mental Readiness

"Mental maturity emerges as perspectives become more adaptable—when responsibility replaces complaint and action replaces excuse."

—Justin Anderson

They say football is a young man's game—and in many ways, that's true.

Watch the NFL Combine and it's easy to believe that the most important number in performance is a 40-yard dash. Speed sells. Scouts drool. Highlight reels get cut, draft boards shift, and seven-figure decisions are made on the basis of millisecond splits.

But spend time in the locker room after a playoff loss—sit across from a 10-year veteran, physically drained, head down but voice steady, when seemingly out of nowhere he says, *"I wish I knew then . . ."*

If you've been around the game long enough, you've heard it: *"I wish I knew then what I know now."* It's not nostalgia talking. It's neuroscience. What we're really acknowledging in hindsight is that the mental operating system we have at 32, 35, or 40 would have made us far more effective at 22. Back then, the physical horsepower was there, but the steering wasn't. We could move fast, but not always in the right direction. Awareness, judgment, and focus simply hadn't caught up to our physical capability.

That steering wheel is made of emotional intelligence, which includes:

- **Attention Control:** directing and sustaining focus under pressure, adversity, and fatigue
- **Motivation Awareness:** knowing what drives you internally versus what hijacks you externally
- **Emotional Regulation:** managing intensity without suppression or emotional outburst
- **Meaning-Making:** interpreting adversity constructively rather than catastrophically

These aren't abstract traits; they're trainable systems of the mind—but few athletes ever get the manual early enough.

The body peaks early. The brain catches up later. And in between? There's a gap that deserves more attention.

The Preconscious Mind, Where Joy Lives

Think about a toddler learning to walk. They don't second-guess. They don't self-condemn. They fall, they wobble, they stumble—and they marvel at the attempt. The attention system is dialed in, laser-focused on the task. No shame. No scoreboard. Just play.

This is the preconscious mind in action. It's performance without performance anxiety. It's raw attention. It's what athletes experience in their earliest developmental stages: see ball, hit ball. Run, jump, shoot, tumble. They engage the task fully, without distraction by outcomes or evaluation.

Renowned developmental psychologist Jean Piaget, whose work shaped much of what we know about how children think and reason, described this stage of cognitive functioning as the preoperational phase—a period dominated by symbolic play and motor exploration, before abstract reasoning fully develops (Piaget, 1952). During this time, the neural networks responsible for executive functioning—particularly in the prefrontal cortex—are not yet fully wired. Paradoxically, this immaturity is an advantage. Freed from constant self-evaluation, the developing brain is primed for curiosity, active experimentation, confidence, and joy.

Then Something Changes

As the brain develops in early adolescence, new cognitive and emotional capacities begin to emerge. Around this time, empathic processing and emotional awareness accelerate (Baron-Cohen et al., 2005), while the prefrontal cortex—responsible for planning, reasoning, and self-reflection—continues to mature (Blakemore & Choudhury, 2006). Meanwhile, limbic structures like the amygdala are firing at full strength, amplifying emotional reactivity and social sensitivity.

Athletes don't just notice the ball anymore. They notice the crowd, the scoreboard, their peers, their coach's expression—and, for the first time, *themselves*.

This cognitive leap—what some in performance psychology call *postconscious attention*—marks the emergence of what we call self-evaluative attention: the awareness of oneself as an object of evaluation. It's not yet about regulating thoughts; it's about *perceiving oneself being perceived*. The brain begins to register social judgment, consequence, and implication—not just action. This developmental shift is well documented: as self-consciousness heightens, attention increasingly orients toward how one is seen by others (Rankin et al., 2004).

In developmental terms, this marks a fundamental change in the attentional system. Early in life, attention is pure—anchored fully in the task itself. But now it splits between *what I'm doing* and *how I'm being seen doing it.* Focus moves from direct engagement to self-evaluative monitoring, and with that subtle shift, performance becomes less consistent.

Consider a child learning to ride a bike. Instruction can explain the basic mechanics and balance required, but experience is what teaches the body how to ride. During early development, skill acquisition happens rapidly—not only because of the neural connections that are forming, but because learning unfolds with minimal interference from internal or external judgment. That's the preconscious mind in action—direct, automatic, and non-judgmental. Young athletes often operate in a similar mode: the ball is all that exists.

This is also the essence of *flow*—the mental state where attention is fully absorbed in the task at hand. Growth and performance thrive here because focus is pure, unfragmented by evaluation or expectation. Learning happens naturally, not through analysis, but through immersion.

Then, in early adolescence, as the brain grows in its complexity, the game changes. Athletes become aware of themselves as performers. In addition to the ball, they begin to register judgment—the coach's tone, social status, rankings, expectations. Their focus becomes divided between *the act* and *the evaluation of the act.*

Girls often enter this shift earlier, due to faster emotional maturation and increased empathic processing (Baron-Cohen et al., 2005). But that seeming advantage can carry a cost: the complexity—and sometimes the burden—arrive sooner.

A Female Gymnast: Talent Meets Turbulence

A 13-year-old gymnast we worked with made the junior elite level by age 12. She was fearlessly throwing full-twisting layouts without blinking. At 13, her technique hadn't declined, but her performance had. Mid-routines, she'd pause. On the beam, she'd hesitate. Her coach said she was "thinking too much."

She was.

What changed wasn't her body. It was her brain.

Her attention was no longer locked on movement patterns. It was split between her form, the judges, her teammates, and her place on the team. She had gained consciousness of herself as a performer. Without a framework to navigate this self-consciousness, her brain—wired for emotional protection and social safety—hijacked her precision.

Her story isn't unique. In a study of elite adolescent gymnasts, researchers found that increased self-awareness and social comparison significantly predicted declines in performance consistency (Harwood et al., 2004). These athletes weren't less skilled—they simply performed with less freedom. And in sport, freedom is oxygen.

This emergence of self-evaluative awareness is a necessary and powerful cognitive upgrade—but it also introduces a potential threat to raw, task-focused attention and performance precision. Attention begins to shift from the task itself to its consequences—to meaning, judgment, and what-ifs. This marks the birth of internal evaluation, a process few athletes are ever taught to recognize or manage. Without training, they are left to navigate it by chance, relying on trial and error rather than deliberate education.

The Cognitive Developmental Gap

What's striking is that many athletes reach their physical peak before their attentional maturity fully develops—certainly before they learn to manage the complexities that come with a more powerfully developed brain.

The gap between those two trajectories—body and brain—is what we call the **Cognitive Developmental Gap** (see Figure 5.1). It

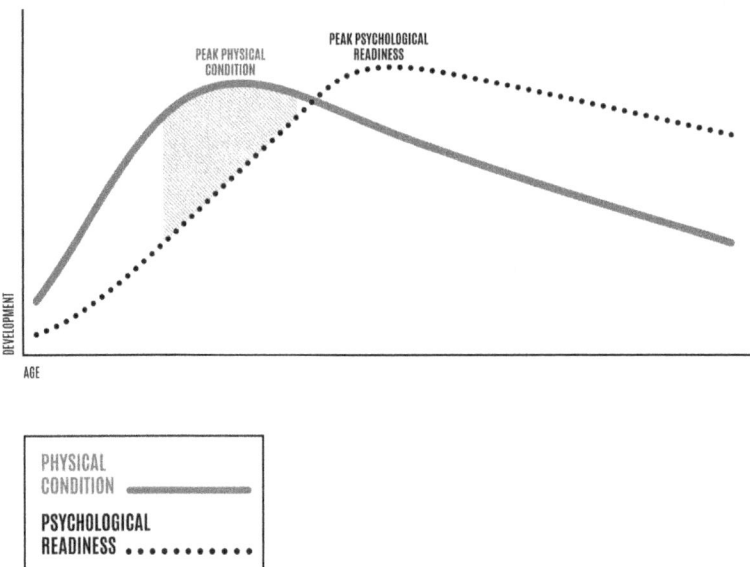

Figure 5.1 The Cognitive Developmental Gap.
Source: Justin Anderson.

remains one of the least addressed challenges in performance psychology today, especially at the professional level. It's a gap that rarely gets discussed, yet it can fundamentally shape consistency, decision-making, and vulnerability under pressure.

Physical development (the solid line in Figure 5.1) surges during adolescence, peaks in the mid to late 20s, and then begins its gradual decline in our 30s—slower recovery, higher injury risk, and greater maintenance demands.

Now overlay a second curve (the dotted line): attentional development. As this system strengthens, the brain becomes better equipped to shift perspectives, adapt approaches, and deploy effort more efficiently. This growth in attentional management supports emotional regulation, impulse management, and meaning-making—ultimately enabling faster psychological recovery after stress or disruption.

That curve doesn't peak in the mid-20s. In many cases, it's still climbing.

Developmental neuroscience helps explain why. The prefrontal cortex does not reach full functional maturity until the mid to late 20s (Casey et al., 2005). At the same time, subcortical systems involved in emotion, reward, and threat detection mature earlier and are highly sensitive to pressure and social evaluation.

This imbalance is central to what Steinberg (2010) describes as the dual systems model of development: a brain that is increasingly powerful in terms of motivation, emotion, and reward-seeking, but not yet fully equipped with the attentional control systems required to consistently regulate those forces under stress. In performance environments, that means physically developed athletes often *feel* ready before they are neurologically prepared to manage pressure reliably.

Compounding the issue, the ability to harness and refine attentional control through deliberate repetition—what we would call attentional training—often lags even further behind structural brain development (Blakemore & Mills, 2014).

The result places many athletes in a paradoxical space: their physical systems reach peak readiness just as their attentional systems are still calibrating how to manage intensity, expectation, and consequence.

The Freshman Captain: Making the Case in Reverse

A number of years ago, we worked with a freshman women's hockey player at a Division I program. She wasn't the fastest or flashiest on the roster, but she'd been exposed to mental training since she was 14—not just breathing exercises or visualization, but true attentional reps: identity and performance values development, motivation mapping, focus training, and cognitive reappraisal techniques to reframe thinking under pressure.

By the start of her sophomore season, she wore the captain's "C."

Why? Because at 15 she could do what few 18- and 19-year-olds can: filter signal from noise. When her coach barked feedback, she separated insight from ego threat. When the pressure of overtime mounted, she didn't lock up—she locked in. And her teammates followed.

Mentally, her maturity was years beyond that of her teammates.

This pattern holds across elite environments: Athletes who are introduced to attentional training early can often more easily harness pressure instead of being hijacked by it. They direct their focus toward performance-relevant data in high-stakes moments. They learn faster, adapt easier, and lead earlier—not because they experience less stress, but because they've learned to respond more effectively.

When Awareness Outpaces Skill

This conscious mind isn't the enemy. It's a gift. But when awareness grows faster than emotional intelligence—when athletes become aware of pressure without the tools to handle it—the result is performance paralysis.

This gap shows up as hesitation, self-criticism, perfectionism, fear of failure, and social anxiety—all of which impair attention. Attention drifts not because athletes don't care, but because they've never been taught how to manage it effectively.

The problem isn't awareness. The problem is untrained awareness.

The sports world has built a performance system that rewards physical prowess while largely neglecting or entirely ignoring their psychological development. As a result, elite athletes are often navigating world-class demands with middle-school-level attention control skills.

By 22, an athlete may be as strong, fast, and explosive as they'll ever be—but their prefrontal cortex won't fully mature until years later (Casey et al., 2008; Giedd et al., 1999). Meanwhile, expectations have never been higher: college scholarships, social media visibility, NIL deals, Olympic trials.

Bridging the Gap

The goal of examining this model isn't to disparage conscious awareness or modern player development. The power of conscious awareness is central to what makes us human. But we are long overdue to better structure and integrate mental training—to teach people how to transition from unconscious reactivity to Intentional Attention.

Our aim is to bridge the developmental gap with frameworks and tools that align cognitive growth with performance demands. Without that alignment, even the most physically gifted athletes remain vulnerable—to burnout, inconsistency, and underperformance.

We also need to stop treating mental development (both mental performance and mental well-being) as remediation—something reserved for athletes "in crisis." These skills are not supplemental; they're structural. They form the scaffolding for athletes and leaders entering the most volatile phase of their development.

Using attentional training as a framework to develop mental skills early and proactively—with the same repetition and intentionality we bring to physical training—builds capacities that extend far beyond sport: into leadership, academics, careers, and relationships. It doesn't just catch us when we fall; it gives us a pathway to grow, preparing us to stand firmer when adversity inevitably hits along the journey.

Because when we train attention early, we're not just shaping performance—we're shaping development itself. We're strengthening the very systems that govern focus, adaptability, and meaning-making.

Yet despite its impact, attention training has been largely absent from most developmental systems.

How we overcome this gap becomes the next part of our story.

In the chapters ahead, we'll explore why traditional approaches to cognitive and emotional development have lagged behind, how attentional skills have been misunderstood or undertrained, and what it takes to build an intentional operating system for high performance within the modern time constraints of development programs.

Chapter 6

We Were Never Taught This

"Education is not the learning of facts, but the training of the mind . . ."

—Albert Einstein

It's been said that sport is a microcosm of life. If that's true, modern sport is also a preview of what's coming for everyone else.

Athletes today don't just play the game—they live inside a fishbowl. Every move, decision, mistake, and facial expression can be captured, clipped, and critiqued by millions in real time. And it's not just athletes—coaches, front offices, and staff live under the same scrutiny. One decision, one post, one rumor, one underperformance—and suddenly everyone weighs in.

Of course, they sign up for it—and they're compensated well. But the pressure to perform isn't abstract. It's real, relentless, and intensifying.

What that kind of constant visibility does—and what most people outside the arena don't realize—is create a subtle but powerful shift in mindset. Slowly, without realizing it, performers stop playing to win—and start playing not to lose. Their attention drifts from growth to survival. From expansion to protection.

And that shift in attention changes everything.

Why Mental Training Has Fallen Short

For years, the field of sport psychology and mental performance training hasn't gotten it quite right. We've told athletes and leaders to be confident, to stay positive, to trust themselves. We've held up traits like *mental toughness* as if they were innate character strengths rather than trainable skills. Despite good intentions, we've built mental training on fragments, not frameworks.

We've taught individual techniques—breath work, self-talk, imagery—but too often we haven't fully connected the dots. When athletes came in with performance anxiety, we often prescribed breathing or activation interventions. But we rarely helped them understand *why* those tools work, how to layer them with deeper psychological training, or how to build those traits in a sequenced and sustainable way—especially when the technique itself isn't effective for the individual. In some cases, breath work isn't the solution—it's a surface-level entry point to much deeper cognitive and emotional patterns that can require deliberate development over time. What's been missing is a cohesive framework—one that explains how mental skills interconnect, how coaches and staff can reinforce them, and how organizations can integrate mental development systematically into player-development systems (Beauchamp et al., 2021; Henriksen et al., 2020).

Instead, sport psychology has largely existed as a series of one-off interventions—a service offered to people who want supplemental tools—rather than being strategically embedded in an organizational structure as part of the developmental core.

The problem with that approach is predictable. When pressure truly peaks and losses accumulate, these isolated, vague concepts often collapse. They're misunderstood, misapplied, or quietly deprioritized. They become Band-Aids—temporary relief rather than long-term solutions. Coaches understandably lose faith, assuming, *"We sent the player to sport psych, and nothing changed."*

While recent league-wide initiatives have expanded access to mental health services—a significant and positive step—many organizations rushed to comply by hiring clinicians without sport or performance-psychology-specific training or credentials. In doing so, teams often conflated *mental health* and *mental performance*, bringing in psychologists and counselors who lacked the specialized competencies, supervision, certifications, and contextual understanding needed to operate effectively in high-performance settings (American Psychological Association, 2019; Lundqvist & Andersen, 2021; Moore et al., 2019).

Meanwhile, some mental skills coaches without clinical training attempted to address deeper mental health concerns with performance tools alone—an equally problematic and potentially unethical practice (Silva et al., 2020). With limited organizational understanding or oversight, clinical models were applied in competitive contexts while performance techniques were misapplied as de facto treatment, eroding trust with coaches, staff, and leadership.

Today, the result is often a fragmented service: mental training has struggled to demonstrate its full organizational impact—not because the science is lacking or the applications aren't effective—but because its delivery has been disjointed or misaligned reactive rather than proactive, integrated, and systemic.

Until recently, most mental training within organizations has been treated as a resource to use primarily when something goes wrong—not as an integral part of performance preparation. As long as it remains reactive rather than embedded, it will continue to underdeliver on its potential—to elevate both individual and team performance while also protecting well-being.

The Training Landscape Is Shifting—and Pressures Are Compounding

When she received her first B– in college, she came into our sport psych offices with swollen eyes and a frantic mind. For days, she'd been drafting the demise of her identity: *"My parents will be devastated. My coaches will be disappointed. My teammates will think I'm dumb."* Her internal working model—stitched together from years of external expectations and internal perfectionistic rules—had already begun to spiral her into a shut down.

Her second line of defense surfaced just as quickly: "This professor is so unfair; how could he be so biased?" In her mind, the pain was being *done to* her, not *experienced by* her.

That's what it looks like when internal coping systems fail—not because someone lacks talent or grit, but because they never developed the scaffolding to navigate the swirl of emotions that setbacks inevitably bring. These situations don't just strain mental health; sustained stress directly undermines performance, recovery, and growth. Over time, a heightened stress response increases vulnerability to injury—further compounding the cycle of pressure and distress (Filaire et al., 2009; Ivarsson et al., 2017).

And today, the competitive environment is only becoming more challenging.

Several forces are converging—and they explain why mental training feels more urgent than ever.

1. *Margins are shrinking—ability is evolving.*

    In elite sport, the difference between competitors is razor thin. More athletes are fast, strong, and explosive. Technical skill, biomechanics, and tactical understanding are being taught at scale, often from earlier developmental ages. The physical ceiling is higher, but the differentiation now lives in the cognitive domain.

2. *Visibility intensifies social pressure.*

    The "fishbowl" effect has gone systemic. Every move is recorded, replayed, and judged. Social media algorithms amplify error and insecurity. Everyone in a performance or leadership space is subject to constant scrutiny. A post, a viral clip, or a review can all be forwarded to thousands within seconds. The external gaze inevitably becomes internalized, driving chronic self-monitoring and threat sensitivity (Nesi et al., 2017; Valkenburg et al., 2022).

3. *Information overload is relentless.*

We all now swim in data: news, stats, medical metrics, social cues, and endless feedback loops. Our minds were not designed to handle this volume. We are assaulted with data from all angles. Without a strong gatekeeper, attention defaults toward emotionally charged or belief-confirming inputs—amplifying reactivity, bias, and cognitive fatigue (Mark et al., 2016; Rosen et al., 2013).

4. *Structured environments replace unstructured growth.*

Childhood, for many, has become increasingly scheduled. More play is adult-directed, coached, and organized. While this shift carries benefits, it also has hidden costs.

Empirical research shows that free play—unstructured, child-led activity—enhances executive function, self-regulation, and emotional flexibility (Barker et al., 2014; Yogman et al., 2018). When structured programs dominate, kids lose opportunities to develop and test ambiguity, self-organize conflict, fail safely, and reset independently. Over time, this minimizes the opportunity to develop healthy scaffolding to manage adversity, improve resilience, and regulate emotions (Burriss and Tsao, 2022; Gray, 2011).

5. *There is a pattern of entitlement, feedback fragility, and the loss of agency.*

Unfortunately, we're seeing this pattern more often. The college athlete who receives a B turns inward, spiraling in a loop of resentment: *"How dare the professor grade like this? He should have offered extra credit. I deserve better."* Instead of running toward the learning, attention runs toward blame and justification. Feedback becomes a threat, rather than a signal.

In many organizations, it looks similar. A seasoned medical director once shared her frustration with a junior staffer who wanted to work in professional sports—but *only if they didn't have to work nights or weekends.* The underlying belief was that fairness should adapt to comfort. That narrative—entitlement mixed with underdeveloped ego strength—weakens internal agency and can fuel anxiety.

The research aligns: high external attribution and perceived unfairness correlate with lower internal locus of control, greater anxiety, and poorer coping under stress (Cheng et al., 2013; Perry et al., 2021; Rotter, 1966). The result isn't empowerment—it's fragility.

The Need for a Cognitive Operating System

Elite teams and organizations are beginning to address the cognitive need. They recognize a pattern—if we want to change outcomes, we must change behaviors—and to sustainably change behaviors, we must change systems.

Not just speeches.

Not just values.

Systems.

This is why athletes, coaches, and leaders are turning to high-performance and organizational psychology—not just for mental-health support (though that matters) and not just for platitudes or motivational "tips and tricks," but for cognitive architecture and organizational design.

They want an integrated, sustainable process—one that can be infused directly into existing player-development systems. They understand that high-functioning professional behaviors aren't innate—they're built through systems that are repeatable, controllable, and trainable.

Research confirms that attentional training can reshape neural networks to support more stable focus, behavioral consistency, and adaptive emotional regulation (Tang et al., 2015).

This is the terrain into which we launch Part II.

The demands are higher. The vulnerabilities are deeper.

In the chapters ahead, we'll introduce the **Intentional Attention Framework**—a structured approach to training the mind's operating system. It's scalable for time-constrained performance environments and integrable within demanding systems. Its aim is to give performers and leaders a foundation of control and agency—so they can move forward, compete, and thrive, not just survive, within the complexity of the modern arena.

Building Intentional Attention: Developing Attentional Management Within the IA Framework

Chapter 7

Introducing the Intentional Attention Framework™

"Give me six hours to chop down a tree and I will spend the first four sharpening the axe."

—Abraham Lincoln

Abraham Lincoln's principle applies as much to the mind as to the blade. The first half of high performance isn't about doing— it's about sharpening. Up to this point, we've uncovered what dulls that edge: the way our minds default under pressure and why instinctual survival strategies, while protective in real danger, can derail us in the performance moments most of us face each day. Now, we turn to the solution—how to sharpen attention deliberately.

Moving to a Solution

Mental skills training has given performers many valuable tools, often with good results. These days there is a developed recognition that mental skills are required for performance success and there's no shortage of strategies aimed at deploying them. But the approach of matching a specific skill to a specific circumstance has a problem in itself.

For the most part, these tools have been treated as isolated tactics rather than an adaptable system. A specific mental skills strategy in a particular moment may work well—but change the circumstance, and it often fails. Moreover, you as a performer may well be at a loss for finding an alternative.

Why Understanding Is Not Enough

I think we'd all agree that simply *understanding* the brain's tendencies is not enough. Declaring, *"Now that I know, I won't do that next time"* is rarely effective. Even adopting popular mantras like *"just be confident"* or *"develop a new mindset"* tends to have sporadic impact. Why? Because we are up against deeply rooted, genetically successful survival tactics—tactics that are nearly impossible to overcome by willpower alone.

Developing an optimal mental game isn't like hitting a light switch. Under acute stress, the brain doesn't respond to slogans—it defaults to what it knows. That's why lasting breakthroughs don't come from quick fixes or motivational mantras. They come from deliberate practice, structure, and repetition over time. Just like strength training, we don't become stronger by lifting once. It can take weeks and months to see significant results. The good news is that we don't have to fight against our wiring—we can work *with* it. By leveraging neuroplasticity and repetition, we can reprogram the attentional system in ways that stick (Jha et al., 2010; Tang et al., 2012).

Not long ago, I worked with a baseball player who had just been called up to the majors—a dream he'd carried since boyhood. He rose fast through the minors, and after dominating at AAA, he suddenly found himself facing big-league pitchers. But like many young players who arrive fast, he didn't have the same volume of at-bats that others had accumulated. The sharpness and deception of major-league pitching exposed that gap immediately. After weeks of success in the minors, he now found himself struggling at the plate.

When we sat down, he told me: "I've lost my confidence. I just need to feel confident again in the box, and everything will take care of itself." He was leaning hard on positive self-talk: reminding himself of how good he was, how hard he'd worked to get here, how he deserved to be in the lineup. And while all of that was true—he was a phenomenal athlete—it wasn't working. In fact, in this case, it may have been making things worse.

Instead of focusing on the ball and executing his plan at the plate, his attention shifted toward chasing the feeling of confidence. Because he loved how it felt to be confident in the batter's box, he convinced himself he couldn't perform until that feeling returned. Confidence had once been a byproduct of his best at-bats. Now it had become the target itself—and his attention had slipped off what mattered most.

The breakthrough came when he realized that he didn't need to feel confident to lock in on the ball. Confidence wasn't the precondition for focus; it was the outcome of sustained attention on the right cue. When he stopped chasing the feeling and started training his attention back onto the ball, his rhythm returned. The lesson was simple but transformative: Confidence comes and goes, but attention is always available.

That distinction—between chasing confidence and training attention—captures the shift this framework is built on.

From Techniques to Architecture: Why Training Needs a Framework

Over the years, mental training has evolved—from proving that thoughts mattered, to teaching discrete mental skills, to embracing mindfulness and acceptance-based work. Each wave added something valuable. But a common thread runs through them all: attention.

Introducing the Intentional Attention Framework™

Every technique requires it, and most breakdowns under pressure trace back to an attention break—the light flickers, shifts, or goes out entirely. Yet, we rarely train performers to keep that light on, to redirect it on command, or to reset it when stress manifests. That is where the Intentional Attention Framework comes into play.

To make change stick, people don't need a longer list of techniques; they need an architecture that organizes and connects them. Frameworks do what the brain loves: simplify complexity into clear pathways and create anchors you can "go to" quickly in the heat of competition (Ericsson et al., 1993).

Think of a skyscraper: We can pour in premium materials all day, but without a strong frame, the building will crumble when the infrastructure is taxed. The same is true of mental performance. Installing new skills without embedding them in an intentional framework invites collapse under stress. In a playoff game, a high-stakes presentation, or a championship putt, there's no time to cobble together strategies. We need a system we can trust—that has been deliberately trained into both conscious and subconscious layers—so high-level focus shows up when the noise is loudest.

This is why we built the Intentional Attention (IA) Framework: a durable architecture that links Awareness, Intention, Execution, Reflection, and Renewal into one organic system. See Figure 7.1.

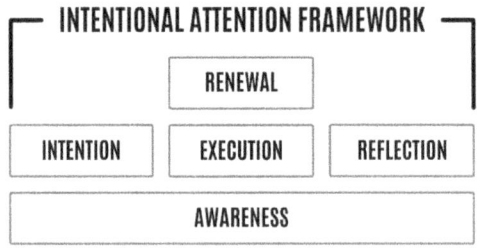

Figure 7.1 The Intentional Attention Framework™.
Source: Justin Anderson.

The IA Framework Model

When we think about attention, it's tempting to picture it as a narrow skill—something we flip on and off. But attention is more like a living system. It has roots, an action zone, and a source of energy. Without all three, it withers.

- **Awareness (Roots):** The foundation. Roots don't produce fruit directly, but they stabilize and feed the system. Awareness functions the same way—anchoring attention by understanding our core attributes and clarifying our attentional patterns, triggers, and tendencies beneath the surface. Without it, the system topples.

- **The Action Zone (Where Performance and Growth Occur):** Intention, Execution, Reflection. These are the core levers of attentional performance—the space in the cycle where targets are set, skills are applied, and experiences are transformed into learning.

- **Renewal (Energy Source):** The sunlight that fuels the system. Without rest, recovery, and energy management, even the deepest roots and strongest trunk eventually burn out.

The IA Framework integrates years of applied lessons and proven methods from elite performers into one practical model for training and managing attention.

A Road Map for What's Ahead

The rest of this book unfolds as a progression through the Intentional Attention Framework—moving from foundations to training, and then into transformation.

Part II: Building Intentional Attention

In the chapters ahead, we'll take the IA Framework one layer at a time, showing how each can be developed, trained, and strengthened. We begin with Awareness—the foundation of everything. Without awareness of identity, values, motivators, fears, and attentional patterns, performers are flying blind. From there, we move into Intention, Attentional Execution, Reflection, and Renewal.

These are the building blocks of a repeatable attentional management system—tools that can be practiced, refined, and relied upon when the pressure to perform is most consequential.

To bring this to life and give readers a feel for how we actually train it, we've included brief reflection prompts and sample exercises—adapted directly from the work we do with athletes, executives, and teams. Think of these as starting points for building a personal practice of attentional management. We've written this part with two types of readers in mind. Some will want to engage with the exercises, using them as a way to begin shaping their own routines and strategies. Others may be more interested in understanding how this kind of training works in practice. We believe both paths are valuable to show what training attention actually looks like in action.

By the end of Part II, readers will not only understand the framework but can also begin to assemble their own attentional playbook—an architecture that can be carried into the environments that matter most.

Part III: Transforming Attention

In Part III, the focus shifts toward integration—bringing all the pieces together to highlight how, when trained and applied, Intentional Attention can be relied upon to transform performance when the stakes are highest. In our work, mastery rarely comes from a single tool or breakthrough. It emerges when skills are woven into routines, layered across environments, and reinforced over time.

This part highlights how many of the world's top performers have built their own "catalog" of attentional strategies—and provides concrete examples that can help anyone build greater consistency in performance over time.

Some have hesitated to put forward a structured model of attention, worrying it might oversimplify something so dynamic. Our perspective is different. A clear framework is not a limitation—it is a guide. It provides enough structure to consistently develop a critical and controllable attribute—attention—while offering the flexibility to adapt to the unpredictable realities of competition, leadership, and life.

By the end of the book, readers will not only understand the IA Framework but will also hold a set of tools to write a personal attentional blueprint—one designed to help individuals, teams, and organizations be better.

Chapter 8

Awareness Is the Foundation: The Personal Attentional Attribute Inventory

"Until you make the unconscious conscious, it will direct your life and you will call it fate."

—Carl Jung

We all want to be "locked in" when it counts. But targeted focus begins long before the opening whistle, the first slide, or the first note. It starts with what we carry into the moment—our beliefs, habits, and hidden scripts—most of it running beneath conscious awareness. If we skip examining these more deeply, we risk building attention on unstable ground. Every mental skill we train and every cue we rely on during performance will falter if it isn't anchored first.

That's why we begin with awareness—specifically targeting a deeper understanding of our core beliefs, values, and scripts. Awareness creates conscious recognition of the attributes that subconsciously shape where our attention drifts and what habits we tend to follow when left undirected. When applied, this awareness can steady the ground beneath us, allowing us to see more clearly the paths we are likely to follow naturally—and whether those paths lead us closer to or further from our goals. With that information, we can choose more clearly where we want to place our focus, how to redirect it, and how to grow from it.

Ultimately, awareness underpins intention and execution. We can set meaningful goals and carry them out with greater efficiency only when we understand what naturally drives us. Awareness is also the foundation of attention itself: Without clarity on what shapes our focus under pressure, attention defaults to fears, biases, or habits (Eysenck et al., 2007). And it is the foundation of efficient growth. Without awareness, we often repeat dysfunctional patterns for days, weeks, or even years—mistaking repetition for preparation.

Therefore, awareness is the first lever in the IA Framework—the starting point for all Intentional Attention training. To make it practical, we will jump to several key attributes that we've found materially influence focus in high-pressure environments.

Core Performance Drivers

When we first start working together, we ask many of our clients to complete a personal inventory as well as meet with us to review their historical performance experiences. It's a structured process to identify the key attributes that influence how their attention operates under pressure. The goal is to efficiently hone-in on performance relevant data that is unique to their personal profile, while also identifying the patterns that will likely pull their focus off course when pressure mounts.

The five key attributes are:

- Identity
- Values
- Personal Biases
- Motivators
- Fears and Insecurities

Each attribute works like a lens, quietly shaping how we interpret situations and dictating where our attention tends to land. Some enhance our focus and others misdirect it, pulling us toward fear, habit, or distraction. In the pages ahead, we'll walk through each attribute—sharing stories from athletes and leaders, the science that explains why it matters, and reflection exercises drawn from our work.

When attention is reactive, it follows old wiring—much of it laid down long before we had any choice in the matter. That wiring, built for protection and energy conservation, served us early on. Yet as demands increase and the stage gets bigger, those same patterns can unintentionally hold us back—reducing cognitive flexibility and making it harder to adjust in real time when the situation demands something different.

I saw this with an NFL player who reached out to me during his second season. His raw talent and competitiveness had carried him to the league, but now opponents had caught up. The film study was deeper, the schemes more complex, and the margin for error thinner. The same intensity and "just go play" mindset that made him successful in college now seemed to work against him—leading to mistakes and mounting frustration. He had reached a new level, but his old operating system was simply outdated for the level of competition he was facing.

This appears to be the truth about advancement in any field: The thinking and behaviors that get us to one level rarely are the ones that carry us to the next. Each new stage demands an internal upgrade. But before we can upgrade, we need to have a clear sense of what we're starting with. We need to clearly understand our personal attributes and how they impact our performance. Conducting what we call the Personal Attentional Attribute Inventory helps us to do just that.

Attribute 1: Identity

Who we think we are shapes what we notice.

We begin with **Identity**. Who we believe we are—and just as importantly, who we believe we are not—subtly shapes what we notice, what we ignore, and how we respond under pressure. A narrow or singular identity can limit growth. It shrinks the field of attention, making us blind to new possibilities or alternative ways forward. A broader, more flexible identity does the opposite—it fuels adaptability and resilience (Brewer et al., 1993; Erikson, 1968).

Much like palm trees that bend and sway through tropical storms that would uproot rigid but mighty oaks, flexibility under pressure creates sustainable strength. Adaptability is what gives the palm tree its resilience, just as adaptability can give our identity its stability. That's why palms thrive along the coasts while most oaks remain inland. If identity is defined only as "I'm a great football player," it becomes fragile if the production isn't there. But if our identity expands to "I'm a great football player, and I'm also someone who grows, learns, and adapts," the foundation becomes broader and more adaptable—enabling performers to rely on their strengths, navigate adversity, and produce steadier, more consistent results. Expanding identity allows us to stretch further, grow deeper, and better withstand the storms that inevitably come.

Before diving into the pitfalls of identity working against us, it's worth grounding ourselves in its positive side. One of the most stabilizing forces in performance is remembering that we are more than any singular role we play.

When we ask clients to identify their core identities, we rarely begin with titles or job descriptions. Instead, we start with the basics: parent, friend, sibling, daughter, son, mentor, learner. These foundations existed long before jerseys, job titles, or stat lines. When people reconnect with them, their attention shifts. They realize their worth isn't confined to the scoreboard, the quarterly report, or the spotlight.

Many athletes we've worked with believed early on that they needed a singular identity—that they had to be only *the athlete* because anything else might detract from achieving their goals. I've often heard: *"I don't want another identity or a Plan B, because it will take away from Plan A."* But athletes who only see themselves as "the swimmer" or "the quarterback" often ride an emotional roller coaster—euphoric when things go well, devastated when they don't.

The Olympic Athlete: Just a Swimmer

A swimmer we worked with carried the weight of an identity defined as being "just a swimmer." Every race was all-or-nothing, as if her entire existence depended on the end result. It wasn't until she embraced her other roles—teammate, daughter, artist—that her attention expanded and her racing loosened up (Brewer et al., 1993). She swam faster not because she cared less, but because she cared differently. Her identity became bigger than the pool, and her attention—and consequently her performance—followed.

When identity narrows to the outcomes of a single role, consistency often suffers. The subconscious treats setbacks as survival threats. Recall the NBA player from the Introduction: His entire existence was wrapped up in being "the basketball player." Every missed shot or poor game wasn't just about performance—it felt like an attack on who he was at his core. And as we've seen, the subconscious is more butcher than surgeon when it comes to perceived attacks. It overprotects. Instead of making small adjustments, it swings wildly to shield us from pain, pulling attention toward fear, doubt, or withdrawal. *If I can't be a basketball player, then who am I?* To the subconscious, that question feels like extinction—and it reacts accordingly.

Expanding identity gives us room to maneuver. If one role falters, others remain to anchor us, and the subconscious believes we can survive even if we fail in this one task. This is why identity expansion is critical for sustainable Intentional Attention: It frees us from constantly battling the threat response that low points tend to deliver. That steadiness shows up as resilience.

A setback in one identity doesn't erase our worth; it simply becomes part of a bigger whole. People who embrace multiple identities are often the steadiest under pressure. They know that a stumble doesn't erase them. They also recognize that growth doesn't happen in a straight upward line—it looks more like a stock market chart: full of ups and downs but advancing over time.

The Business Leader: Defined by Success

We once worked with a business leader whose entire sense of worth was tied to her division's success. When her business unit didn't perform as well as another within the company, her confidence shrank. Her attention was constantly caught in a compare-despair spiral—watching what other division leaders were doing and magnifying what her own staff wasn't doing. Instead of focusing on balanced problem-solving, she became quick to point out shortcomings, frustrated that her team wasn't measuring up.

Much of this stemmed from her identity being significantly over-indexed into her job. Because her identity was so tightly tied to performance, every downturn felt like a personal failure. And as often happens, her subconscious acted like the butcher, not the surgeon—overprotecting by pushing her attention toward emotion, comparison, and frustration instead of clarity.

When we explored it through the IA Framework, she reconnected with other identities she had undervalued: mentor, problem-solver, learner. When she leaned into being a mentor, her perspective on her staff shifted—instead of judging them against others, she began investing in their growth. When she embraced her identity as a problem-solver, she shifted from ruminating on outcomes to engaging in solutions.

That reframing steadied her. Her attention shifted from the insecurity of "I'm failing as a leader" to the opportunity of "I can lead us through this." Her division eventually turned the corner, but the bigger change was how she showed up: steadier, more emotionally balanced, and increasingly respected by her team. By broadening her identity, she not only improved outcomes but also grew her credibility as a leader worth following.

That's the performance advantage of multiple identities: they transform pressure from a threat into a challenge. They don't erase the stakes, but they steady the hands on the attentional steering wheel. One way we can strengthen this performance advantage is to intentionally expand one's own identity using a tool we call an identity map.

Exercise: Expanding Your Identity Map

Step 1: Write down your primary performance role (athlete, leader, coach, parent, etc.) in the center of a page.

Step 2: Around it, list at least five other roles or identities you hold outside of that role (for example, parent, sibling, friend, mentor, learner, artist, adventurer, community member).

Step 3: For each identity, jot down one way that it positively influences your performance.

- Example: "Being a parent strengthens my patience."

- Example: "Being a friend reminds me I don't need to be perfect to be valued."

Reflection Prompts

1. Which identities have you underappreciated or forgotten?

2. How might these identities help steady you when performance pressure rises?

3. Which identity do you want to lean on more intentionally in your next high-stakes moment?

Exercise: The "Get To" Reappraisal

Expanding identities also helps shift the mindset from needing to perform (identity under threat) to getting to perform (identity as opportunity).

> **Step 1:** Write down a high-pressure situation you're preparing for.
>
> **Step 2:** Next to it, finish this sentence from three different identities you hold:
>
> - As a parent/friend/mentor, I get to . . .
> - As a learner/problem-solver/teammate, I get to . . .
> - As a [performance role], I get to . . .

Reflection Prompts

1. How does the "get to" attentional perspective change how you feel about the moment?
2. Which identity do you most want to bring with you into that performance?
3. If the performance doesn't go well, which identities will remain untouched and still matter most?

The Division I Golfer: The 70-Shot Barrier

Of course, identity doesn't always serve us. Just as powerful as the stabilizing effect of multiple identities is the destabilizing effect of a narrow or negative one.

We were working with a talented Division I golfer who, in practice rounds, could hit shots like no one else on his team. Yet when it came to collegiate matches, he couldn't break 70. Over and over, he'd play himself into position for a final score in the 60s, only to watch it slip away in the last few holes—bogeys, even double bogeys, down the stretch.

It wasn't for lack of effort. He'd been through mental skills training before: breathing strategies, visualization, pre-shot routines. He applied them with discipline. But no matter how much we fine-tuned the skills, they didn't have the pull to change the outcome. Something deeper was running the show.

Through the IA Awareness framework, he discovered it. As we worked through the Identity section, he named an internal belief that had been imperceptibly guiding his attention: *"I'm the guy things go well for at first, but they never last."* That belief was not random—it traced back to a formative event at age 13 when he lost a junior tournament after holding a four-stroke lead. What he had dismissed as a disappointing afternoon had, without his realizing it, become part of his identity.

He was surprised by how deeply that single event had embedded itself. It wasn't just a memory—it had become a "failure script" that his subconscious replayed in the background, almost as a form of protection: *Prepare yourself to fall short so it won't hurt as much when it happens.* Of course, that protective script became a self-fulfilling prophecy. His attention, locked onto the familiar pattern, began scanning for signs it was about to happen again . . . and found them.

Once he named it, everything shifted. He could see the script for what it was—just another distraction, a past event that, while disappointing, didn't define who he was and certainly who he planned to become. In his case, the distraction was a deep-rooted subconscious one, disguised as a safety net. From there, we could work on treating it like any other irrelevant performance data. As later chapters will explore, he began building a plan for what to do in those late-round moments when his attention started listening to the failure script.

By recognizing it, he could redirect it—and eventually, he indeed was able to break the 70-shot barrier.

The Impact Timeline: Making the Invisible Visible

In our work with athletes and leaders, we often use a tool called the Impact Timeline—usually in immersive retreat settings where there's enough space to slow down and reflect. The exercise is simple but powerful: We ask individuals to walk back through their life, from earliest memory to present day, and write down any moment that carried an emotional charge.

The exercise has positive experiences listed on the right and negative experiences listed on the left, creating a T-shaped chart. We separate early childhood, childhood, teenage, early adult, and adult stages.

What unfolds is often unexpected. People begin to see patterns they've never noticed. A "throwaway" moment from age 12 suddenly explains why they shut down in team meetings. A victory that felt small at the time reveals itself as a lasting anchor of confidence. These discoveries don't just tell stories—they uncover the scripts that have been shaping identity and attention all along.

Exercise: Identity Inventory

Note: If you've experienced trauma in the past, consider consulting a mental health provider before beginning this exercise. Reflecting on past experiences can sometimes stir up strong emotions or symptoms that may be difficult to manage. Proceed with care.

Step 1: Using the Impact Timeline, write down moments from your life—in both performance and personal contexts—that carried a strong emotional charge. Include both the positive (joy, pride, accomplishment) and the negative (shame, embarrassment, sadness).

Step 2: Organize them by life stage: early childhood, childhood, preteen, teenage, early adult, adult, etc. List positive experiences on the right and negative experiences on the left.

Reflection Prompts

1. Which events on your negative list do you feel still influence how you see yourself today?

2. What personal "scripts" or identities might have formed from these moments?

3. Are there positive events you've underappreciated that could serve as anchors for confidence or direction?

4. Which scripts serve you, and which might be holding you back at your current "level" of performance?

Attribute 2: Values

What we believe guides where we look, and where we look guides what we believe.

The next step we often recommend in building a Personal Attentional Attribute Inventory is reflecting on what seems to really matter to us: values. Values, of course, can range from deeply held religious or political beliefs to more immediate views of what's important. Most of the values we see impacting performance are the more immediate ones. When the moment gets chaotic, values act like an internal compass. They're not usually about winning or losing— most often they're about how we want to show up. They function like actionable "themes" for behavior. Those values shape the lens we use to interpret stress. They don't erase pressure, but they

75

provide a stable reference point when circumstances threaten to hijack attention.

The NFL Quarterback: Values Reset

Late in the season, a divisional matchup with playoff implications loomed. The stadium noise was deafening, the media had spent all week questioning his poise, and he could feel the weight of the moment settling in his chest. In the past, these conditions had pulled his mind toward proving himself—obsessing over stat lines, ownership reactions, or what the postgame headlines might say, along with the flip side of what might happen if he didn't produce.

This season was different. He had started working on strengthening his mindset with us during the offseason. We guided him through a values exercise and emphasized how important it was to anchor both his behaviors and his attention to what he valued most in his performance. I asked him to reflect on what mattered to him and what he admired in other quarterbacks he respected. He came back with three things: their **hard work**, **eye discipline** (getting his eyes across his progressions quickly), and the way they **attack**.

That last one, he said, came from a Rich Gannon (a former NFL MVP) quote he had read over the summer: *"There are two types of quarterbacks in this league—the ones who feel the pressure and the others who apply the pressure."* Given how often attention drifts toward fear and distraction, the quote hit him hard. It became an anchor for how he wanted to compete.

From this, he started to incorporate these simple phrases and wrote them in block letters on the first page of his notebook, which he used daily to learn the playbook and prepare each week: **Prepared and Present. Eye Discipline. Attack.** These weren't motivational slogans; they were performance standards designed to direct his attention.

Intentional Attention

1. **Prepared and Present:** Trust his preparation and place his attention fully in the moment.

2. **Disciplined:** "The ball will go where the eyes go"; moving quickly through keys/progression allows for more decisive decision-making.

3. **Attack:** Let the defense react to him instead of always feeling on his heels.

The cool thing about these values was that they were largely controllable. They could be lived no matter the score, the last play, or the game's circumstances. And they gave his attention something firm to return to—a way through the chaos that gave him the best chance to compete up to his physical potential.

He visualized these values in pregame prep routines throughout the week, reminding himself of them anytime his attention drifted. He rehearsed them in weekly team sessions so they became second nature. By the time he stepped into the huddle, the external noise had been reduced to background static. When the defense brought unexpected pressure, he didn't panic. He stayed disciplined, trusted what his eyes showed him, and attacked. And when adversity hit— like when a receiver dropped a sure touchdown—he didn't spiral. His values gave him a compass to guide his attention back to what mattered most, even in the middle of chaos.

The Entrepreneur: Getting Out of a Downward Spiral

We were working with an entrepreneur who was expanding her accounting practice. She was hiring a lot of younger professionals to keep costs lower while she grew. In practice, though, that meant she was doing most of the heavy lifting. In the middle of serving her key clients, she also had to secure new business to sustain the growth she wanted and support the junior professionals she had just brought on.

When she came to me, she shared that she had been in a very frustrating space for quite some time. She was working 70–80 hours a week, which was taking a toll on her health, her relationships, and her ability to be the kind of parent she wanted to be. She felt stuck. She wanted to build so that she could ultimately have more time for family, friends, and even a few hobbies she had always dreamed of. But the paradox was maddening: the more she built, the more work landed on her plate.

"How can this be?" she told me. "These younger employees don't want to work. I come back from days on the road with clients, and the office is a mess. The coffee station isn't stocked; the conference room isn't clean. I'm paying them good money, and they have such opportunity here if they would just lean in. Instead of preparing for a critical client meeting, I'm the one cleaning, setting up, and then delivering the service. And my staff looks at me like I'm crazy for working this hard."

Eventually, she hit her breaking point. She began to lose her temper with her staff, labeling them as lazy, entitled, and ungrateful. Her attention was consumed by frustration and comparison—focusing on what she didn't have rather than the leader she wanted to be. Of course, this had a negative impact on her team. Several left her firm, and others talked negatively in the community. She knew that her responses were detrimental to her goals, but she didn't know how to get out of the spiral.

One of the first things we did was walk her through the same values reflection exercise we had used with athletes. The question was simple: What's most important for you to be as a leader? And what do other leaders you've respected value the most? Reflect on this for a while and come back with at least three important values.

She came back with three answers: **mentor**, **builder**, and **joyful**.

From there, she defined those values with controllable performance standards—much like the quarterback had done with his notebook.

1. **Mentor:** Invest in the growth of our young staff, even when it's easier to just do the work myself.

2. **Builder:** Keep my attention on creating systems and practices that we can scale, not just patching the momentary holes.

3. **Joyful:** Set my intention each day to look for and nurture things that bring energy and optimism; model to my team that even while carrying significantly more responsibilities, I can find moments of appreciation and enjoyment. By focusing on joy, I'll recharge and have more energy to deal with the inevitable challenges.

Those values became her compass. Instead of spending her mornings frustrated about small office details, she started scheduling short development meetings with her staff, teaching them how to prepare the space and handle client transitions. Instead of cleaning the coffee station herself, she delegated it as part of a "client readiness" checklist her team co-created. She approached these adjustments proactively, with a building perspective, instead of the negative or passive-aggressive tone she had been using before.

Her attention shifted from anger to alignment. Instead of ruminating on "Why don't they care as much as I do?" she began asking, "How can I mentor them to see the fruits of hard work?" Instead of pushing herself into exhaustion, she began guarding time for her family—because being joyful meant showing up with presence and perspective.

From this foundational work, she reported to us years later that her practice had grown significantly, but more importantly, her leadership steadied and her enjoyment returned. The same workload that once left her angry and overwhelmed now felt purposeful because her attention was anchored to her values.

Exercise: Values Clarification

Step 1: Identify three values that matter most to you under pressure—not outcomes, but how you want to show up.

Step 2: For each value, define at least one controllable behavior or standard (something you can do regardless of score, client reactions, or circumstances).

Reflection Prompts

1. What qualities do I want others to consistently feel from me under pressure?

2. When have I been proud, not because of the outcome, but because of how I lived my values?

3. Complete the sentence: "In moments of pressure, I want to be the kind of person who _____."

Attribute 3: Personal Biases

"We don't see things as they are. We see them as we are."

—Anaïs Nin

The next personal inventory area we often recommend performers address to build their foundation is identifying significant personal biases. Every one of us carries biases. They are shortcuts the brain uses to interpret the world—filters shaped by the experiences we've lived, the people who've influenced us, and the cultures we've grown up in. These filters are not inherently bad. They often form from real experiences. They can help us. And they can also limit us. The danger is when we don't know they're there. Without awareness, we often don't realize how they impact us. That's why personal bias is one of the most important building blocks in the IA Awareness phase of the Intentional Attention Framework. If we want to train our attention with intention, we have to understand what it's already reacting to.

Biases are invisible filters that quietly influence where our attention goes, and sometimes that can be detrimental to our goals. Instead of us steering attention, the bias steers us. Biases don't just influence decisions—they often direct our attention before we even realize it. That's what makes them so powerful. Therefore, if we want to train our attention with intention, we have to understand what it's already reacting to.

The NBA Athlete: Experience-Driven Bias

An NBA player we worked with was a force of nature when he played loose—attacking the rim, leading fast breaks, lifting his teammates. But after a few standout games, his performance would often dip. Coaches became frustrated, and he couldn't put a finger on why he was so inconsistent. What was consistent was his pattern: The higher the praise, the more tentative he became—until he was nearly losing his coaches' and teammates' confidence. Then he'd flash games of incredible talent again, leaving everyone in the organization asking, "Where did that come from?" He had the ability to be a starter in the league, but his inconsistency eventually cost him meaningful minutes.

After working together for some time, we were able to move past surface-level mental-skill adjustments and dig into the deeper root.

We discovered a personal bias shaped by grief. His father, who had passed away years earlier, had been his biggest supporter. To simplify a very complex mixture of emotions: Somewhere deep down, success triggered a fear that he couldn't live up to his father's memory. The more he succeeded, the more pressure he felt to make his dad proud. His subconscious started filtering for data that made "falling short" easier to justify: *If I don't climb too high, I won't fall too far.* This bias shifted his attention toward mistakes and deficits instead of opportunities.

Once he named this bias, he was able to identify behaviors and attentional cues that countered it. He reframed the connection: playing aggressively wasn't a risk to his father's opinion of him—it was a tribute to it. By pairing that reframing with in-game reset cues, he began practicing those pairings consistently. Unfortunately, in the harsh reality of the league, he had already lost the trust of his current team, and other organizations weren't willing to take a chance when younger, cheaper players were available. These short runways are one reason we hope to get this information out to performers earlier in their careers. If he had discovered this sooner, he may have had a longer career in the NBA. So many young athletes believe they'll have years to figure themselves out, but in reality, they often have less than two years to prove they can compete consistently at the highest levels.

The Business Leader: A Different Experience-Driven Bias

These types of experience-driven biases happen with all of us, yet many rarely stop to reflect on what may be contributing to behaviors we find limiting. One senior executive of a large family-owned business shared that he tended to avoid speaking in high-level meetings or in front of large groups. He had no problem speaking in smaller circles or managing his team, but when he advanced into senior leadership and was in the room with the Founder, the President, and other executives, he often remained silent. It wasn't that he lacked ideas or opinions—he had plenty. But something about those high-authority settings left him hesitant.

After reflection, he traced the hesitation back to an experience when he was 12 years old. His teacher had been trying to demonstrate the power of social influence. The teacher asked him to wait in the hallway while the class was instructed to answer a simple question incorrectly: "Which line is longer, A or B?" The longer line was clearly B, but the teacher instructed the class to raise their hand for A. When the boy walked back in, the teacher repeated the question, and the entire class raised their hands for A. The boy thought he had misheard, but feeling uncertain, he raised his hand for A as well. The teacher used the moment to make a point to the class, but for the boy, it triggered deep embarrassment and shame. He never forgot the sting of that moment and how foolish he felt in front of his classmates. That single experience quietly created a strong bias: directing his attention to the risk of being embarrassed rather than the opportunity to contribute. Decades later, that bias still shaped his participation in executive meetings.

When he finally recognized this as a bias—not an objective truth—we worked on gradually re-engaging in low-risk settings, pairing each contribution with a specific message he wanted to land. Over time, awareness loosened the old narrative's grip, and his voice became a steady presence in the company's most important conversations.

Attentional Biases Are Real

In working with high performers, we've observed a range of attentional bias "filters" that show up consistently and effect performance:

- **Confirmation Bias:** We notice what confirms our existing beliefs—especially about ourselves (Nickerson, 1998).

- **Negativity Bias:** Our brains prioritize negative information over positive (Baumeister et al., 2001a).

- **Social Evaluation Bias:** We over-focus on how others perceive us, especially in status-driven environments (Dickerson & Kemeny, 2004).

- **Cultural and Familial Scripts:** We carry inherited beliefs about performance, leadership, gender roles, and emotional expression.

These biases are features—designed by evolution or experience to help us survive. But when they operate below the surface, they can subconsciously redirect our attention away from the precise goal we're trying to accomplish.

The takeaway is that biases can't be eliminated—but if we can identify those that impact our goals, they can be managed. Awareness turns them from invisible distractions into visible data. And once they're conscious, we can intentionally choose where to direct our attention instead of letting the bias choose it for us.

By becoming aware of the lenses we're looking through, we give ourselves the freedom to see more clearly. Not to erase our past—but to understand it well enough to move forward with intention.

Exercise: Bias Awareness Reflection

1. Go back to your Impact Timeline exercise provided in the Identity section of this chapter and reflect on the moments from your life—big or small—that still carry emotional weight.

2. For each, ask: "What belief about myself or others came from this experience?"

3. Ask yourself: "How do I carry this experience today?"

4. Does this experience impact how you think or react to similar situations that you experience today?

5. Do you notice patterns in what catches your attention based on this experience (pay particular attention to experiences that were embarrassing, you experienced loss, regret, or you felt shame)? How do those experiences impact your thoughts or beliefs today?

6. Then take it one step further: "How do these experiences, and the bias they created, pull my attention away from my current goals?"

7. What would it look like to redirect it back toward performance-relevant information that you can control and will lead you to achieving your goals?

Attribute 4: Motivators

"Sometimes, you need to do the things you don't want to do, to do the things you do want to do."

—Jon Gruden

If identity answers, *"Who am I?"* and values answer *"How do I want to show up?"* then motivators answer, *"Why am I doing this in the first place?"* They are the fuel for our attention—whether intrinsic (curiosity, growth, mastery, love of the game), extrinsic (money, recognition, approval, contracts), or self-transcendent (a purpose that serves something larger than ourselves).

Intrinsic Versus Extrinsic Motivation: What the Research Tells Us

Psychologists Edward Deci and Richard Ryan developed Self-Determination Theory in the 1980s, which has become one of the most influential frameworks for understanding human motivation. At its core, the theory suggests that human beings are most likely to thrive when three basic psychological needs are supported: autonomy (a sense of choice and ownership), competence (a sense of mastery and effectiveness), and relatedness (a sense of connection and belonging) (Deci & Ryan, 2000; Ryan & Deci, 2005). When these needs are met, motivation becomes more stable, internal, and sustainable—less dependent on external conditions and more rooted in personal meaning. This is where intrinsic motivators—curiosity, growth, mastery—become so powerful. They tend to anchor attention inward, toward learning, execution, and process. In contrast, extrinsic motivators—rewards, approval, contracts, recognition—can be highly effective in elite performance environments, but they may also pull attention outward toward evaluation, comparison, and outcome monitoring (Cerasoli et al., 2014). Under pressure, that outward shift matters. Attention drifts from what we can control to what we hope others will think.

But extrinsic motivators aren't the enemy. In fact, they can fuel effort in high-stakes environments (Cerasoli et al., 2014). The key is not to reject extrinsic motivation. Money and achievements matter—to both the athlete and those they care for. We often encourage athletes to acknowledge the importance of these external motivators. In many cases, extrinsic motivation helps define the destination—a Super Bowl win, an Olympic medal, an eight-figure contract.

The challenge is that focusing too much on the destination during performance can be detrimental. Outcomes are seductive, especially when the entire world is directing its attention to them. We often remind athletes that because nearly everyone else is focused on the outcome, they need to be even more disciplined in holding their attention on the process.

What sustains performance in the moment is attention to the journey—the daily controllables, the process, the small choices that compound. Those who anchor their attention there tend to feel less threatened, enjoy the journey more, and grow through the process regardless of the outcome. Many come to realize that even if they don't ultimately reach the destination, they've gained so much along the way that they will be okay. That realization is freeing—and it leads to better performance in the moment.

The key is awareness: knowing when to focus on each type of motivator. Used wisely, extrinsic motivators set direction. Intrinsic motivators provide daily fuel. Together, they not only help us determine where we want to go but ensure we don't lose sight of the details that make us capable of getting there.

The NFL Kicker: Intrinsic and Extrinsic Motivators Shift

We worked with an NFL kicker who, as a teenager, loved nothing more than seeing how far he could kick a football. The joy came from growth—watching the ball sail farther and straighter each season. When he helped his high school and college teams win games with last-minute field goals, those were some of the most joyous moments of his career. But once he began earning a paycheck in the NFL, his motivation shifted. Now it was about the next contract, his coaches' approval, and the outcomes of each performance. Anxiety followed, and inconsistency crept in.

Through awareness work, he realized that while extrinsic motivators mattered, they couldn't be where he anchored his attention. Returning to the intrinsic motivators of precision and growth steadied both his attention and consequently, his performance.

Transcendent Motivators: Doing What Is Worthwhile Turns Out to Be Effective

"He who has a why to live can bear almost any how."
—Friedrich Nietzsche

Another level of motivation we often introduce to leaders and performers is self-transcendence motivation. Abraham Maslow, one of the most influential psychologists of the 20th century, is best known for his *hierarchy of needs*. He argued that humans are first driven by physiological and safety needs, then by belonging, esteem, and self-actualization. His model reflects what we outlined in earlier chapters—and what performers often feel under pressure: Attention first pulls toward survival and protection. Only once those needs are stabilized can attention expand to growth.

Late in his career, Maslow proposed a stage beyond self-actualization: self-transcendence (Maslow, 1969). Here, individuals find fulfillment not in personal achievement alone, but in serving causes greater than themselves. This idea parallels the writings of Viktor Frankl, a psychiatrist and Holocaust survivor, who argued in *Man's Search for Meaning* (1946/2006) that purpose and meaning—often found in service to others—are what allow humans to endure suffering.

This concept is especially relevant for today's performers. Life isn't always pleasant or easy. Many of us are grinding—doing difficult things not because they bring happiness, but because we feel compelled to. Yet when that effort is tied to something larger than ourselves—our children's future, our family's security, our community's well-being—it shifts our attention. Instead of fixating on what hurts about the present struggle, attention re-anchors to what the effort will provide. Self-transcendence is motivation anchored in meaning. It's the recognition that *why* we act often matters more than how it feels in the moment.

Research supports this. Frank Martela and Michael Steger (2016) found that prosocial, self-transcendent motives predicted greater perseverance and well-being than either intrinsic or extrinsic motives alone. When tasks are framed as serving others or advancing a larger purpose, people endure longer and perform better—even under discomfort.

Intentional Attention

Self-transcendent motivation continuously directs attention away from fear, fatigue, and self-doubt, and toward contribution and purpose. It helps performers reframe pressure moments not as threats to self, but as opportunities to serve something bigger. That attentional shift is often the difference between collapsing under stress and finding another gear.

A Broader Lens on Worthwhileness

Philosopher Sebastian Purcell captures this powerfully in his essay *"What the Aztecs Can Teach Us About Happiness and the Good Life"* (Purcell, 2018). He wrote that each semester, he asks his students two questions:

1. *"How many of you want to be happy in life?"* Every hand goes up.
2. *"How many of you plan to have children?"* Nearly every hand stays up.

Then he pauses and says, half-coy and half-serious: *"Wait, I thought you said you wanted to be happy?"*

Next, he presents the evidence: Research shows that having children decreases day-to-day happiness for most people, with consistent joy only returning after the last child leaves home. Then he asks again: *"How many of you still want children?"*—and the same hands rise.

His students reveal something the Aztecs knew centuries ago: We don't organize our lives around happiness. We organize them around worthwhileness. And if that's true, then attention must be redirected as well.

Purcell shared that the Aztecs called this *neltiliztli*—a "rooted" life. Not a life of constant joy or comfort, but one anchored in what is worthwhile: body, character, balance, community. The Earth, they said, is "slippery, slick"—a place of constant difficulty. The good life wasn't about avoiding hardship, but about rooting ourselves in what truly matters so we could withstand it.

This kind of thinking is an attentional guide. When we expect adversity and don't equate failure with erasure of identity, attention can be more quickly redirected to what matters most—the act of standing back up, of learning, of responding to setbacks with growth.

Self-transcendence is the modern echo of *neltiliztli*. When our motivator is to live a rooted, worthwhile life—whether that's raising children, contributing to a team, or playing a game for something larger than ourselves—our attention shifts. We don't perform because it feels good. We perform because it *is* good. And when we act in service of that larger good, the brain often rewards us with a reinforcing sense of meaning and vitality that sustains behavior over time.

The Uncertain NFL Quarterback

We worked with an NFL quarterback who admitted that much of his preseason anxiety came from uncertainty about being named the starter. As the weeks went on, his attention increasingly locked on the body language of teammates and coaches. "I'd be lying if I said it didn't affect me," he shared. "When I see receivers frustrated after a play, or a coach shaking his head, it impacts my confidence and my belief that they have my back."

When I asked what happened to his attention in those moments, he was honest: "I withdraw. I get quieter. My body language drops. My head goes down." This was his brain's natural survival response—attention gravitating toward what he lacked, what he had failed to do, and what that might mean for his future. None of those questions led his attention anywhere constructive for the next series or the next snap.

We reframed the challenge. If he expected those reactions—just as the Aztecs expected life to be "slippery and slick"—could he prepare his attention to respond differently? Instead of asking *What does their frustration mean about me?* we explored a more transcendent question: *How can I serve my teammates right now?*

He began experimenting with this shift. After a mistake, rather than retreating inward, he looked for ways to pour into those around him—finding a teammate to encourage, offering a fist bump, or picking someone else up with a quick word of support. His attention moved from fear of rejection to intentional acts of leadership. Not only did it lift his own confidence, but teammates noticed. Coaches noticed. His credibility as a leader grew 10-fold. This was someone people could count on. He wasn't lost in his own stuff, he was picking others up constantly, even when he was facing some adversity.

That shift—anchoring attention not in outcome or approval, but in the purpose of being a great teammate—was self-transcendence in action. It transformed mistakes from identity threats into opportunities to reinforce trust. And it showed him that when leaders transcend the self, they don't just steady their own attention—they steady everyone else's too.

The Nonprofit Director: A Change in Perspective

A nonprofit director once described fundraising as the part of the job she dreaded most. Cold calls, rejections, endless proposals—it all felt draining, and her attention locked on how unpleasant it was. The more she focused on the grind, the heavier it became.

But over time, she reappraised her motivation. Each ask wasn't just about dollars—it was about creating opportunities for the kids in her community who otherwise wouldn't have them. When she began to tie her effort to that larger purpose, her attention shifted. The fatigue didn't disappear, but it stopped being the center of her focus. What replaced it was the worthwhileness of the mission.

That shift made her more resilient. Rejection still stung, but it no longer defined her energy or her self-worth. Her attention now returned more quickly to the next conversation, the next opportunity to make a difference. As she put it, *"I stopped hearing no as a failure. I started hearing it as one step closer to a yes for the kids we serve."* The change didn't just improve her mindset—it improved her results.

Why Motivation Matters for Attention

Motivation is the engine that drives our attention. Extrinsic motivators set the destination. Intrinsic motivators provide the attentional cues that sustain our process and keep us on an efficient path toward our goals. And self-transcendent motivators—those anchored in worthwhileness—root attention in resilience.

That way, when setbacks come—and they inevitably will if we're pursuing something great—we don't ask "What's wrong with me?" or "Why bother?" We already know why. We know what deserves our attention and what doesn't. And that our "why" is bigger than us.

Exercise: Surfacing Self-Transcendent Motivators

Take a few minutes to consider these prompts:

1. Recall a time when you endured something difficult. What allowed you to keep going—was it for yourself, or for someone or something beyond you?

2. List three roles you play that matter beyond personal gain. (For example: parent, mentor, teammate, citizen.) How do these roles give you a sense of contribution?

3. Imagine your life at age 80. People are celebrating you. What do you hope they say you stood for? What felt most worthwhile about how you lived and worked?

4. Complete this sentence: "Even if it's hard, I will give my attention to this because _____."

These questions aren't about happiness or reward. They're about rooting your attention in what makes the struggle worthwhile.

Attribute 5: Fears and Insecurities

"The cave you fear to enter holds the treasure you seek."

—Joseph Campbell

Alas, we must follow the uplifting transcendent motivators discussion with a rather extended discussion of the other side of the coin, so to speak. That discussion affords us the opportunity to begin to see directly how awareness leads to successful attention management. This final layer of our core awareness profile is fears and insecurities. We've included this section because no performer is immune to them. We all carry fears and insecurities, and when they're triggered, they often flip our personal threat-response cycle to the full-on position.

In sport—and in many high-performance organizations—the conversation about fear is often the one people avoid most. When we were asked to lead a training for a large group of senior leaders at a major financial institution, I suggested we spend some time exploring fear—what it looks like, how it influences decision-making, and how awareness of it might sharpen leadership. The person coordinating the session paused and said, *"No, I don't think that would go well with this group. I've brought up the idea of doing more reflection on fear before, and the response was, 'We're not afraid of anything.'"*

His tone wasn't defensive as much as certain—strong, declarative, absolute. It reminded me of what I've seen across countless professional sport organizations: strength projected so completely that it crowds out self-awareness and obscures reality.

This kind of over-certainty can feel like confidence, but it often conceals unexamined fear. In performance settings, that defensiveness quietly handcuffs growth. For athletes, it can create a hypersensitivity to anything that might expose their fears—failure, letting others down, mistakes, or looking foolish. That vigilance can fuel judgmental self-talk and overanalysis in the very moments that demand clarity. In leadership, it can create significant blind spots in decision-making, leading to reactive choices, emotional contagion, and, at its worst, reckless leadership disguised as conviction.

The paradox is that fear denied becomes the most powerful form of fear—it runs the system subconsciously from the background. The best way to manage it is to name it, understand what it is and what it isn't, and face it directly so we can make choices grounded in our truth. Everyone has fears. Everyone has insecurities. If someone insists they don't, it usually means they haven't yet done the deeper intentional work.

That's why becoming aware of these triggers is critical. If we can predict where our fears will try to send our attention, we can plan in advance where we want it to go instead. Without awareness, fear steers attention automatically. With awareness, we regain the option of choice.

Fear and Insecurity Narrow Focus

Our fears and insecurities narrow our attentional options. They're designed to. The amygdala prioritizes survival over performance, scanning for danger long before it considers goals. For most of human history, missing a threat could mean death.

In today's performance arenas, as we noted earlier, that same wiring works against us. Attention drifts toward hazards, judgment, insecurities, and imagined failure. The brain doesn't distinguish between a charging bear and the fear of embarrassment in a classroom. Both trigger the same alarm system. And that alarm is efficient. If there's a bear and a pizza in the room, we won't notice the pizza no matter how hungry we are.

The problem isn't that fear or insecurity shows up. It's that our attention treats them as more relevant than our goals. Left unchecked, the subconscious hands fear the steering wheel—and performance follows whoever decides to drive.

The Neurobiology of Attentional Hijacking

It may be helpful here to review what we discussed in Part I: the human brain is wired for survival, not performance. When the amygdala detects a threat, it triggers a cascade: Cortisol and adrenaline flood the body, sharpening vigilance and narrowing focus. That helps in the wild. But in modern contexts—a free throw, a sales call, an audition—it hijacks attention away from what's performance-relevant and toward threat monitoring.

The prefrontal cortex, which handles decision-making and logic, loses access. Our system prioritizes protection over execution. Under pressure, attention defaults to the most emotionally charged variable in the room. Awareness gives us the chance to see that hijack happening and redirect before it takes over.

The Collegiate Golfer: Awareness of Threat Leads to "Managed" Attention

A collegiate golfer entered the Big Ten Championship with a polished swing and months of preparation. But in the days leading up to it, he started noticing something odd: His misses weren't predictable. First a hook. Then a slice. For him, missing on both sides of the fairway was the real red flag—it wasn't mechanics. It was mental.

On the first tee, his eyes wandered to the hazards—the water on the left, the bunkers on the right. His mechanics hadn't broken down. His directional attention had. The more the stakes mattered, the more his subconscious scanned for what could go wrong, steering his eyes—without him realizing it—toward danger on the hole. In a

95

Awareness Is the Foundation

sense, his brain was directing his eyes to stop searching for the shot and start searching for the miss.

We reminded him: His brain was doing exactly what it was designed to do—scan for threats. That didn't mean he had to follow where it wanted to send his attention. Those signals weren't useful for execution toward his goal of winning the event.

Now, because he had elevated his awareness and learned to expect threat thoughts to show up, he had a plan for when he noticed them. Instead of trying to suppress the anxiety or the fear of missing, he acknowledged it and redirected to a simple cue that grounded him: *"Yup, danger on both sides. And the 150-yard mark—that's my target. I want to attack that mark. Aim small, miss small."* He picked the target, visualized the shot, and striped his drive within feet of it.

He repeated that process every round of the Big Ten Championship—acknowledging the threats, redirecting his attention, and committing to his cue. By the end of the week, he finished in second place. The result exceeded his expectations. He was surprised by the outcome, but not by the process that made it possible.

The Sales Exec Presenting: Threat Awareness Leads to a Highly Successful Attention Shift

A leading sales executive came to us because she struggled when presenting to larger groups. This was especially embarrassing for her because she excelled in most other settings—she was extroverted, talented, emotionally intelligent, and knowledgeable in her service. Yet when the audience grew, she would clam up. Ironically, her success meant more and more people wanted to see her present, which only amplified the problem. She admitted feeling anxious before every big presentation. That's when she reached out to us.

As we explored the root of her anxiety, a pattern emerged: Her attention was glued to the skeptical faces in the room. Each time she noticed someone who looked bored or disapproving, her delivery faltered. The threat wasn't physical; it was social—the possibility of judgment. And it had been dogging her since she started presenting to larger audiences, where she no longer had the time or space to personally win people over one-on-one. She had to do it with her presentation, and that didn't always land.

Our first step was to help her understand what her brain was doing and why. With the elevated stress of public speaking, her attentional system went into automatic threat-scanning mode. In her case, the perceived danger was an old insecurity: *"What if I'm not good enough?"* She realized that she consistently locked onto the skeptical third of the room. She simply didn't even notice the positive feedback cues—likely another third of the audience—such as nodding heads, smiles, or engaged eyes.

We taught her the science behind the brain's natural threat response. We also shared a group-dynamics principle that applies in most settings where the audience doesn't know you well: the 1/3 rule. In any group, roughly a third will be skeptical, a third undecided, and a third supportive. So now she knew that critics would always be present in larger audiences. She also grasped a key reality: The higher one climbs, the more visible the critics become. Not necessarily because of anything she had done wrong, but because people bring their own biases and insecurities into the room.

We explained how this often plays out: some audience members will focus on what's wrong or frustrating in their own lives, and the unaware or uninformed tend to project that onto others instead of looking in the mirror. It's easier—and more ego-protective—to blame someone else than to acknowledge one's own role (attribution error). The irony, of course, is that this persecutor behavior is actually a form of victim projection. It leaves the critic stuck, with no influence over their situation, and damages their own well-being and aspirations

97

Awareness Is the Foundation

because their locus of control remains external. (A topic of another book, perhaps.)

When she began to understand this dynamic, she had an *a-ha* moment. She recognized why her attention had been so strongly glued to the skeptics. She also realized that many of those skeptics were dealing with the same insecurities she herself had been experiencing. Reappraising the meaning behind their expressions gave her freedom. Instead of assuming *"I'm not good enough,"* she began to reframe: *"They may be projecting their own doubts, just like I've done."* That reappraisal freed her from taking their expressions as truth and gave her more choice in where to send her attention. It was a deeper shift than positive self-talk or visualization alone could provide, because it addressed the source of the distraction rather than just trying to place a band-aid on it.

We then connected her awareness to her values. Her transcendent value became: *"Serve the room, not the critic."* She believed deeply that there were people in the room who could benefit from the services her firm provided. That belief helped her prioritize her attention on the message, not on the audience's negative cues.

After our interventions, she admitted she still felt nervous before big presentations. But the difference was dramatic. Her performance no longer tanked as it once did. She could now understand the nerves, recognize her natural tendencies, and use a few focus cues to stay on message. Since then, her career has taken big leaps. Today, she is doing public speaking events all over the country. What once felt like a self-imposed ceiling became the very barrier she broke through.

Like many of us, her brain was wired to fixate on the skeptical third. Their expressions triggered insecurity and spiraled into doubt—questioning her abilities, her message, even her career path. In time, she came to see that nothing was wrong with her. What she experienced was both natural—her attentional system scanning for threat, amplified by the anxiety of performing in front of larger crowds—and predictable, since every audience will include skeptics for reasons that often have little to do with the presenter.

Her plan became simple: expect the skeptics, notice the pull toward them, and redirect. Each time she felt her attention snag on a critic, she shifted toward the supportive faces in the room. Their energy reinforced her message and grounded her confidence.

Her composure returned—not because fear disappeared, but because her attention had somewhere else to go.

Putting It All Together: Employing All Five Core Attributes

The story of the presenting sales exec captures why awareness is so powerful and why understanding our own personal inventory is critical. Her identity as a capable leader was undermined by insecurity. Her values gave her a transcendent anchor ("serve the room, not the critic"). Her biases—and the audience's biases—shaped what she noticed. Her motivators reconnected her to why her message mattered. And her fears revealed the patterns that hijacked her attention.

By surfacing and integrating all five, she transformed a paralyzing weakness into a platform for growth. And that's the point: The work isn't erasing these forces. The work is learning how to navigate through them. The performers who thrive under pressure don't conquer fear, erase insecurities, or strip away motivators. They learn to see them clearly, name them honestly, and build systems to work with them instead of being controlled by them.

Awareness as the Anchor for Training Attention

You'll notice the last two awareness cases dealt with the link between hidden limitations and attention management. That's why we say awareness is the core anchor. Sometimes just seeing a limitation clearly can spark change. More often, it becomes the root system for growth.

In this chapter, we surfaced the five attributes that most often steer focus in performance settings without us realizing it: identity, values, biases, motivators, and fears. The performers who thrive under pressure don't erase these forces; they learn to work with them. Fear, threat, and insecurity will always be part of the equation. The win is anticipating their pull on attention—and building a plan to direct that attention where it helps instead of where it harms.

Kevin Hart captured this idea well in a widely shared interview on the Joe Rogan Experience—a message that resonated deeply with many professional athletes we consult:

> *"In this life, the moves we make allow us to do more, see more, experience more . . . Some people are dealt a tougher hand, but if you find a way out, you realize—it's a game. That doesn't mean you play with it. It means you can do what you put your mind to, and if you keep at it, the game opens up new levels . . . The only person I'm competing with is me. If I keep beating the me from yesterday, I'm winning the game. That's my battle. That's the new energy I've found in life: Keep leveling up, no matter what the last level took out of you."*

Hart's perspective mirrors what we've seen in the best athletes, executives, and leaders across domains: Each new level—whether it's a promotion, a championship season, or a comeback from injury—demands an internal upgrade that never has to cease. Awareness is what makes that upgrade possible, because what we believe shapes what we notice, what we ignore, and how we respond when the pressure rises.

Intentional Attention

Wherever the arena—sports, leadership, or daily life—the same principle applies: Awareness gives us choice, and choice opens the door to thriving rather than just surviving.

In Chapter 9, we'll shift from uncovering the roots to observing them in action—mapping how attentional patterns emerge in real time and shape how we think, feel, and behave in performance environments.

Exercise: Fear and Insecurity Pattern Spotting

Take a few minutes to surface your own fear and insecurity patterns. Don't try to change them yet—just notice them.

1. **Top triggers:** What high-stakes moments tend to bring up the most fear or insecurity for you? (for example, visible critics, public evaluation, late-game mistakes, letting others down)

2. **Body tells:** Where do you feel it first in your body? (Circle or rate: chest, stomach, jaw, hands, breathing)

3. **Attentional pull:** Complete: *"When the stakes rise, my attention jumps to _____."* Add specifics if you can (people, places, thoughts).

4. **Self-talk under doubt:** What questions do you quietly ask yourself when insecurity hits? (For example, *"Do I belong here?" "What if I fail?" "What will they think of me?"*)

5. **Predictable context:** Where and when does this pattern show up most? (for example, in presentations, at the free-throw line, during big decisions)

Reflection Prompts (In the Moment)

- "In high pressure, I tend to focus on _____. The part that deserves attention is _____."
- "What would 'serve the room, not the critic' look like in the next 10 seconds?"

You don't need to solve these yet. Simply spotting the patterns is the win here. In Chapter 9, we'll show you how to map these attentional shifts in real time and redirect them toward execution.

Intentional Attention

Awareness of Attentional Patterns

"Knowing yourself is the beginning of all wisdom."

—Aristotle

In Chapter 8, we uncovered several personal attributes that serve as the roots of our inherent attentional patterns. We highlighted how identity, values, biases, motivators, fears, and insecurities can subconsciously channel where attention lands. But knowing those attributes is only the first step in optimizing attention. The next step is mapping where attention actually goes in real time—especially when it matters most. When the heat rises, where does attention land? Is it moving us closer to the goal, or pulling us away from what matters most? Answering those questions gives us a more tangible level of attentional awareness.

To make this visible, we'll use three lenses for assessment:

- First, Metacognition helps us notice attention in real time rather than only in hindsight.

- Second, the Mindset Matrix lets us map how attention cascades into thoughts, emotions, physiology, and behavior.

- Third, the Focus Window gives us a way to filter the stream of information so we can decide what deserves to be inside and what stays out.

Together these lenses turn self-knowledge into a concrete scouting report on our mind—so we can choose the cues that matter and prepare for the ones that don't.

We begin by tracing the trail of our attention. Attention is never invisible—it leaves footprints. We can see it in the behaviors we repeat without thinking, the way our eyes track a room, or the habits that surface when pressure mounts. Sometimes those patterns provide positive performance-relevant information, sharpening our ability to respond to what matters most. Other times they siphon our focus and energy toward distractions that seem important only because they echo an insecurity, a bias, or an overextended value—one that we identified in our previous awareness work.

A leader who fears not being respected may find themselves scanning faces for subtle reactions after every meeting. An athlete tied tightly to outcomes may feel pulled to check the scoreboard stats rather than focus on the next play. The heart of attentional awareness is learning to recognize these patterns and ask a simple but powerful question: Is my attention serving my goal or pulling me away from it?

To make that question actionable, we need better lenses. Brain knowledge and self-knowledge are not enough; we need tools that help us capture our attentional tendencies in performance environments to evaluate whether they are helping or hindering us. The three models in this chapter—Metacognition, the Mindset Matrix, and the Focus Window—do exactly that.

The point of these tools and exercises is to provide an additional step of clarity for how attention directly impacts all that we do. Once we can see our patterns more tangibly in the real-world arena, we can begin to decide which ones serve our performance purpose and which ones need to be redirected. That is the move from unconscious habits and protective reflexes to Intentional Attention.

Metacognition: The Window of Awareness

To make that move, we need a way to better understand some basics. Metacognition is an important element in that understanding. In psychology, the concept of metacognition—the ability to "observe our thinking"—has become a cornerstone of adaptive performance (Flavell, 1979). It gives us a window into what is happening in our own mind. Instead of being swept along by thoughts and emotions, we can pause and observe where our focus is, what thoughts follow, how those thoughts generate emotions, what sensations ripple through the body, and ultimately, what behaviors emerge. The observation doesn't stop thoughts from appearing, but it lets us see them more clearly.

When we activate our metacognition—by observing our thinking and attention during or shortly after a performance—we often discover something surprising: We are more than just the thoughts that run through our minds. Many athletes and performers are shocked by how often doubts or criticisms show up once they start observing their stream of thoughts. They often think there is something wrong with them or that they are the only athlete to think that way. In addition, before practicing metacognition, many assumed their thoughts were their "true selves." Looking through the window reveals something different: Our thoughts are just events or ideas that pass through the mind; they are not our identity.

This suggests there are, in effect, two selves layered together: the acting self that performs and the observing self that can step back and watch what the acting self is doing. This observing self is a highly sophisticated capacity of the human brain, one that few, if any, other species on this planet appear to share. It gives us the ability to notice our attention while it is happening, rather than only after the fact. That ability is nothing short of a performance superpower—because it means we are not bound to every thought that arises.

Without utilizing this capacity, we are often pulled into every passing thought as if it defines us. With it, we begin to choose which thoughts deserve our attention and which ones we allow to drift past. The greatest performers are not the ones who never experience doubt or distraction; they are the ones who have trained their observing self to notice the drift and redirect attention toward what serves their goals.

Neuroscience reinforces this. The prefrontal cortex (PFC)—the brain's "air traffic control tower"—monitors, directs, and reallocates attention. Under stress, this system can dim while the amygdala takes over, primed to scan for threats and keep us safe. That survival mechanism was critical in our evolutionary past but often hijacks our attention in modern performance arenas. Building metacognitive awareness strengthens the PFC's ability to step back into control—to notice where attention has gone and to redirect it toward what matters most.

The evidence is consistent across fields. In education, students who pause to reflect on how they studied—rather than simply logging more hours—perform better on exams. In sport, athletes who have thoughts of fatigue and pain during a tough workout, but who choose to nurture alternative thoughts that recognize effort and growth, build stronger motivation and greater focus on development rather than pain. In clinical psychology, metacognitive therapies help people identify unhelpful thought loops before they spiral and more negatively impact our mental health. And in performance psychology, metacognition is the foundation of attentional training.

However, it's not enough to know what to focus on. We must also recognize when our focus drifts, what distractions that drift follows, and how to bring our attention back. That is the essence of studying our attentional patterns. By looking through the window of metacognition, we build the skill of noticing the footprints attention leaves behind, so we can separate those that serve performance from those that quietly sabotage it.

Pause for a moment and recall a recent performance—a specific event at work, in sport, or in daily life. What thoughts do you remember most clearly? Did you assume those thoughts were *you*, or can you see them as events that passed through your mind?

The Mindset Matrix: Mapping the Trail of Attention

If metacognition gives us a scope into our minds, the Mindset Matrix gives us a structure of what we see through it. The Matrix is an applied model we use with performers to capture how attention cascades into the rest of experience. It organizes five interconnected components:

- Where the spotlight of attention is directed
- The thoughts tied to that focus
- The emotions that follow those thoughts
- The body sensations that ripple through
- The behaviors that can be observed

These components are always linked. Change in one area of the Matrix will naturally impact other areas. The performance that results then is not random—it is the visible outcome of this invisible chain. See Figure 9.1.

The value of the Matrix is in contrast. When we map a time when our performance flowed and a time when it did not, the differences can tell us more than results alone ever could. We begin to see patterns: how attention narrowed to certain sets of data points, how

Figure 9.1 The Mindset Matrix™.

Source: Justin Anderson.

self-talk shifted, how emotions tightened or released, and how behaviors changed before outcomes did.

This process turns performance from something mysterious—where we say things like *"I just didn't have it"*—into something we can study, track, and ultimately train. The Matrix doesn't broadly define a performance as "good" or "bad." Instead, it forces us to look at performance as more of a continuum. Starting with, *What was my attention doing? And how did that shape what followed?*

For many performers, this becomes a breakthrough. Instead of chasing confidence or waiting for "the zone" to appear, we start to understand performance as patterns of attention playing out in predictable ways. With the Mindset Matrix, the observing self now has a more surgical and structured way to study the acting self in motion—and we can begin reshaping those mental patterns with intention.

The NBA Player Who Tried to Feel His Way Out of a Slump

Consider the NBA All-Star introduced earlier who found himself stuck—confidence fading, rhythm gone, performance inconsistent.

Like many athletes, his instinct was to try to *feel* his way back into form. He told himself he needed to feel confident, to feel strong, to feel like the player he once was. But every time he looked at his shooting percentage or noticed defenders sagging off him, it reinforced the opposite. The harder he chased the result, the further it slipped away.

When we mapped his Mindset Matrix, the contrast between his best games and his worst games revealed what was really happening.

- **Focus:** At his best, his attention was outward—locked on finding efficient pathways to attack the hoop, on defensive rotations, and on building up his teammates. In his worst, his focus was directed inward, circling around thoughts of what his stats meant, which created a fairly negative internal dialogue and birthed more doubt.

- **Thoughts:** When thriving, his self-talk was simple and task-oriented: *"Attack the gap . . . find the open man. Get out quickly in transition."* In struggle, it shifted to self-consciousness: *"Don't miss . . . what if I'm letting people down? What is going on, do I still have it?"*

- **Emotions:** In rhythm, he carried energy and urgency, a feeling of being loose or free, coupled with connection to teammates. In slumps, frustration crept in, doubt, along with an embarrassing fear of losing respect.

- **Body Sensations:** At his peak, his body was energized, loose, fluid, and springy. Under pressure, he had felt tightness in his chest, his legs felt heavy, and he generally expressed feeling more fatigued.

- **Behaviors:** When playing well, he was animated—communicating loudly, fist-bumping, the first to encourage others. He also noticed he was smiling a lot more. When struggling, his energy withdrew—shoulders were slumped, eyes on the floor, voice quiet. He wasn't building up his teammates, and he noticed effort muted, especially in transition as he was often running slower and with his head down.

What the Matrix revealed was simple but profound: The slump wasn't about mechanics, and it wasn't even about confidence. It was about attention. His acting self was pulled inward by an identity-level threat—*What if I lose the respect of others?* Once his focus narrowed around that fear, the cascade unfolded: negative thoughts, anxious emotions, tight physiology, withdrawn behaviors. The box score wasn't the cause—but it reinforced this loop. He was caught in a downward attentional pattern.

Through metacognition, his observing self could finally see this trail clearly. And with the Mindset Matrix as a guide, he began to understand how to intervene. His plan became simple:

Intentional Attention → Identify and focus on task-relevant behaviors, give maximum effort in transitions and get back on defense, and exhibit connecting behaviors to teammates, which includes smiling and being the first to pick up teammates when they hit the floor. The prescription was that by focusing on these cues, it would give him a much better rhythm, and his rhythm would give him better results.

Notice the order. Results came last. Also note that his plan was not to try to conjure up confidence or chase stats, but to direct attention outward—onto task-relevant or what we call performance-relevant behaviors including his teammates. When he did that, rhythm returned. When rhythm returned, his production and shooting percentages shot back up. As a result, confidence followed. Now his attentional loop was moving in a more productive pattern, but perhaps more importantly, he now understood how to quickly intervene should he find his performance dip again.

This is the power of the Mindset Matrix. It helps us step into the observing self, study the acting self, and see performance for what it really is: the outcome of attentional patterns. And once those patterns are visible, they can be outlined, redirected, and trained.

Beyond the Court: Why the Mindset Matrix Matters Everywhere

What we saw with the NBA All-Star is not unique to basketball. The same cascades play out wherever performance lives. Whether we are in a classroom, conference room, hospital, or locker room, the sequence is familiar: When our attention is outward—anchored to the task, to others, and to relevant cues—performance tends to rise. When our attention collapses inward toward doubts, insecurities, or identity threats—performance suffers, often before we even realize what's happening.

Someone preparing to speak up in a meeting may find their attention pulled toward how they might be judged rather than the idea they want to contribute. A person on a first date may notice their mind scanning for signs of rejection instead of being present in the conversation. A student may experience their emotions shift from curiosity to panic the moment they see the first difficult exam question. In each case, the cascade follows the same pattern: Focus narrows inward, thoughts turn self-conscious, emotions constrict, the body responds, and behaviors shift.

The Mindset Matrix helps us capture this process in a way that is both systematic and personal. By stepping into the observing self, we can map what the acting self is doing in those moments and make the invisible trail of attention visible. Instead of chalking performance up to "confidence," "momentum," or "having it," we begin to see the real controllable mental levers: what we noticed, how we interpreted it, and what cascaded from there.

In short, the Matrix makes it possible to study ourselves the way we would study film or data: not to judge, but to understand. It gives the observing self a structured way to track the acting self—and with that, the power to redirect attention toward what truly matters.

Reflection Prompt

Think of two contrasting performances—one where you thrived and one where you struggled. Map the five components (Focus, Thoughts, Emotions, Body Sensations, Behaviors) for each. What shifted between the two? What patterns do you notice?

The Focus Window: Sorting Relevant from Irrelevant

Imagine standing on the shoulder of a busy freeway. Cars whip by—each one representing a thought, memory, temptation, distraction, or piece of performance-relevant data. Metacognition is the ability to notice the traffic rather than being swept along by it. But here's the catch: We can ride in only one car at a time. Wherever we climb in, that's where our attention goes.

Some cars carry performance-relevant data that move us forward—closer to our goals. Others are filled with irrelevant noise, from simple detours to more complex ones like insecurities and fears. Without awareness, we often find ourselves in the wrong car before we realize it—speeding down an off-ramp leading us away from our goals and into judgment, doubt, or distraction.

This is why the **Focus Window** matters. The Focus Window is the tool that helps us choose which car to step into. It's a simple but powerful model for filtering the endless stream of information the brain encounters in performance settings deciding what we want in, and what drives by (see Figure 9.2).

Figure 9.2 The Focus Window™.
Source: Justin Anderson.

The brain is constantly sorting through data, deciding what to let into conscious awareness and what to ignore. But it can concentrate on only one thing at a time. Right now, for instance, we are using our eyes to process these words. Meanwhile, parts of our body—our right foot, for example—are also sending signals to the brain. Normally that data is filtered out as irrelevant. But if something suddenly crawled across the foot, attention would snap to it—because the brain flagged it as different and potentially threatening.

That initial pull is not a choice. It reflects the brain's natural wiring that we explored in Part I: survival systems designed to prioritize novelty, threat, or discomfort over neutral information. Without awareness, we may not even realize our focus has shifted—or whether that shift is helping or hindering performance.

Here's where the controllable aspect of attention comes in. We can't stop the brain from reacting. But we can train ourselves to notice when attention gets pulled, and we can decide how long we want it to stay there. Unlike thoughts, beliefs, or emotions—which are often harder to override in the moment—attention is more malleable. With practice, we can more quickly and intentionally bring it back to the task, behavior, cue, or the information that matters most. That's the essence of Intentional Attention: not eliminating distraction, but shortening its duration and redirecting focus back to performance-relevant targets.

The Focus Window helps us take charge of that process. It reminds us that while countless signals and thoughts will always be present, concentration can sit in only one window at a time. What sits inside the window receives our full concentration; everything else becomes background noise. The challenge—and the opportunity—is to decide what deserves to be inside.

For a quarterback, this model is invaluable. In a single play, countless cues compete for attention: the crowd noise, the defensive line's movement, an awareness of the last mistake. The Focus Window helps them decide what belongs inside: the play call, the formation, the protection scheme, the snap count, their footwork to depth, and then moving their eyes through progression keys. Everything else— how the defense celebrates, what the scoreboard says, even stray self-doubts—may still appear, but they let them go by quickly and stay outside the window. By choosing what to attend to, the quarterback invests their limited concentration energy in the cues most likely to produce success.

The same principle can apply in very different arenas. A surgeon may be aware of dozens of competing stimuli—the beeping of monitors, the chatter of staff, the tension of time pressure, or even self-doubt about the complexity of the procedure. But when the scalpel is in hand, only certain cues belong in the Focus Window: the patient's vital signs, the precision of their movements, and the next surgical step. Everything else is irrelevant and needs to stay out. The ability to keep the window locked allows the surgeon to concentrate fully on what preserves life and ensures success.

And perhaps most importantly, the Focus Window matters at home. Imagine a parent walking through the door after a long day. The pull of unfinished emails, buzzing text messages, and unresolved decisions can easily slip into the window. But in that moment, what belongs inside is different: the faces of their children, the conversation at dinner, the chance to be present in the limited minutes

Intentional Attention

together. Many of the leaders and athletes we've worked with have said this model has been just as transformative for their family life as it has been for their performance arenas. By keeping their Focus Window locked on what matters most from moment to moment, they learn to bring the same level of intentional attention home that they once reserved only for the field, stage, or boardroom.

The Focus Window is both a mindfulness exercise and a performance tool. It reminds us that we can only concentrate fully on one thing at a time—and therefore, we must be intentional about what car we choose to step into. Over time, this process helps us pinpoint the specific cues that anchor our best performances, while also alerting us when irrelevant distractions start to take us for another ride.

Reflection Prompts

Take some time to address these points.

- What's in your Focus Window right now?
- Is it controllable and performance-relevant—or irrelevant noise?
- How long can you keep one piece of data within your Focus Window without your attention wandering to another piece of data/information?
- Are you aware of what's in your window when you're performing?

Controllable and Performance-Relevant Data Versus Everything Else

With the three models in place, we can sharpen the filter. A simple two-question test helps performers spot information worth their time and energy: Is it controllable? Is it performance-relevant? If both answers are yes, it belongs in the window. If not, it is a distraction.

Looking back at the Mindset Matrix—Focus, Thoughts, Emotions, Body Sensations, and Behaviors—only two of those categories are reliably controllable: attention (focus) and behavior. These are the best levers to pull in real time.

Thoughts, emotions, and body sensations all matter deeply, but they shift constantly and often outside our direct influence. Research shows that trying to forcefully control them—like telling ourselves to "calm down"—tends to backfire. This is a classic case of ironic process theory: the harder we try to suppress or control a thought, the more dominant it becomes (Wegner, 1994).

That's why we encourage performers to reframe. Instead of "I need to be calm," which draws us into a losing battle with anxiety, we can try "I'm excited" or "I'm ready." Studies show that reappraising anxiety as excitement improves performance in public speaking, math, and even athletic tasks (Brooks, 2014; Moore et al., 2015). Unlike suppression, reappraisal doesn't demand that the emotion vanish; it shifts attention toward action and engagement (Gross & John, 2003).

There's a reason this happens. Attention tends to amplify whatever it touches. If our focus rests on an emotion, we magnify that emotion. We see it in sport all the time: a golfer standing on the tee box, eyes locked onto the water hazard, thinking, "Don't miss left," and then doing exactly that. The mind doesn't process the "don't." It processes the image, and the ball follows. The same principle applies to emotion—"don't be anxious" points our focus toward anxiety, and anxiety spikes.

This is why we encourage athletes and leaders to redirect their focus toward controllable, performance-relevant cues instead. It doesn't mean ignoring emotions or thoughts; it means acknowledging them but placing our limited attentional energy on the factors we can actually influence.

Stories from the Field

A collegiate softball infielder once came to us in a slump, again desperate to "feel confident" at the plate. But when we walked through her Mindset Matrix, she noticed something important: her thoughts, emotions, and body sensations shifted constantly—out of her control. What didn't shift were the behaviors she could repeat and the focus she could choose.

When she returned her attention to her plan and approach at the plate and anchored her routine—tapping the plate, taking three practice swings, verbalizing "ready, ball, ball, ball"—her rhythm returned. Not because she willed herself into feeling confident, but because she directed her attention and behavior toward controllable cues. Confidence, positive emotions, and belief followed later.

This is the heart of performance-relevant attention.

Applying the Lens

So what does this look like in practice? We can start by sorting cues into four buckets:

1. **Controllable + Performance-Relevant:** Where we want to spend most of our attention (for example, play call, breathing rhythm, body posture, words we choose, task at hand).

2. **Controllable + Irrelevant:** Distractions we control but that don't serve us (for example, fidgeting, overanalyzing stats mid-play, playing out what if scenarios).

3. **Uncontrollable + Relevant:** Things that matter but we can't influence directly (for example, weather, referee calls, opponent's game plan, audience reactions).

4. **Uncontrollable + Irrelevant:** Pure noise (for example, crowd heckling, social media chatter).

Awareness of Attentional Patterns

The bullseye—the sweet spot—is to maximize controllable and performance-relevant data. That's where our attention and behaviors combine to give us the greatest leverage.

Distractions: Preparing for the Pull

Distractions deserve their own discussion for one reason: preparation. It's not enough to know what belongs in the Focus Window; we also need to know what is most likely to compete for that space.

The reason we highlight distractions as a separate attentional pattern is not to eliminate them—that is impossible. We don't want performers spending energy trying to banish every distraction that shows up in the Focus Window. It will happen. That's the nature of the mind. The key is not to be surprised by distractions and, just as importantly, not dwell on them. What matters is having a clear plan to return to performance-relevant data as soon as we notice we've been pulled away.

One important step in doing this effectively is preparation. Knowing what to focus on is only half the equation. The other half is anticipating what will try to pull us away—so that when a distraction sneaks in, we're ready. This is where the "car" analogy we introduced earlier comes back into play. Imagine standing on the shoulder of a freeway, watching data points—thoughts, sensations, emotions, external cues—rush past like cars. Inevitably, some of those cars will cut into our Focus Window. We might even find ourselves riding in the wrong one before we realize it. Preparation gives us the ability to notice when we've jumped into a distraction-car, step back out, and redirect into one carrying the performance-relevant data.

Distractions, in other words, are not signs of weakness. They are part of being human. What separates elite performers from everyone else is not the absence of distraction, but the ability to expect it, recognize it quickly, and move back to what matters most.

The Firecracker Effect

Imagine a firecracker explodes unexpectedly behind us.

BAM!

Without warning our amygdala jumps into action instantly. Heart rate spikes. Breathing shortens. Muscles flinch. Our attention frantically and scans the environment for potential threats: *Where did that come from? Am I in danger?* Protection drives the reaction.

Now imagine the same firecracker, but this time the only difference is that we *know* it's coming. Someone tells us it will explode in 10 seconds. When it goes off, our reflexes still jump—but our body and mind appraise the situation very differently. The reaction is far less intense, and more importantly, without the amygdala hijacking control, our prefrontal cortex stays online. Instead of spiraling into panic or hyper-vigilance, we can return more quickly to what we were doing. Preparation is what makes the difference.

Elite performers use this principle and don't rely on emotional control in the moment. They rely on attentional preparation in advance.

How Special Forces Train for Chaos

Nowhere is this clearer than in how U.S. Special Forces are trained. Navy SEALs, Army Rangers, and other elite units don't train to avoid stress—they train to expect it. They use a process called stress inoculation training (SIT), deliberately flooding training with distractions, chaos, and fear-inducing stimuli so the brain learns not to hand the keys over to the amygdala when pressure peaks under duress (United States Air Force Reserve Command, 2024). In these environments, operators must maintain focus on performance-relevant data to execute protocols while being blasted by sirens, navigating through smoke, responding amid loud explosions, and sometimes continuing through simulated injuries. It isn't just rehearsing what to do when everything goes right—it's rehearsing what to do when everything goes wrong.

The 2011 raid on Osama bin Laden's compound is a vivid example of this playing out in a life or death situation. Mid-operation, one of the helicopters carrying SEALs crashed just as they were about to land inside the compound walls. For most teams, this kind of catastrophic distraction would create paralysis. A crash like that is loud, violent, and unexpected—every instinct screams to turn attention toward the wreck. But the operators didn't freeze. They didn't flood their Focus Window with "What just happened?" or spiraling thoughts like "Are we doomed?" Instead, they fell back on what had been rehearsed thousands of times and their performance-relevant data: *clear the corner, cover the door, execute formation.*

Their attention wasn't on the crash. It was on the next controllable cue.

That wasn't superhuman calm. It wasn't the absence of fear. It was trained attentional control. By preparing for distractions—anticipating chaos rather than hoping to avoid it—they ensured their attention would go where it needed to, not where the noise of the moment naturally wanted to pull it.

This is the same principle that elite athletes, executives, and parents can use. We can't stop distractions from showing up. But with preparation, we can train our minds to recognize them, let them pass, and redirect into the cars that actually move us toward our goals.

Internal Distractions

We saw this with a quarterback early in his career. In high school and college, he was known as a "gamer"—calm under pressure, thriving in late-game moments. But in the pros, after a few rough starts, his window became filled with irrelevant and uncontrollable questions:

- "Am I blowing my shot?"

- "What will the media say?"
- "Does the staff trust me anymore?"

These weren't weak-minded thoughts; they were normal for any human going through what he was experiencing. But they were also distractions and would detract from him from his ultimate goal. Instead of directing attention to controllable, performance-relevant cues (reads, leverage, progressions), he had jumped into the wrong car—one heading away from his goals. Once we laid it out visually with the Focus Window and Bullseye (covered later in this chapter), he could see it clearly. His job wasn't to fight the thoughts, but to step out of the car and redirect toward performance-relevant cues.

External Distractions

External distractions are often easier to see, but no less powerful. They show up in stadiums, stages, offices, and homes.

Consider Wisconsin's Camp Randall Stadium. At the start of the fourth quarter, 80,000 fans jump in unison to "Jump Around." The stadium shakes. The intention is clear: to rattle the opponent. Without preparation, it works. The same with the Minnesota Vikings' Skol Chant—designed to overwhelm, destabilize, and distract.

But the principle holds far beyond sport. Take a leader heading into a performance review, or worse, having to let someone go. Their Focus Window can easily get hijacked by the ping of email notifications, a buzzing phone, or a colleague dropping by with urgent questions—interrupting their preparation or derailing their delivery. Yet what belongs inside the window are controllable and relevant cues: being clear, respectful, present, and aligned with values. Without awareness, it's easy to jump into the wrong car. With awareness, the leader can anchor their attention on what matters most.

Not All Relevant Data Is Equal: We Need to Find Our Bullseye

There's one final nuance. Even when we identify controllable, performance-relevant data, not all cues are equally impactful.

Take the quarterback again. In training camp, he recognized he could direct his attention toward mechanics—his footwork, his reads, his technique. All of these were controllable and relevant. But what shifted his performance most was a different cue: intentionally picking up and encouraging teammates. That behavior created rhythm, restored confidence, and reconnected him with the bigger purpose of leading the team.

Both footwork and encouragement were controllable and relevant. But one was more impactful than the other. This is why attentional training doesn't end with awareness; it must progress to intention, execution, and reflection. In later chapters, we'll explore how to set intentions, direct and hold our attention on chosen cues, and reflect afterward to see if those choices had the impact we hoped for. That cycle is how we sharpen our ability to apply Intentional Attention at the highest level.

After going through the process and refining our performance-relevant data as well as preparing for our distractions, we gain a clearer sense of which information deserves the center of our focus. Many of our clients visualize this using a simple circle diagram like the one in Figure 9.3, mapping their most impactful performance-relevant cues in the bullseye and identifying the internal and external distractions that tend to pull them away.

This is why awareness alone isn't enough. As we discussed in Chapter 7, training attention means moving from noticing (awareness) to intentionally selecting, directing, and holding our attention on the cues that matter most—and then reflecting afterward to see if they delivered the effect we hoped for. That cycle is how we sharpen our ability to apply Intentional Attention at the highest level.

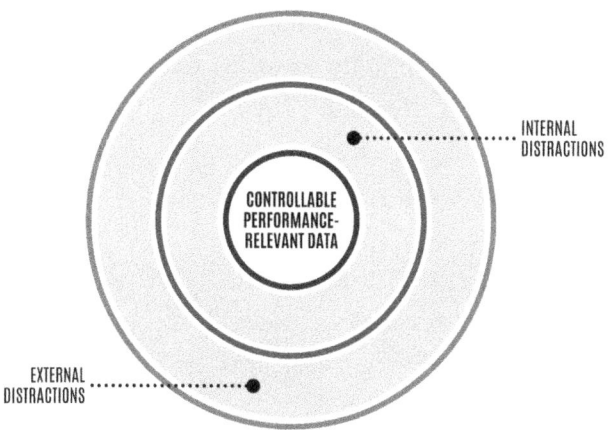

Figure 9.3 The Focus Bullseye™.
Source: Justin Anderson.

Exercise: Performance-Relevant Data

In this chapter, we moved beyond inner awareness to study attentional patterns in action. Through Metacognition, the Mindset Matrix, and the Focus Window, we built tools to trace where attention lands in real time—and to assess whether those patterns serve or sabotage performance.

We learned to filter cues through a simple lens: Is it controllable? Is it performance-relevant? The cues that pass both tests deserve space in the Focus Window and can be outlined in the Focus Bullseye. Everything else is a performance distraction—forces that compete for attention and pull us away from our goals. Distractions can come from within (doubts, emotions, self-judgment) or from without (crowds, environments, reactions). The key is not to waste energy trying to eliminate them, but to prepare for them—so that when they inevitably appear, we can notice, step out of the wrong car, and redirect toward what matters most.

Finally, even among controllable, performance-relevant cues, some will have greater impact than others. The real power of Intentional

Attention lies in identifying those most effective cues, directing focus toward them, and reflecting afterward to determine their true influence. That process sets the stage for what's ahead, as we move from awareness into intention, execution, reflection, and renewal—the full cycle of the IA Framework.

■ ■ ■

Patterns in performance don't just appear; they reflect where our attention has been.

Take a moment to apply these tools to your own world:

1. List three controllable and performance-relevant cues that consistently help you perform well (for example, eye contact, pre-task routine, scanning key data, posture).

2. List three distractions that regularly compete for your attention—both internal (doubts, self-criticism, outcome focus) and external (environmental noise, reactions of others, technology).

3. For each distraction, ask: When it sneaks into my Focus Window, what thought or "car" have I jumped into (am I attending to)? And what car do I want to step into instead?

4. Circle the one controllable, performance-relevant cue that is most impactful for you. Write down one way you will intentionally hold your attention on it this week.

This simple exercise begins to transform awareness into a practical scouting report—helping us prepare not only for what we want to focus on, but also for what will inevitably try to compete for our focus.

Chapter 10

Intention: The Bridge from Awareness to Action

"It's not the will to win that matters—everyone has that. It's the will to prepare to win that matters."

—Paul "Bear" Bryant

It was the middle of training camp, and one of the quarterbacks we worked with was on the edge of making the roster. Every rep felt like a test. Every throw was being dissected by coaches, teammates, and media. He wasn't the strongest arm in the room, nor the fastest runner. He knew his value was being measured: decisive, disciplined, and consistency in his leadership—and in that moment, he wasn't delivering.

The previous practice had been brutal. A couple of late reads, an interception, some frustrated body language. He walked off the field replaying mistakes in his head, each one magnified under the spotlight of competition. By the time he got home that night, his thoughts were racing: *Am I losing ground? Do the coaches trust me? What if this is slipping away?* His attention wasn't on tomorrow's game plan—it was trapped in fear of falling behind.

The next morning, he decided to try something different. Before heading back to the facility, he sat down at the kitchen table with a notebook. Instead of writing out plays or stat goals, he wrote three intentions for the day:

- Encourage my teammates with energy.
- Move quickly through my progressions.
- Let mistakes go—keep head up and shoulders back, and reset immediately.

It wasn't about feeling confident or being perfect. It was about anchoring his attention to behaviors he could control, no matter what else happened.

That day at practice, nothing magical erased the adversity. He still threw incompletions. He still felt the weight of the defense collapsing the pocket. But when his attention started to drift toward frustration, he returned to his intentions. He patted a receiver on the helmet. He hustled back to the huddle with his chin up. He reset his eyes on the next progression. Slowly, his rhythm returned. His body loosened. His presence lifted. Coaches noticed. Teammates noticed.

"I didn't control every play," he told us later, "but I controlled how I showed up."

That single practice didn't win him the roster spot on its own. But it gave him something more powerful: a repeatable plan for directing his attention when pressure tried to hijack it—a plan that ultimately helped him secure a contract and a place on the roster.

Goals to Intention

A goal defines what we want to achieve. An intention defines how we want to show up in pursuit of it. A lot has been written about the science of goal setting, so we won't linger there, but the evidence is clear: Setting specific, challenging, and measurable goals enhances motivation and performance far more than vague or generalized ones (Locke & Latham, 2002, 2019). The act of setting a goal activates the brain's reward and planning networks, increasing dopamine and stimulating the prefrontal cortex to organize behavior toward that target (Oettingen & Gollwitzer, 2010).

But while goals clarify direction, they don't necessarily shape *attention* in the moment. Once we know who we are (awareness), we can outline where we want to go (goals), but intention determines *how* we move through the process—especially when conditions change or pressure rises.

Most performers we work with have well-defined goals. They can tell you exactly what they're chasing: a Super Bowl ring, a Hall of Fame career, a CEO title, or a seven-figure salary. Yet far fewer have articulated their intentions for how they plan to get there. And that's where performance often breaks down. Goals give us targets; intentions give us traction. They connect awareness to action and keep attention anchored to controllable behaviors when the outcome feels far away.

That's why we spend the majority of this chapter not on *what* we pursue, but *how* we pursue it. Because goals alone don't hold focus under pressure—intentions do.

Why Intention Matters

Stories like the quarterback's reveal a universal truth: Across sports, business, and the performing arts, intention is one of the most reliable ways to direct attention toward controllable, performance-relevant cues.

Psychologist Peter Gollwitzer's research on *implementation intentions* shows that if–then planning ("If I make a mistake, then I reset my posture and look to the next cue") significantly improves follow-through and performance under stress (Gollwitzer, 1999). Athletes who set process-based intentions demonstrate greater resilience and consistency than those who focus only on outcomes (Weinberg & Gould, 2019).

Intention: The Bridge from Awareness to Action

Neuroscience reinforces this. Setting intentions primes the prefrontal cortex—the brain's executive control center—to stay active under pressure, allowing us to override emotional interference when stress peaks (Holroyd & Yeung, 2012; Braver, 2012). When we've chosen in advance where to direct our attention, we're less likely to hand the steering wheel over to the amygdala when something unexpected happens.

Even the way we frame intention can change performance. Alison Wood Brooks (2014) showed that reappraising pre-performance anxiety as excitement improved results in public speaking, math, and athletic tasks. Intentionally choosing which perspectives we want to engage doesn't erase nerves, but it gives the mind a constructive cue to ride with instead of fighting emotions directly.

In sport, intention-setting has often taken the form of pre-performance routines. These are powerful. Research across golf, tennis, and other self-paced sports shows that when athletes consistently set and follow intentional routines, their performance becomes more stable and resilient under pressure (Cotterill, 2010; Singer, 2002). We believe, however, that these routines can go even further.

When pre-performance routines are informed by deeper self-awareness—the values, biases, motivators, threats, and attentional patterns identified through the IA Framework—they become more than rituals. They become *personalized attentional plans*. Rather than simply rehearsing mechanics, the performer draws on self-knowledge to anticipate where attention might drift and to set anchors that align with both control and purpose.

This is an essential step if an athlete or a leader wants to be "mentally tough" and "clutch" when the heat is turned up.

This is where intention-setting moves beyond "routine" into something transformational. Awareness gives us the raw data; intention translates it into action. That's why we encourage performers to go beyond pre-performance routines and establish a discipline of

Primary Intention Setting (or priming their mind)—a daily practice of defining how they want to direct their attention before the day begins.

In short: Intention gives us a blueprint for our attention. Without it, we drift toward whatever feels loudest—fear, frustration, fatigue, or other distractions. With it, we can anchor to our performance-relevant controllable drivers—guiding our energy, attitude, effort, and behaviors.

Primary Intention Setting: Our Daily Mindset Prep

Athletes spend hours on movement prep—warming up muscles, stretching joints, activating the body before competition. Yet very few prepare their minds with the same discipline.

We call this process Primary Intention Setting: a short, structured mental warm-up designed to set the trajectory of the day. Its goal isn't to predict every outcome but to prime the mind for how we want to meet the moments ahead. Done consistently, it becomes a form of daily mental conditioning—training the brain to start from a centered, deliberate state rather than a reactive one.

We recommend performers in all arenas adopt a simple five-minute mindset prep ritual every morning, just as naturally as making coffee or lacing up shoes.

Five steps for Primary Intention Setting:

1. **Grounding (Breath + Body Scan)**

   Begin by anchoring in the present. A slow, deep breath and body scan releases tension and cues the brain to shift into intentional focus.

2. **Love (Oxytocin Priming)**

   High performance isn't just cognitive—it's emotional. Bring to mind the face of someone you love—your child, partner, parent, pet. This simple imagery releases oxytocin, a neurochemical that fosters creativity, connection, and growth orientation (Carter, 2014; Feldman, 2017). Entering intention-setting with love primes openness and adaptability rather than defensiveness.

3. Work Through the Day

Visualize the day in segments—meetings, workouts, classes, rehearsals. For each period, imagine bringing ideal energy, effort, and focus.

4. Anticipate Adversity

Identify likely challenges and mentally rehearse intentional responses using the SERR model (Situation, Emotion, Response, Results) described later in this chapter. This inoculates the brain against surprise hijacks by pre-selecting adaptive responses (Mellalieu et al., 2006).

5. Close in Gratitude

Picture yourself at day's end, lying in bed with gratitude—for the effort you gave, the people who supported you, and the opportunity to pursue your goals. Gratitude broadens perspective and stabilizes emotional regulation (Emmons & McCullough, 2003).

A women's professional basketball player we worked with writes down the three things that come out of her primary intention setting. She writes three daily intentions each morning. They often tend to be something like: "Compete with effort. Encourage others. Hunt for your rhythm." No matter how the competition unfolds, she has a road map for her attention.

Performers who sustain this ritual report fewer emotional hooks, smoother resets, and more creativity under pressure. By priming the subconscious each morning, they're programming the brain's attentional filters to notice what matters most.

Neuroscience confirms that the brain doesn't process information neutrally—it relies on selective attention networks (especially in the prefrontal and parietal cortices) to decide what data deserves focus (Corbetta & Shulman, 2002; Petersen & Posner, 2012). Once an intention is set, the subconscious begins scanning the environment for cues aligned with that plan while filtering out irrelevant noise.

Psychologists call this attentional bias—our tendency to preferentially notice information matches our goals, fears, or expectations (Yiend, 2010). Through consistent intention-setting, we shift that bias from default threat- or ego-based scanning toward performance-relevant cues. Over time, these neural filters strengthen, making it easier to notice opportunities, recover from distractions, and sustain focus under pressure.

This is why athletes and executives alike often say that after adopting this discipline, "the day feels different." Their minds are no longer passively reacting to whatever grabs attention—they're actively scanning for what aligns with who they want to be and how they want to show up.

Performance Intention: Locking In Before, During, and After

Our Primary Intention each morning sets the compass for the day. But as performance approaches, we need to reconnect and sharpen that focus. Intention should never be treated as a one-time act—it's a mindset renewed across the key windows of performance: before, during, and after. Each phase plays a unique role in guiding where our attention goes.

Research on the recency effect shows that we remember best what we encounter last (Ebbinghaus, 1885; Murdock, 1962). In education, students who review material right before a test recall it

Intention: The Bridge from Awareness to Action

more effectively (Baddeley & Hitch, 1993; Roediger & Karpicke, 2006). The same applies to performance. When we refresh intentions just before competition, in breaks between action, or immediately afterward, we make them more accessible when pressure peaks. This is where pre-performance intention setting comes in.

Pre-Performance Intention: Locking In Before the Event

Unlike the morning ritual, pre-performance intention should happen within a few hours of competition or performance to maximize the impact of the recency effect. For athletes, this often happens during pre-practice or pre-game routines and can be naturally combined with their movement prep. For business leaders, it might happen during the commute to the office or just before a major presentation.

The goal is to bring the daily compass back to the specific demands of the upcoming performance window. In this moment, performers recall their primary intention for the day and translate it into concrete cues for how they want to show up.

They deliberately reconnect their attention with several other controllables:

- **Energy:** Choosing their activation level. Do they need to be more amped and aggressive, or calm and steady?
- **Attitude:** Re-centering in a positive, engaging frame of mind.
- **Effort:** Committing to presence and engagement, even when fatigue, pain, or distractions pull attention away.
- **Behavior:** Turning intention into action through body language, communication, and executional habits that reinforce focus.

From there, attention can be directed to the **performance-relevant data:**

- For a sales consultant, it could be listening closely for the client's pain points and reflecting them back with empathy.
- For the NFL coach, it might be focusing on staying cool, calm, and collected during the chaos of the game to communicate more clearly and methodically to their players.

Reflection Prompt

Think of an upcoming performance moment. What behaviors, energy, and attitude will you anchor to before you begin?

During Performance Intention: Redirecting During Breaks in the Action

Even with preparation, attention drifts. Intention during performance functions like a reset button—a moment to realign focus when the noise takes over.

One professional hockey player we worked with described how learning about during-competition intention setting completely changed his consistency. He recalled someone once telling him about Mark Messier's routine—how between shifts Messier would put his head down, reflect quickly on what had just happened, take the lesson, let the rest go (a practice hockey players call "shift amnesia"), and then set his intention for what he wanted to do on the next shift.

Our player adopted a similar process. Each time he came back to the bench, he went through a quick cycle: head down, review, release, reset with a clear intention for the next shift. He reported that this ritual made his game cleaner and his decisions sharper.

Instead of carrying frustration or overthinking mistakes, he re-entered the ice with clarity and purpose.

> ### Reflection Prompt
>
> What process could you use during a break in your day/performance to reconnect with your primary intention, checking in with yourself to see if you're on the path toward your goals or not?

Post-Performance Intention: Defining Success Beyond the Scoreboard

Post-performance intentions are just as critical as the ones we set before and during. Without them, attention tends to drift toward outcome evaluation—typically the stat sheet, the scoreboard, or the social media praise and criticism. While outcomes can provide useful feedback, letting them dominate reflection often erodes confidence and distracts us from efficient long-term growth.

Therefore, post-performance intention setting is highly encouraged. It's about deciding in advance how we will evaluate ourselves. Instead of letting the mind chase external validation, we anchor our attention during reflection to controllables: energy, attitude, effort, and behaviors.

- **In Athletics:** A college basketball player finishes a game by asking herself, "Did I bring energy, did I compete, did I encourage my teammates?" By grounding her reflection in these intentions, she prevents her attention from spiraling into frustration about shooting percentages.

- **In Business:** A CEO walking out of a quarterly meeting doesn't just replay shareholder reactions. Instead, he asks, "Did I stay aligned with my values? Did I communicate our vision clearly?"

He measures success by whether he showed up in the way he intended, not by the immediate applause or critique.

- **In The Classroom:** A teacher might leave class reflecting, "Did I stay patient? Did I create space for student voices? Did I bring curiosity into the room?" This intentional reflection protects against being defined only by test scores or student feedback.

By framing evaluation around intentions instead of outcomes, we create a feedback loop that sustains motivation, builds resilience, and reinforces the habits that drive long-term success.

Reflection Prompt

After your next performance moment, how will you measure success beyond outcome? Which controllable actions—energy, attitude, effort, or behaviors—will you review to judge whether you stayed aligned with your intentions?

Deepening Intention: The Four Controllables

Earlier, we identified **Energy, Attitude, Effort, and Behaviors** as the controllables most directly tied to performance. Here, we take them deeper—not as motivational clichés, but as four actionable types of attention that can be trained and directed under pressure.

If awareness shows us the map and intention points us toward a destination, these controllables are the stabilizers that keep our plan steady when the storm hits. When performers ground their intentions in these anchors, they become far more adaptable and consistent— able to adjust without losing alignment.

Intentions built around controllables are powerful because they are *always available*. We can't control outcomes, referees, or whether anxiety shows up before the big meeting. But we can control the energy we bring into the room, the attitude we project, the effort we give, and the behaviors that express those choices. Selecting these qualities in advance helps us show up with *all-pro consistency* when it matters most.

- **Energy:** Our level of activation. Some athletes use a simple cue: "Bring juice today." Energy isn't about hype; it's about bringing life to the performance moment—whether that means intensity or composure.

- **Attitude:** The lens through which we engage. Intention directs attitude toward openness, curiosity, and gratitude—qualities that invite flow—rather than defensiveness or judgment. A baseball player stuck in a slump once told us his turning point came when he wrote one phrase on his glove: *"Stay grateful for the opportunity."*

- **Effort:** The deliberate choice to give our best in this moment. Effort is the antidote to perfectionism. A swimmer preparing for Olympic Trials reframed her pre-race plan from "Swim a perfect race" to "Attack the first 50 with full effort."

- **Behaviors:** The visible expression of intention. This includes posture (head up, chest open), communication (encouragement, clarity), and task cues (eyes on target). Behaviors are where intention becomes observable.

These controllables aren't reserved for spotlight moments—they apply to training sessions, meetings, classrooms, and conversations. Intention-setting means we choose these variables rather than leaving them to chance.

Such controllables have become the backbone of many pre-performance routines studied across sport. Whether it's a golfer's pre-shot sequence, a tennis player's serving ritual, or a basketball player's free-throw routine, each is an expression of energy, attitude, effort, or behavior intentionally crystallized into action (Cotterill et al., 2010).

When performers consistently anchor to these four controllables, two things happen:

1. Their attention more easily locks on what they can influence.

2. Positive outcomes follow—not because they were chased, but because they emerged from controllable consistency.

Reflection Prompt

Look back at a recent performance moment. Which of the four controllables—Energy, Attitude, Effort, or Behaviors—shaped your experience most, for better or worse? What does that reveal about your natural tendencies under pressure? Choose one to prioritize in your next performance. How will you bring it to life through your actions, tone, or preparation?

The SERR Model™: An Intentional Tool to Manage Adversity

The SERR Model™—*Situation, Emotion, Response, Result*—has become one of the most consistently impactful tools we teach (see Figure 10.1). Leaders across sport, business, and the military describe it as the single most practical framework for handling setbacks. Several professional organizations have since invited us to train entire staffs on its use.

Adapted from cognitive-control methods originally developed within U.S. Special Forces and refined through our applied work with elite performers, SERR provides a simple, repeatable structure for staying composed when emotion hits. Its strength lies in clarity: it gives us a direct plan for how to move through adversity instead of reacting to it.

SERR MODEL

| SITUATION | EMOTION | RESPONSE | RESULT |

Figure 10.1 The SERR Model.
Source: Justin Anderson.

| SITUATION | EMOTION | NATURAL RESPONSE | LIKELY RESULT |

Figure 10.2 SERR: Natural Response Before Training.
Source: Justin Anderson.

Here's how it works in practice before training (see Figure 10.2).

- **Situation:** A quarterback throws an interception.

- **Emotion (Default):** Frustration, embarrassment, or anger.

- **Response (Default):** Without preparation, attention spirals inward. He slams his helmet, curses, withdraws. His body language closes, teammates disconnect, focus is gone.

- **Result (Default):** The emotional hijack lingers, performance declines further as he goes out and plays more tentatively.

Now with intentional preparation (see Figure 10.3):

- **Situation:** "If I throw a pick. . ."
- **Emotion (Expected):** "I'll feel angry and frustrated."

| SITUATION | EMOTION | TRAINED RESPONSE | OPTIMAL RESULT |

Figure 10.3 SERR: With Intentional Preparation.
Source: Justin Anderson.

- **Response (Planned):** "Keep my head up. Look coaches in the eye. Talk with receivers. Reset my focus on the next drive."
- **Result (Optimized):** The mistake isn't erased, but it doesn't multiply. Attention returns to controllables: footwork, rhythm, progressions.

Here's how to apply SERR:

1. **Map the Situation:** Identify recurring adversity moments— errors, rejections, tough conversations that you have gone through or that you anticipate could happen again.
2. **Name the Emotion:** Anticipate or recall the emotions and body sensations that show up as a result of that situation.
3. **Spot the Default Response:** Be honest about the untrained, knee-jerk reactions (behaviors) that come when the emotion is felt.
4. **Note the Result:** What happens when you follow the default script?
5. **Reverse Engineer:** Define the *ideal result*, then plan intentional behaviors likely to get you closer.
6. **Rehearse with Imagery:** Each day or before performance, mentally simulate the situation, the emotion rising, and yourself executing the trained response. (See the next section.)

Intention: The Bridge from Awareness to Action

Imagery: Rehearsing How to Get Through Adversity

Once we know our intentional response, the next step is to rehearse it. Imagery turns a plan into neural rehearsal.

We often think of visualization as replaying highlight reels—the perfect shot, the flawless performance. But when paired with SERR, its most powerful use is practicing *how* we'll respond when things don't go as planned.

We encourage performers to go beyond "seeing the highlight reel." That can be helpful, but it doesn't prepare them for the many adverse experiences that likely emerge in high-pressure settings. Instead, we ask them to imagine the full sensory experience:

- What will the arena sound like?

- What will it smell like?

- What will my body feel like as adrenaline spikes?

- Which distractions or setbacks could appear, and if they do, how will I respond (using the SERR model)?

Seeing themselves walking through adversity in an optimal way can be an incredibly powerful tool for building consistency and resilience.

An NBA Player Using SERR Plus Imagery

A professional basketball player we worked with began using the SERR model and imagery to prepare for missing the first three shots of a game. This was a situation that occurred from time to time, and when it did, his natural response was, *"I just don't have it tonight."* Of course, players at his level don't suddenly lose their ability. He had it; he just wasn't accessing it. Most of that came from focusing on his negative self-talk.

Instead of listening to that default voice, he decided—after reconstructing his response with the SERR model—to imagine talking to himself instead of listening. During his pre-performance intention setting, he would picture himself "calibrating" to find his rhythm if the first few shots didn't fall. He imagined feeling the frustration of the misses, but instead of collapsing into the binary judgment of *"I don't have it tonight,"* he simply named the miss: *"That one was long. That one was wide."*

This naming process allowed him to work through the immediate knee-jerk emotion and reset his attention on seeing the spot and hitting the spot. Once he trained this imagery routine, his confidence took off. He realized that tough starts or cold stretches no longer defined him, because he now had a plan—and he had practiced that plan in advance.

It's important to note that imagery is effective because the brain doesn't fully distinguish between vivid mental rehearsal and lived experience. Mental rehearsal strengthens the same neural networks that are activated in reality. Applied research has consistently shown that imagery enhances attentional control and confidence, especially when it integrates multiple senses and rehearses adversity as well as success (Vealey & Greenleaf, 2010; Moran, 2009).

By running through both the ideal scenarios and the adversity scenarios, performers inoculate themselves against the firecracker moments. When the real distractions hit, it feels less like a shock and more like something they've already prepared for.

Exercise: Refine and Repeat

Think of a recurring setback that tends to pull you off course. Walk it through the SERR model:

- What situation reliably triggers you?
- What emotions and body signals usually show up?

- What default response do you tend to fall into?

- What result does that create?

Now, rewrite the script: Choose the behaviors you want to execute the next time this situation arises, regardless of how you feel. How will this intentional response create a better result? (See Figure 10.3 for an example.)

Every SERR plan is a draft. After performance, revisit it: Did the response (behaviors) get me closer to my goal? Did it keep me aligned with my controllables? If not, adjust and refine. As we say: If we hit, we build. If we miss, we learn. Either way, we're growing.

Exercise: Building Your Intentional System

We view Intention as the bridge between awareness and action. It takes the self-knowledge we build in the IA Framework—our values, motivators, biases, fears, and strengths—and translates it into controllable plan of action we can carry into performance.

We saw how:

- **Primary Intention Setting** (our daily mindset prep) primes the brain's attentional filters to notice what matters most.

- **Performance Intention Setting** (Pre, During, and Post performance) sharpens that compass and leverages the recency effect to make our chosen cues easier to recall under pressure.

- **Controllable Intention Cues—Energy, Attitude, Effort, and Behaviors**—provide structural supports that are always within our control, no matter the situation.

- **The SERR Model** equips us to navigate adversity by planning intentional behaviors that keep us aligned with our goals when emotions are strong.

- **Imagery** strengthens these tools, training both ideal scenarios and adversity responses into the brain's neural networks so that when the real noise hits, we're not surprised—we're prepared.

The throughline of all these tools is simple: We don't control outcomes, but we can control how we show up. Intention-setting makes sure that when the spotlight turns on or the pressure spikes, our attention is anchored to the behaviors most likely to produce consistency, resilience, and growth.

But setting intentions is not the same as holding them. A blueprint matters only if we can execute on it. Chapter 11 is about **Attentional Execution**—the real-time skill of sustaining focus on our intentions, resisting the pull of distractions, and resetting quickly when attention drifts. Where intention sets the plan, attentional execution is about carrying it out when the heat is on.

In Chapter 11, we'll step directly into the fire of performance and explore how to strengthen the attentional muscle—so that when pressure hits, we don't just know what we *want* to do, we actually *do it*.

Take 10 minutes to map out your personal intention system across the three performance phases:

1. **Primary Intention (Daily Mindset Prep):**

    Write down one intention for how you want to show up tomorrow morning. Anchor it in Energy, Attitude, Effort, or Behaviors.

2. **Pre-Performance Intention:**

    Think of an upcoming performance moment (practice, presentation, meeting). Within a few hours of it, what cues will you lock in on to sharpen your focus?

3. During-Performance Intention:

Identify one simple process you can use to reset during breaks or mistakes (for example, Mark Messier's head-down reset, a breath, or a key word).

4. Post-Performance Intention:

Decide in advance how you will evaluate yourself afterward. Which controllables—Energy, Attitude, Effort, or Behaviors—will you review instead of defaulting to outcome?

5. Adversity Plan (SERR):

Pick one recurring setback. Walk it through the SERR model and write down your intentional response and use imagery to see yourself successfully navigate your plan.

Chapter 11

Attentional Execution: Winning the Moment

"You can't stop the waves, but you can learn to surf."

—Jon Kabat-Zinn

It was early in the second quarter of a playoff game when one of the point guards we worked with turned the ball over twice in back-to-back possessions. He jogged back on defense with his head down, frustration flashing across his face. The crowd roared, the opposing team's momentum surged, and his teammates' body language began to sink.

But something different happened on the third possession. After the whistle, he crouched, tied his shoe, and took a slow breath. He gave himself a cue—"Eyes up, run the team"—then slapped his chest twice before jogging back to the huddle. That small ritual was his reset. Instead of spiraling into frustration, he redirected his attention to what he could control: pace, energy, leadership.

The shift wasn't magic. He didn't suddenly drop 20 points like we might see in a Hollywood movie. But he steadied the team, kept them connected, and made sure the game didn't slip away by focusing on his energy, attitude, and effort.

This is the essence of Attentional Execution: the ability to direct and hold focus on performance-relevant data—and, when attention drifts, to reset quickly and re-anchor to the cues that drive performance.

Attentional Execution is the centerpiece of the IA Framework. Everything before it is meant to prepare us to execute optimally, and everything after it is designed for us to learn from it and recharge our attentional systems so we can be our best for extended periods of time.

Awareness tells us where our attention tends to go. Intention sets the blueprint for where we want it to go. But neither matters unless we can translate them into deliberate behaviors in the fire of performance. Attentional Execution is that translation—the moment where attention stops being a concept and becomes a skill.

To be clear, Attentional Execution doesn't mean "perfect focus" or "never distracted." It means catching drift faster, redirecting more efficiently, and staying anchored to performance-relevant data long enough to win the moment.

Performance doesn't happen when we are learning in the classroom or in the mirror—it often happens in the arena of chaos, when stress is high, emotions are loud, and distractions compete for our focus.

One leader we worked with described how easily her attention drifted during high-stakes owner meetings. Instead of listening, she found herself mentally rehearsing what she was going to say next. After learning Attentional Execution skills, she began using a personal cue—"Listen first"—whenever she noticed herself drifting. It didn't eliminate distractions, but it sure helped. It kept her anchored to what mattered: hearing the question behind the question. It also helped her stay curious, following up with more questions instead of rushing to provide answers. Over time, that shift created greater clarity and alignment with the owners' vision. Within a year, her executive evaluations reflected noticeable change—"a step up" in her leadership presence, openness to others' ideas, and composure under pressure.

Neuroscience helps explain why this is so difficult. The prefrontal cortex—the brain's control tower—has limited bandwidth. Under stress, it competes with the amygdala and emotional circuits for control. Mistakes and unexpected stressors trigger error-monitoring systems in the anterior cingulate cortex, which can either guide adaptive adjustment or, if unmanaged, flood attention with noise. What separates elite performers isn't the absence of distraction but the efficiency of their recovery—the speed and precision with which they reset and re-engage with controllable cues.

The Focus Window™: Cars on the Freeway

In Chapter 9, we introduced the Focus Window—the space where performance-relevant data lives. During Attentional Execution, this model shifts from awareness tool to tactical system. It becomes how we manage the moment in real time.

We described attention as a freeway filled with cars rushing by—each car representing a thought, sensation, or cue. Some carry information that matters; most don't. We can't stop traffic. Thoughts will always come and go—mistakes, crowd noise, frustration, judgment, even hope. The goal isn't to control the flow; it's to notice which car we've climbed into and decide whether to stay in it or step out.

In performance, drifting into the wrong car is inevitable. A missed shot triggers self-talk: *Don't mess up again.* A leader's attention shifts to how their words sound instead of who they're speaking to. These are normal human reactions—but staying in those cars too long pulls us off course.

The skill lies in catching the drift early and redirecting back to performance-relevant data—the cues that drive action in the present moment. For the quarterback, that might mean moving from *"I can't throw another pick"* to *"Find leverage, trust the read."* For the student, it's shifting from *"I'm going to fail this test"* to *"One question at a time. Read carefully. Execute."*

One common attentional error many performers make during the execution phase is believing that distracting thoughts shouldn't show up in competition—and then get frustrated when they do. That fight with the thought often becomes more disruptive than the thought itself. Instead, this is where the *observer stance*, metacognition, and our Focus Window model matter most: noticing the thought, labeling it as distraction, and letting it pass without judgment. You don't fight traffic—you just choose which car to ride with.

Because of the groundwork built in Awareness and Intention, we shouldn't need to reprocess or overanalyze in the moment. By then, we already know which thoughts and cues belong in our Focus Window. Execution simply becomes this: Noise, Name, Redirect.

Without that preparatory work, however, attentional management is far from simple. Precious time and focus get hijacked by unanticipated, disruptive thoughts. Lacking a prescreened set of intentions, trying to choose the right car from dozens racing by can feel insurmountable, especially in the heat of pressure. But with a pre-trained blueprint—our performance-relevant data and intentional cues—the mind can act with speed and clarity.

When this skill becomes embodied, something remarkable can happen. A tennis player feels anger after a double fault but steps back into a more productive thought labeled "feet set, toss high." A manager might catch the drift into worry about direct reports' reactions and step back into "clarify and connect" thought.

And it's not just for athletes or executives. A parent once told us about bedtime with his two young kids. He often caught himself sitting in the wrong "car" on the freeway—thinking about work emails or frustrations from the day—while reading them a story. Then he started concentrating instead on the wonderment in his kids' eyes as he turned each page.

After practicing with the Focus Window, he started catching those drifts and stepping back into the "present car"—fully engaged in the moment: voices, laughter, and warmth. *"Be where my feet are,"* he'd quietly remind himself. His kids didn't know the science, but they knew the difference. They felt his presence, because he truly noticed them.

Attentional Execution isn't about controlling thoughts—it's about mastering choice. The freeway is always full. The power is deciding which lane to travel in. To train that choice under pressure, we need to strengthen the system that directs it—the brain itself.

Harnessing the Brain's Strength: Training Focus Execution

Like strength and conditioning, Attentional Execution can be trained. The more deliberate reps we give our attentional system, the stronger—and less easily disrupted—it becomes. This is supported by decades of research showing that attentional management is plastic and can be improved through deliberate practice (Eysenck et al., 2007; Klingberg, 2010).

One of the most effective gateways into training attention is through *vision*. The human brain is a visually dominant organ. Roughly one-third of the cerebral cortex is devoted to processing what we see—more than to hearing, touch, taste, and smell combined (Zeki, 1993; Kastner & Ungerleider, 2000; Wandell et al., 2007). The occipital lobe, our visual hub, is the largest of all sensory regions.

Evolution favored this design. Humans are navigators and interpreters—creatures built to orient, predict, and connect through sight. By comparison, a dog's brain devotes similar real estate to smell—in a lineup, simply by scent, dogs can distinguish one individual out of millions—humans prioritize vision in much the same way. We can distinguish faces with remarkable accuracy, determining one person from the next in an instant. As a result, *human eyes don't just see—they lead.*

Every glance, fixation, and scan pattern sends a signal that ripples through attentional and motor networks. Neuroscience shows that where our eyes go, attention and motor planning follow within milliseconds (Posner, 1980; Corbetta & Shulman, 2002). That's why stabilizing the gaze can stabilize the mind.

Training the visual system, therefore, is one of the most direct ways to train attention. The exercises that follow help us strengthen two essential attentional skills:

1. **Holding focus** on what matters.

2. **Letting go** when distraction arises.

The Flashlight Exercise: Training to Hold Focus

The flashlight exercise strengthens external attention by treating the eyes like a beam of light. The task is simple: Hold attention on a specific object and notice what emerges. Because the eyes lead the mind, this simple exercise strengthens both systems at once.

Many performers start by focusing on their hand at arm's length, noticing details they've never really seen before—skin tone, pores, indentations, wrinkles. The challenge is to keep attention locked there for more than 30 seconds. Inevitably, the mind wanders. Many are surprised by how quickly their minds wander, normally within seconds. But with all training, each time attention drifts and is brought back to the target, the attentional muscle strengthens.

The next step is to have athletes practice at different depths: a picture across the room, a tree outside, or eventually, sport-specific distances. A baseball hitter might focus on an object 60 ft away to simulate the important distance where pitcher releases the ball. A basketball player might lock onto the rim from 15 ft—the distance of a free throw. Over time, this practice strengthens the neural pathways that sustain focus at the precise distances competition demands.

We also teach a "zoom-out" variation, broadening the flashlight beam to take in a wider visual field without locking on a single point. This panoramic gaze has been proven to lower arousal and reduce anxiety (Kaplan, 1995; Felisberti & Currie, 2019). Perhaps it's the same reason panoramic views—a sunset over the ocean or a valley from a mountaintop—feel inherently calming. We can harness this natural human neurology to regulate our activation levels under stress. For example, golfers use it by scanning the horizon of a course as a reset routine after a poor shot. A softball player might trace the meeting point of sky and stadium before stepping into the box. In both cases, the athlete is managing activation through attentional control—using vision to regulate physiology before performance. In this case, expanding the visual field calms the system, creating a relaxed attentional state before execution.

Visual Priority: Where the Eyes Go, the Mind Follows

If the flashlight exercise helps us train the attentional muscle, *visual priority* explains why those reps matter.

As noted earlier, the human brain devotes more cortical real estate to vision than to any other sense (Kastner & Ungerleider, 2000). This dominance means that the eyes are not passive receivers—they're active directors of attention. Neuroscience shows that every shift in gaze triggers downstream activity across attentional and motor networks, steering both what we perceive and how we move (Posner, 1980; Corbetta & Shulman, 2002).

That's why a steady gaze often equals a steady mind. Visual control offers a powerful entry point for attentional control. But it also explains why visual distractions—screens, movement, flashes of light—capture us so easily. Our attentional wiring still treats motion and novelty as potential threats. In modern environments, that instinct often works against us.

A clear example of visual priority in action comes from sport science through what's known as the Quiet Eye phenomenon. First identified by Joan Vickers (2007), the Quiet Eye describes the final visual fixation on a task-relevant target just before movement execution. Across sports—golf, basketball, field-goal kicking—elite performers consistently maintain longer, steadier fixations than less-experienced peers. That final half-second of visual stillness acts as an anchor point for the brain and body—and many seasoned performers have incorporated it into their pre-performance routines.

When a basketball player lines up for a free throw, she may dribble three times while locking her gaze on a precise spot at the back of the rim for an extra beat. If she's a sharpshooter, she's not merely "looking"—she's stabilizing her attentional system. The steady gaze filters noise, sharpens focus, and synchronizes neural timing between perception and action. In essence, the eyes become a metronome for execution.

We've seen this firsthand using eye-tracking with professional athletes. Many less consistent free throw shooters' eyes darted around the rim before release—brief, reactive, scattered fixations. After visual-focus training, those same athletes developed longer, calmer gazes. The result wasn't just more made shots. It was steadier composure, more consistent rhythm, and greater confidence that their attention would hold when pressure peaked.

By steadying our eyes, we steady perception—and with it, the coordination between mind and body. This is the essence of Attentional Execution—stabilizing what we see so that the mind and body can operate in sync.

Vision is one of the strongest levers we have for directing focus; where the eyes lead, the mind follows. But not all distractions enter through sight. Some arise internally—emotions, doubts, intrusive thoughts, or body sensations competing for bandwidth.

The next layer of Attentional Execution addresses this inner terrain: learning to observe, release, and re-anchor focus when the distraction comes from within.

The Drift-Through Exercise: Training to Release Thoughts

As we've discussed throughout, distractions to our attention can be a significant barrier to living up to our potential and achieving our goals. And we know that not all distractions come from external stimuli. Many arise within: the swirl of thoughts, judgments, emotions, and physiological sensations that pull focus away from what matters.

The Drift-Through Exercise is an intervention we use to train how to move through these distractions. It strengthens what we call *selective non-attachment*—the ability to notice thoughts and feelings without being owned by them. This allows performers to recover from ruminating thoughts and emotional noise more quickly and efficiently.

We begin by again using our Focus Window and the cars on a freeway metaphor. This time, the task is to simply not climb into any of them. Observe each car as it enters your Focus Window—your field of consciousness—and let it pass without judgment. At times, you'll notice you've jumped in and started riding with one. The moment you realize that, step out, watch it drive by, and return to observing. Inevitably, another thought will enter. Each time you notice and release, you strengthen the skill of *letting go*—a cornerstone of mental agility across every performance domain.

Most clients practice this exercise for no more than 10 minutes a day, often as part of their evening routine. Over time, it trains detachment from thought and emotion. Many describe the process as "popping popcorn"—thoughts continuously bubbling up, one after another. Some are familiar, others random or absurd. All of this is normal. The point isn't to stop the popcorn from popping; it's to realize that *we are not the popcorn*. We are the observer.

Research on mindfulness-based attention training shows that such practices improve cognitive flexibility, emotional regulation, and sustained performance under pressure (Kabat-Zinn, 1990; Jha et al., 2007). One Olympic swimmer told us that her pre-race nerves used to hijack her in the ready room. After practicing the exercises in this section, she learned to redirect her attention from the noise around the outcome of her race back to her breath, then to her lane, then back again to her breath. The effect was liberating: "I realized my attention didn't control me—I controlled it."

Together, these exercises highlight two essential sides of Attentional Execution: the ability to choose what to hold on to and what to let go. Both remind us that distractions—whether external or internal—will always appear. What matters is not stopping them, but recognizing where they pull our attention and deliberately redirecting it toward the data that move us closer to our goals.

Perspective-Taking and Reappraisal

Often, what derails performance is not the distraction itself, but the meaning we attach to it. A stumble, a critical comment, or a spike of nerves isn't inherently destructive—it's how we interpret it that determines its impact. Perspective-taking and reappraisal are the skills that allow us to reinterpret the moment in constructive ways.

But timing matters. We don't recommend that performers try to think through complicated reappraisals in the middle of competition. For example, if a presenter notices a member of the audience dozing off during a presentation, that's not the moment to pause and mentally generate potential explanations. Trying to solve the "why" in real time just pulls attention further away from the task.

That work—surfacing and reframing limiting appraisals—belongs in the Awareness and Intention phases. In training, a performer might recognize that their default appraisal is, *"They're sleeping because I'm boring,"* and deliberately replace it with alternatives: *"Maybe they had a long night. Maybe they trust me enough to relax. My job is to deliver the message with clarity."* Doing that work beforehand means execution stays anchored to the goal.

Still, surprises will arise. That's why we encourage every performer to have a catch-all reframe ready: *"Back to my behaviors and values."* If an unexpected distraction surfaces, the reframe isn't to solve it—it's to return attention to controllables. Reset posture. Stick to the task cue. Reconnect with a core value. Deep reappraisal can wait for reflection and can happen afterward; in the moment, the most effective reframe is simply to get back to performance-relevant behaviors.

One of the most important reappraisals to complete ahead of time is how we view anxiety. Many performers assume that anxiety is a "bad" signal, something to fight off or eliminate. That's why phrases like "calm down" tend to backfire: They frame anxiety as evidence of weakness, which increases self-focus and undermines confidence (Brooks, 2014). In contrast, when performers reappraise anxiety as excitement—as the body's way of gearing up for performance—the same physiological arousal becomes fuel rather than friction.

This is because anxiety and excitement share the same underlying physiological signatures—elevated heart rate, quickened breathing, increased adrenaline. The difference lies not in the body's state but in the story the mind attaches to it (Jamieson et al., 2010). If the appraisal is *"this means I'm nervous, and nervous is bad,"* attention drifts to threat and performance suffers. If the appraisal is *"this means I'm ready, and this energy can help me perform,"* attention stays on performance-relevant data.

We've seen this single reframe change careers. A track athlete preparing for Olympic Trials told us she used to interpret pre-race nerves as proof that she wasn't ready. After working on reappraisal, she began telling herself, "Of course I'm nervous—this is my body generating energy and letting me know it's ready." The nerves didn't disappear, but her attention shifted back to her race plan. The result: She converted that energy into an explosive start, smoother rhythm, and her fastest qualifying time.

Perspective shifts don't erase pressure—but they give the brain a constructive lens to ride with instead of fighting against. And the best time to build those shifts is before the spotlight is on.

The Actual Test of Attention

The actual training of our attentional skill is critical, but our ability to evaluate that skill comes when the whistle blows, the meeting starts, or the lights go on. Performance execution is where the attentional muscle gets activated—applied to the controllable behaviors that help us win the moment.

Focus Cues

When we step into performance, the most effective thing we can do is tether our attention to what we already know matters most. Focus cues—short, repeatable anchors—are the bridge from intention to execution. They work because they're simple, behavioral, and memorable under pressure. In many cases, they take the form of self-talk: the words we choose to say to ourselves in the moment.

Examples:

- A golfer whispering, "Commit to the target."
- A quarterback muttering, "Chin up, reset."
- An executive repeating, "Listen first."

One NFL kicker uses the cue *"strike"* before every attempt, funneling his entire focus into contact and follow-through. A Fortune

500 sales leader we worked with enters negotiations with the cue *"curiosity"*—a single word that shifts her from performance anxiety into genuine engagement.

The best cues share three characteristics:

- **Short:** one to four words.

- **Present tense:** tied to the immediate moment.

- **Behavioral and instructional:** "Eyes on target" is stronger than "Be confident."

We often coach performers to build two or three cues tied to the four controllable pillars described in Chapter 10—Energy, Attitude, Effort, and Behaviors. When distraction inevitably arises, the cue becomes the rope that pulls attention back. The time for self-talk like "Be confident" is before the competition. In execution, cues in most cases ought to be instructional, specific, and actionable.

Not all cues are verbal. Some should be visual—letters inscribed on gear, initials taped to a glove, or a symbol that reconnects focus. Steve Kerr famously wrote *FI* ("F*ck It") on his sneakers—a cue to free himself from judgment and let the ball fly. Baseball players will often lock onto a foul pole or a dot on their bat after a missed swing. Each cue serves the same purpose: tethering attention to what's next, not what's past.

Post-Mistake Response: The AAA Model

Even with strong cues, mistakes are inevitable. What separates elite execution isn't whether errors occur—it's how quickly performers respond afterward.

One professional golfer told us that his post-mistake response became as important as his swing. He built a deliberate plan, practiced it during training rounds, and visualized it each night until it became automatic. After every offline shot, he stepped back, cleaned his club, exhaled, and walked to the ball with his head up. "The walk," he said, "is my reset—it's the line between what just happened and what I want to happen next."

That reset was more than ritual. Within it was an intentional post-mistake process—a model we've found to be highly effective across high-pressure environments: **we call it the AAA Model—Awareness, Acceptance, and Action.**

- **Awareness (Nonjudgmental)**

  The first step is simply naming what we observe without judgment: *"I pulled that left"* rather than *"That was a horrible shot—I'm in the rough, and this round's slipping away."*

  This kind of awareness fills the Focus Window with clear, factual data—like a play-by-play commentator calling the moment, not a color commentator analyzing it. We just name what we see: *"The ball went left." "I hit it thin."*

  These acknowledgments keep the brain in a calmer state by allowing the prefrontal cortex to focus on facts instead of emotions. Labeling what happened, rather than qualifying it as "good" or "bad," limits the emotional charge and provides the brain useful feedback for subtle correction on the next attempt. In our experience, this process helps the subconscious *solve* the performance problem instead of getting stuck in the identity problem—"I don't belong" or "I'm bad." Judgment triggers the brain's anxiety-driven threat spiral, sending attention down a dozen distracting off-ramps.

- **Acceptance**

  The next step is acceptance—acknowledging reality without analyzing what it means. For the golfer, this meant noting both the situation and the emotion: *"I'm frustrated—and I still have an opportunity to make a shot here."*

Naming the emotion reduces its power. It moves us from *being* the emotion to *observing* it. That shift reopens bandwidth for choice, letting the brain see options rather than locking onto the feeling itself. Without acceptance, the mind generates noise and distraction, making calibration nearly impossible.

- **Action**

    Finally comes action—resetting attention to the next performance-relevant behavior. Self-talk becomes present, specific, and instructional: *"Okay, in the fairway trap—dig in, right side of the green."*

This sequence—**Awareness, Acceptance, Action**—is the AAA Model in practice: a fast, repeatable post-mistake reset that moves attention away from rumination and back toward what's real, present, and controllable.

In the golfer's case, by reviewing the facts and naming what he felt—without judgment—he stripped power from the emotional fallout. That prevented the brain's protective mechanisms from overreacting. Shots were no longer "good" or "bad"; they were simply "left" or "long." That objectivity freed his attention from compounding the past and turned the moment into data. The shot was simply long—useful information that could be used to calibrate the next swing.

This same approach shows up across sports and domains. Serena Williams embodied it with her signature "next point" posture: a brief pause after an error (*awareness*), an exhale to release the outcome (*acceptance*), and an immediate refocus on the serve or return ahead (*action*). Quick release. Reset. Intentional focus.

Research helps explain why this works. Studies on *post-error slowing* show that untrained minds often linger on mistakes—ruminating, overcorrecting, and burning attentional bandwidth that could be used

Attentional Execution: Winning the Moment

to recover (Rabbitt, 1966; Danielmeier & Ullsperger, 2011; Houtman et al., 2012). Reset rituals like the golfer's walk or Serena's next-point routine counter this by building an automatic pathway back to performance-relevant cues. They train the brain to simply focus on the facts of "what is" to *let go faster*—which means the prefrontal cortex can re-engage before the emotional system takes over.

In practice, the principle is simple but powerful: Mistakes are inevitable, judgment is optional, and recovery is trainable. The AAA Model isn't just about composure—it's about reclaiming cognitive bandwidth when it counts.

Flow: The Focus Bullseye

When Attentional Execution reaches its highest form, we enter what psychologists call **flow**—a state of deep immersion where action and rhythm merge and distractions fade to the edges. It's not mystical; it's mechanical. Flow represents the optimal synchronization between attention, emotion, and performance.

Athletes in flow often say they're "not thinking." What they really mean is that their attention is so fully absorbed in performance-relevant cues that the usual interference—self-judgment, outcome anxiety, or overanalysis—goes quiet. Cognitive scientist Arne Dietrich (2004) describes this as *transient hypofrontality*: a temporary down-regulation of the brain's judgment function, which frees motor and perceptual systems to operate fluidly and without interruption. Mihaly Csikszentmihalyi (1990), who first formalized the concept, found that flow arises when challenge and skill are balanced—when we're stretched just beyond comfort but still within reach of mastery.

In flow, attention moves with precision and efficiency. The brain's error-monitoring systems stay active, but they signal adjustments automatically rather than triggering emotional interference. Time can distort, movements smooth out, and decisions accelerate. The prefrontal cortex still plays a role—it monitors and directs—but it doesn't micromanage.

Importantly, flow isn't the absence of distraction; it's the *byproduct* of a trained attentional system. Because the performer has rehearsed awareness, intention, and execution, the irrelevant "cars" on the freeway fade into the periphery. What remains in the Focus Window are only the cues that matter.

We see this across contexts:

- A basketball player in rhythm stops tracking stats and starts tracking space.

- A musician on stage stops analyzing technique and becomes fully immersed in the sound.

- A parent reading to their kids stops evaluating the day and simply inhabits the moment.

Flow isn't something we chase—it's something that *emerges* when attention is trained, intention is clear, and execution becomes automatic. It's the internal reward for all the unseen mental reps that came before—the moment when all systems align and performance falls into rhythm. It reminds us of what's possible when attention, intention, and execution operate as one. The next step is to make that level of focus more repeatable.

Exercise: Building Your Attentional Execution Plan

Attentional Execution is about *winning moments*, not eliminating distractions. The goal is to create a personal system that helps you return to performance-relevant data more efficiently and consistently.

Use the following prompts to begin shaping your own execution plan and training the attentional muscle.

1. Focus Window Check

- What kinds of "cars" most often pull your attention off track in your performance environment? (Distractions)
- Which cues consistently carry performance-relevant information that you want to include in your Focus Window more often?

2. Attentional Muscle Training

- Which practice feels most relevant right now: *holding attention* (Flashlight Exercise) or *letting go of distraction* (Drift-Through Exercise)? Why?
- Where could you integrate two to three minutes of deliberate attentional training into your daily or weekly rhythm?

3. Reappraisal Readiness

- What common triggers—nerves, feedback, mistakes—tend to derail your attention?
- Write one reframe you can prepare ahead of time to keep attention on controllable behaviors when that trigger appears.

4. Focus Cues

- What short, actionable cue will you use to anchor attention at the start of performance?
- What second cue will help you recover quickly if drift or distraction sets in?

5. Post-Mistake Reset (AAA Model)

- What mistake tends to hook you most strongly (for example, missed shot, critical comment, small slip in execution)?

- What physical or verbal reset will you use to release it (movement, breath, phrase)?

- How can you apply the AAA Model—**Awareness** → **Acceptance** → **Action**—in that moment to return attention to what's controllable?

6. **Integration: Building Your Reset System**

- If you built your personal "reset system" today, which two or three tools from this chapter—Focus Window, Flashlight, Quiet Eye, Drift-Through, Focus Cues, AAA, or Nonjudgmental Awareness—would form its core?

- How will you rehearse these tools so they become automatic when pressure peaks?

Attentional Execution sits at the center of performance, but growth doesn't stop when the lights go off. The real gains come in what happens next—how we review, learn, and refine after performance ends.

In Chapter 12, we'll explore *Reflection*: how to evaluate performance not through outcomes alone, but through alignment—between our intentions, our attention, and our actions. We'll also see how feeding that reflection back into the IA Framework—awareness, intention, and execution—creates a continuous loop of growth and adaptability.

Reflection: Learning Beyond the Whistle

"We do not learn from experience . . . we learn from reflecting on experience."

—John Dewey

In professional sport, film sessions are the backbone of postgame analysis. They often zero in on scheme and technique—missed rotations, blown coverages, poor shot selection. Traditional review nails what happened but rarely digs into the root cause of *why*. Without that deeper layer, the same mistakes surface again and again.

Was a player forcing shots because of motivation—chasing production? Was it a misunderstanding of the scheme? A physical gap, where execution simply wasn't possible? Or was it mental—attention slipping, poor decisions, the game speeding up in the moment? These are significant differences, and they require very different interventions. Standard review rarely distinguishes between them. And when it doesn't, the most important lessons slip away.

Many coaches stop there. However, more are now going further—building reflection processes that not only correct tactics but also uncover the psychological drivers of performance by examining mindset, decision-making, and, just as importantly, the levers for improvement. This is reflection through the lens of attention—identifying not just what happened, but where attention was directed and how it shaped execution.

One head coach we worked with refused to let his staff settle for surface-level review. After every game, he required assistants to submit written reflections in a simple, consistent format:

- What stood out today?
- What needs to carry forward?
- What drove the gaps in execution?
  - Scheme/Tactics/Technique
  - Physical Ability (strength, size, speed)
  - Mental/Emotional Skills (processing speed, confidence, attention)
- What does each player need to improve?
  - List
  - Prioritize
  - Plan

At first, assistants saw it as busy work. After the grind of an 82-game season, the extra layer felt like another box to check. But the head coach insisted. For him, this wasn't about venting—it was about training his staff to hunt for performance-relevant data: the actions that helped the team win, the behaviors worth reinforcing, and the true gaps worth addressing.

He pushed them past labels like "selfish play" toward causal drivers: motivation, scheme clarity, physical limits, or attentional drift under pressure.

Reflection wasn't just about players, either—it extended to coaches. Before the season began, he set out staff nonnegotiables:

1. Bring positive energy into the building.
2. Regulate emotions: Teach, don't yell.

3. Problem-solve: Help players adjust within the system.

4. Grow and learn yourself.

Over time, the culture shifted. Staff meetings became less about critique and more about concrete, prioritized development plans. As assistants shared what worked, a feedback loop formed. Tactics that proved effective spread across the staff. Players noticed, too. When they saw teammates improving, they wanted to engage in the same process.

By season's end, the team was sharper, the players more efficient, and—just as striking—the coaches had become better teachers and communicators. Through structured reflection, they adapted their approach to connect with players' preferred learning styles and delivered more impactful coaching. The lesson was clear: Intentional reflection wasn't just maintenance—it was a competitive advantage. And this isn't just true in sport.

The Science of Reflection

Reflection provides a competitive edge in learning and performance. The science backs this up. In a large-scale study, Di Stefano et al. (2014) examined reflection's impact across lab and field settings with more than 4,000 participants. In one field experiment at a technology support call center, employees in training were divided into three groups:

- **Practice group:** Spent the final 15 minutes of each session completing more problem-solving exercises.

- **Reflection group:** Spent those 15 minutes reflecting on what they had just learned—writing down what worked, what didn't, and what they would do differently.

- **Sharing group:** Reflected individually and then shared their reflections with peers.

The results were striking. On a subsequent training test, the reflection group outperformed the practice group by 23%, despite having done *less* additional practice. The sharing group performed slightly better than the reflection-only group (about 25% improvement), showing that the performance gains primarily came from the act of reflection itself—but sharing didn't hurt either.

The benefits appear across industries as well. Ellwood and Abrams (2017) found that medical students who reflected after clinical exercises demonstrated significantly stronger long-term recall and skill transfer compared to peers who only practiced more. In other words, reflection didn't just help participants remember—it helped them *apply* learning to new, complex situations.

These studies highlight a powerful truth: reflection consistently accelerates learning. It is a core mechanism for turning experience into expertise. And critically, it is one of the most effective tools we have for improving attentional control under pressure.

Why? Because reflection strengthens metacognition—our ability to think about our thinking. It creates the space to notice themes, encode lessons more deeply, and connect actions and attentional patterns to values, goals, and performance-relevant data. Across domains the evidence is consistent: Deliberate reflection consolidates learning and strengthens metacognitive control in ways extra reps cannot. In time-scarce environments, the fastest way forward is often looking backwards.

The Problem: Too Much Prep, Not Enough Reflection

In both sport and business, the bias is always toward *what's next*: the next opponent, the next pitch, the next client meeting. What often gets skipped is the last rep, the last game, the last presentation. Without intentional reflection, valuable data slips away, mistakes repeat, and lessons scatter.

Reflection doesn't need to be lengthy. But it does need to be structured. Which brings us to the simple framework we teach leaders and athletes:

- **What Went Well?**
- **What's Worth Improving?**
- **What's the Priority for Tomorrow?**

We saw this firsthand with an NFL quarterback we worked with. Prior to learning a structured reflection process, his film reviews were harsh and judgmental. After a missed throw, his default reflection sounded like: *"That was a horrible play. Such a bad pass."* That kind of evaluation didn't help him—it only reinforced self-criticism and threat-based thinking.

During a particularly important intersquad practice, he attempted this structured reflection for the first time. On a crossing route, he missed his receiver's hands by about 10 inches. At first glance, his judgment labeled it a disaster. But when he slowed down and reviewed it systematically, the picture changed:

- **What Went Well?** He began with controllables—values, energy, and attitude. He noted that his energy was strong and alert, his attitude open and positive, and that he had been a good teammate—encouraging others throughout practice. Then he reviewed execution: He had called the play correctly, aligned the team, triggered motions on time, reset protections, executed his dropback, worked through his progression, and released the ball on time. That was a long chain of successful actions.

- **What's Worth Improving?** The miss came down to one technical detail: He shortened his step, limiting hip rotation and causing the ball to drift behind the receiver. A small, correctable issue—not an indictment of his ability. More importantly, he noticed how quickly judgmental self-talk crept in. In the past, a few consecutive misses would have triggered a spiral. Now, instead of "That was terrible," he shifted to more precise reflections like, *"That throw was behind"* or *"I didn't get my eyes over to the route quickly enough."*

- **What's the Priority for Tomorrow?** His plan was simple: rehearse full step-and-rotation footwork in individual drills, while replacing judgmental self-talk with the cue, *"Feet, follow-through."* He also carried forward his values of hard work and leadership—he was still the first in the building, still encouraging teammates on the sideline, and he wanted to reinforce those behaviors alongside his technical adjustments.

The reflection didn't erase the misses. But it reframed them. Instead of spiraling into judgment, he left with clarity: emphasize footwork, get eyes on the read quicker, reset attention faster, and carry forward what was already working. Over time, this structured process helped him see how attention connected to judgments, emotions, and body tension—and more importantly, how to interrupt the old spirals that used to hijack his season. Like the research shows, the look back made him better, faster, than mindlessly "repping it out" ever could.

Reflection as Release: Breaking the Cycle of Rumination

One of the biggest traps for elite performers isn't a lack of preparation—it's rumination. Many athletes, executives, and performers replay mistakes over and over, long after the game or meeting is done. They lie in bed at night rehashing every detail, convinced that the extra mental churn will somehow lead to better outcomes tomorrow. In reality, it rarely does. Rumination magnifies judgment, drains energy, and disrupts recovery. Extensive research distinguishes reflection from rumination—while reflection promotes adaptive learning, rumination reinforces negative emotion and impairs performance recovery (Nolen-Hoeksema et al., 2008).

This is where structured reflection makes the difference. Our quarterback learned that once he had gone through the reflection process—capturing what went well, what was worth improving, and what his priorities were for tomorrow—he didn't need to keep thinking about it. The lessons were already stored. The plan was already in place. Reflection became a container: a deliberate, time-bound process that gave him clarity and then freed him to let go.

Without structure, reflection can feel endless—an open loop of "what ifs" and "should haves." With structure, the loop closes: Clarity replaces judgment, a plan replaces worry, and release replaces rumination. This release isn't a luxury; it's a performance necessity. Just as a surgeon doesn't keep operating on the same incision once the work is done, performers don't need to keep dissecting the same play, pitch, or meeting once the reflection is complete. The most important step after structured reflection is to trust the process, shut the mental book, and allow the body and mind to recover.

For high achievers who are often their own harshest critics, this is one of the most valuable outcomes of intentional reflection. It gives them permission to stop. To know they've captured what matters, built a plan, and can now turn the page—freeing their attention for rest, recovery, and what's next. Once they reflected and built tomorrow's plan, they can close the loop: *Reflect, Plan, Release.*

Why Structured Reflection Matters

Reflection is powerful, but structured reflection is what makes it transformational. Without structure, reflection can easily drift into judgment or endless rumination—a trap that many high-level performers know all too well. Structure creates boundaries, much like a surgeon's process: identify the issue, address it with precision, and then close up so the body can recover. We don't ask surgeons to operate on the same spot again and again; the same principle applies to performance. Once we've reflected, learned, and built a plan, the best next step is to let go, recover, and allow growth to take root.

A structured reflection process does four critical things:

1. **Directs Attention.** It narrows the focus onto performance-relevant information instead of vague judgments.

2. **Reinforces Strengths.** By highlighting what went well, it strengthens the attentional patterns and behaviors that drive success.

3. **Identifies Constructive Improvements.** By assessing "what's worth improving" through controllable levers (not just outcomes), performers use nonjudgmental, data-driven reflection to identify the adjustments that truly make a difference.

4. **Closes the Loop.** Ending with a clear plan signals to the brain that the reflection is complete. For perfectionist performers who tend to overthink, this is crucial: The process allows them to capture lessons, commit to tomorrow's plan, and then release lingering judgment.

Research supports this. Reflection transforms experience into learning (Kolb, 1984), deliberate practice accelerates growth when it incorporates feedback and adjustment (Ericsson et al., 1993), and structured reflection enhances coaching effectiveness and athlete learning (Gilbert & Trudel, 2001). In other words, it's not reflection alone that fuels growth—it's reflection done with intentional structure.

Structured reflection turns experience into information, and information into adjustment. It helps performers extract the lesson, commit to the next plan, and release the moment—so attention stays anchored on what comes next, not what already happened.

A Five-Minute Performance Reflection (End of Day/Game/Meeting)

Much like the QB, we encourage all performers to take five minutes at the end of their activities to move through three prompts:

1. **What Went Well?**
   - Begin with values/energy/attitude you lived.
   - Note attention and behaviors (what you noticed, what you did).
   - End with outcomes: completions, first-pitch strikes, opening remarks, warm greetings (briefly).

2. **What's Worth Improving?**
   - Where did attention drift? What triggered it?
   - Which specific behaviors would better align with values/plan next time?

3. **What's the Priority for Tomorrow?**
   - Choose one or two controllable levers—not outcomes.

- Technical or attentional cue (for example, *"Practice non-judgmental observation after a miss," "Lock on target and trust quick release," "Give a teammate a compliment when I'm not feeling confident," "Listen first," "Ask one clarifying question in the meeting"*).
- Decide when and how you'll implement it.

4. **Release (Close the loop to relax)**

- Example: One breath + one line: "Captured and planned. Book closed."

This process doesn't take long. But the compound effect is enormous: reflection turns experience into usable information. Just as we lift weights to build physical strength, these brief reflections build attentional strength. Over time, people stop carrying mistakes forward and start converting each day into clearer execution.

An Example of an Actual Intentional Reflection Journal Entry After a Preseason Game

1. **What Went Well?**

Begin by identifying strengths and wins. Start with controllables—values, energy, attitude—before moving to attention, behaviors, and outcomes.

- *Case Example (NFL QB):*
  - Values: Showed up early, prepared, and supported three teammates on the sideline.
  - Energy and Attitude: Entered the game calm and steady, found early rhythm.
  - Attention: Stayed locked into progressions, avoided distraction after the tipped ball.

- Behaviors/Outcomes: 4 of 5 completions on the first series, protection adjustments correct.

  → These become anchors worth carrying forward.

2. What's Worth Improving?

Next, identify opportunities. The key here is specificity and honesty without judgment.

- *Case Example (NFL QB):*

  - Judgmental self-talk after misses pulled attention away.

  - Throw behind receiver traced back to shortened step and under-rotated hips.

  - Emotional spike after second incompletion distracted focus for two plays.

3. What's the Priority for Tomorrow?

Finally, distill the review into one or two controllable priorities for the next day.

- *Case Example (NFL QB):*

  - Technical Priority: Emphasize full step and hip rotation in crossing-route throws during practice.

  - Attentional Priority: Use the cue *"Feet, follow-through"* after misses instead of judgmental self-talk.

    → These priorities shape the next practice and reinforce growth without adding complexity or distraction.

Chapter 13

Renewal: Recharging the Attentional System

"Almost everything will work again if you unplug it for a few minutes, including you."

—Anne Lamott

In today's world of nonstop data and unending demands, performance is often assumed to depend on pushing harder. Yet one of the most critical drivers remains overlooked. It isn't preparation, repetition, or even reflection—it's renewal.

This is especially true for our attentional systems. High performers often pride themselves on their grind, and while we've never seen anyone reach the top without working harder than most, the very best also work more intentionally. Contrary to the belief that the harder we push the sharper we become, attention doesn't operate that way. Like a muscle, our attentional system is an energy system—one that can be trained for greater strength and endurance, but one that must also be renewed.

We see this every day in the people we work with. Leaders, athletes, and professionals describe days so full that it feels like they're running an ultra-marathon—balancing careers that demand constant output, the weight of family and life stressors, and the pressure to keep growing year after year on top of it all. Burnout, or at least fatigue, has become almost a baseline condition for many high performers. That's why finding healthy, sustainable renewal practices matters. Not as another box to check, but as small, intentional resets—like a runner taking an energy pack mid-race—that help sustain performance when stopping isn't an option. Renewal offers something rare: a way to refuel while still running, so people can keep growing, juggling, and showing up at their best.

And here's the good news: Science has shown us that renewal doesn't have to mean long breaks or wholesale lifestyle changes. Some of the highest performers in the world weave short, practical renewal practices into their daily routines—tools that don't feel like "one more thing" to do, but instead make them more present, efficient, and productive in meaningful moments. This chapter explores what the research teaches us and, more importantly, the practical strategies we can apply—physically, cognitively, and behaviorally—along with common pitfalls to avoid, so we can approach life's marathon with greater intention, energy, and sustainability.

The Neuroscience of Attentional Restoration

Over the past few decades, neuroscience has uncovered much more about how the brain functions, including how our attentional systems are shaped by biology and activity. Because this book is designed to be applied rather than overly technical, we'll keep this overview brief. But it's important to emphasize that our models are built on this science, and while there is far more depth to explore, here we highlight the mechanisms most relevant to applied performance.

Think of each of these systems as different kinds of "energy packs" for the attentional marathon. Some deliver quick boosts, some rebuild reserves for the long haul, but all are essential for sustaining performance under pressure.

The Default Mode Network: Offloading and Integration

When we're not engaged in a directed task—daydreaming, letting the mind wander, or simply reflecting—the brain's default mode network (DMN) activates. Far from being wasted time, this state consolidates memories, integrates experiences, and links information in novel ways, which explains why creativity and problem-solving often arise when we're "zoned out." It also helps regulate emotions by reprocessing events and building coherence in our personal "story."

The DMN itself doesn't refuel the brain in the same way that sleep or nutrition do, but it does offload the task-directed network—our executive, Intentional Attention system. That offloading reduces cognitive fatigue and restores capacity for sustained focus. In fact, fMRI studies show that alternating between task-directed work and DMN activity throughout the day can be essential for sustainable cognition (Christoff et al., 2009).

This is why finding moments throughout the day where attention isn't tightly directed—non-directed attention states—can make our Intentional Attention sharper and more resilient when we return to task.

Attention Restoration Theory: The Power of Nature

Recent neuroscience supports the core insight of Attention Restoration Theory (ART): restorative, natural environments lighten the load on our executive attention systems. Bratman et al. (2015) found that after a 90-minute walk in nature, participants reported less rumination and showed reduced activation in the subgenual prefrontal cortex—a region linked with internal distraction and self-focus. Similarly, Piedimonte et al. (2025) demonstrated that natural visual contexts altered electrophysiological markers of attentional control, suggesting that brief exposure to natural environments reduces demand on certain regions of the brain connected to the central-executive network. A recent systematic review by Zhang et al. (2025)

confirmed these effects, showing decreased prefrontal activation and increased connectivity between the default mode network (DMN) and attentional networks when individuals were exposed to natural versus urban environments. Nature, in other words, doesn't just *feel* restorative—it biologically frees the brain's control tower so attention can reset, integrate, and rejuvenate.

If the DMN shows how the brain rests when focus is undirected, ART explains why the environment matters in that recovery process. Kaplan (1995) described how natural settings evoke *soft fascination*— a broad, effortless focus that engages our senses without demanding active control. This shift gives the brain's "control tower," a much-needed rest while promoting integration across the DMN and limbic regions.

The results are striking. In a landmark study, Ulrich (1984) found that hospital patients recovering from gallbladder surgery healed faster and required less pain medication when their window overlooked trees instead of a brick wall. More recent neuroimaging extends those findings: Green environments reduce amygdala activity (the brain's threat scanner) and strengthen prefrontal networks for emotion regulation and attentional control (Bratman et al., 2015; Sudimac et al., 2022).

Berman et al. (2008) studied similar brain relationships in this area through controlled experiments. In one study, adults who walked for just 50 minutes in an arboretum performed roughly 20% better on working memory and attention tasks than those who walked in an urban environment. The benefit wasn't dependent on comfort; similar gains appeared even when participants walked in winter conditions or merely viewed photos or videos of natural scenes. Berman attributes this effect to fractal fluency—the repeating patterns found in trees, leaves, and rivers. It's believed that these natural fractals are processed efficiently by the visual system, lowering cognitive load and calming the nervous system.

Even short breaks can make a measurable difference. Bratman et al. (2015) found that a 15-minute walk in nature reduced rumination and improved mood compared to an urban walk. Studies of "green micro-breaks" show consistent boosts in mood, working memory, and attentional performance after exposures as brief as 10 minutes (Lee et al., 2015; Ohly et al., 2016).

All of this helps explain why a short walk outside—or even a moment spent gazing at trees, water, or sky—restores concentration far more effectively than scrolling through our social media. Natural settings create *nondirectional attention*: broad, open awareness unhooked from any single stimulus. In the attentional marathon, nature is one of our most accessible energy packs—and unlike most others, it carries no side effects.

Movement and the Amygdala: Resetting the Threat Scanner

While environment sets the conditions for recovery, movement directly shifts physiology. The amygdala, the brain's threat scanner, is constantly monitoring for danger. When overactive, it narrows attention and fuels anxiety. Physical activity—especially walking—has been shown to downregulate the amygdala and increase activity in prefrontal regions that regulate emotion (Li et al., 2019).

These effects are not environment-dependent; they come from physiology itself. Even walking indoors or on a treadmill can provide a reset. Just 5–10 minutes of low- to moderate-intensity movement improves executive functioning and working memory (Hillman et al., 2008). Over time, consistent aerobic exercise restructures the brain, enlarging the hippocampus and strengthening attentional networks (Erickson et al., 2011).

For performers, the takeaway is simple: A short walk through a park, around an office, or even in a hotel hallway before a big meeting can lower stress reactivity and sharpen focus for the hours ahead.

Movement is another energy pack—sometimes the quickest one available.

Mind-Wandering Versus Fixation: The Fine Line

Not all mental drift is created equal. Mind-wandering in non-judgmental states supports creativity, problem-solving, and memory consolidation. In contrast, a fixated or ruminating mind can lock attention into loops of self-criticism and perceived threat.

Neuroscience helps explain the difference. Productive mind-wandering activates both the DMN and the frontoparietal control network, allowing ideas to flow freely while maintaining a light scaffolding of control (Christoff et al., 2016). Rumination, on the other hand, is linked to hyperactivation in the subgenual prefrontal cortex and heightened amygdala activity, which reinforce negative mood states (Hamilton et al., 2011).

In applied terms: Letting your mind drift during a walk or even a shower can spark insights, but replaying a missed shot or awkward meeting comment in a loop only drains energy. Renewal practices—structured reflection, meditation, or simple awareness cues—help create the boundary between healthy drift and harmful rumination.

Sleep and the Glymphatic System: Housekeeping for the Brain

Perhaps the most powerful restoration mechanism is sleep. During deep, slow-wave sleep, the brain's glymphatic system flushes out metabolic waste like beta-amyloid, restoring efficiency in the prefrontal cortex and stabilizing attention the next day (Xie et al., 2013).

Even short naps provide partial glymphatic clearance, boosting alertness and cognitive flexibility (Leminen et al., 2017). For high performers, this reframes sleep as more than rest—it is literal "neural housekeeping," resetting the hardware that attention runs on. In marathon terms, sleep isn't an energy gel; it's where our ability to focus is rebuilt.

Neurotransmitter Cycling: Refueling the Chemistry of Focus

Finally, attention depends on the availability of two key neurotransmitters: dopamine and norepinephrine. Sustained focus depletes them, weakening motivation, executive control, and working memory. When levels dip too low, errors spike—even when people feel they're still performing adequately (van der Linden et al., 2003).

Recovery activities like sleep, nutrition, and relaxation restore these systems to baseline, enabling sharper control and steadier focus (Robbins & Arnsten, 2009). This is why endlessly pushing through fatigue doesn't always work—the brain's chemistry simply won't allow sustained executive function without renewal.

Permission to Shut Off: Renewal in Action

Understanding the neuroscience makes one thing clear: Renewal isn't passive, it's active biology at work. The question then becomes, how do we actually put this science into seamlessly into practice? The answer lies in the levers we can pull every day. Some are external, shaped by the environments we occupy. Others are internal, grounded in how we fuel, move, and regulate our physiology. Together, these levers create the conditions for sharper attention and faster recovery.

With so many of the highest achievers, motivation to be the best is off the charts. Their drive pushes them through grueling hours and endless sacrifices. But we've found that many don't struggle from a lack of effort—they struggle because they lack an "off switch." They replay mistakes endlessly, analyzing what they should have done differently and what it might cost them.

As we discussed in Chapter 12, structured reflection helps manage this tendency by channeling analysis into learnings and plans. Renewal takes it one step further. If done well, it signals to the brain that the surgery is complete, the lessons are captured, the corrections are planned. The most important thing now is not more thinking, but to quiet the mind and allow the attentional muscle to rest.

This permission to shut off is crucial. Just as surgeons don't keep reopening the same incision once the work is done, performers don't need to keep dissecting the same mistake. High performers will tell you this is easier said than done. That's why effective renewal requires an intentional process:

- **Environmental Tools:** sunlight, time in nature, natural views.
- **Physiological Levers:** exercise, movement, sleep.
- **Cognitive Levers:** broad, nondirectional focus—watching the horizon, noticing trees, letting thoughts drift without attachment.
- **Self-talk:** internal cues like, *"The lessons are captured. Tonight, the best way forward is to recover."*

Even five minutes of quiet rest—eyes closed, letting the mind wander freely—can improve memory consolidation and reduce cognitive fatigue (Brokaw et al., 2016). Sometimes renewal is as simple as allowing yourself to check out: doing a mindless chore, listening to familiar music, walking to the bathroom to splash water on the face, or stepping away from performance space to grab some water can be a mental reset. These seemingly small acts shift the brain out of directed focus and give the attentional system the break it needs to come back sharper.

Taking this a step further, the ability to shut off isn't only internal. Our environment, our physiology, and even the substances we consume play a major role in whether attention is restored or drained. Let's begin with the environment.

Shaping Attention Through Environment

Our environment is one of the most overlooked tools for renewal. The spaces we occupy can either drain or restore attentional energy. Research shows that even small adjustments to light, views, or sensory inputs can reset the brain's focus in surprisingly powerful ways. Here are four environmental levers high performers use to recharge attention:

- **Morning Sunlight.** Light is the strongest cue for the circadian rhythm, anchoring our internal clock and setting the brain's chemistry for the day. Morning sunlight boosts serotonin, elevates mood, and primes attentional systems for sharper focus throughout the day (Czeisler, 2013). For athletes, this means better energy regulation at practice; for executives, it reduces the dreaded mid-afternoon crash. One NFL coach we worked with made a habit of stepping outside with his coffee at sunrise—to literally "train his rhythm." He swore the ritual gave him a calmer edge heading into meetings and practices.

- **Natural Views.** Nature offers one of the most potent forms of attentional recovery. As we learned from the previous section, people can recover faster and require less pain medication when they are exposed to nature—even pictures of nature. Today, a few progressive performance environments are starting to apply this principle. An NFL team we worked with redesigned part of its facility into a meditation room with windows, plants, and non-fluorescent lighting. It was impressive to see how many players began utilizing the space before meetings, after practices, and between sessions to unplug. The lesson was clear: If we create these types of spaces, people will gravitate toward them, likely because of the natural feeling of renewal it generates within us.

- **Music.** Sound has a powerful effect on both physiology and attention. Music reduces stress responses and can entrain brain rhythms, shifting attentional states in predictable ways (Thoma et al., 2013). Slower, melodic tempos can support recovery, while upbeat, rhythmic tracks can generate optimal energy. One Olympic swimmer told us she used calming instrumental playlists before bed to slow her mind, and heavy bass tracks before races to push her activation into the "sweet spot." For her, the right sound wasn't just about mood—it was about driving activation to the optimal level that matched the performance demands and attentional energy required to execute.

- **Micro-breaks.** Even a few minutes of non-directed attention can restore executive capacity. Looking at water, greenery, or a horizon creates broad focus—an antidote to the narrow, effortful focus of performance tasks. We encouraged a Fortune 100 executive to replace phone scrolling during breaks with five-minute walks in her courtyard, or at minimum standing at her office window overlooking the horizon. Over time, she noticed those moments became her most reliable reset button, improving both her focus and patience with her team.

Many of these actions may seem small, but their cumulative impact on the brain's attentional energy systems can be significant. Micro-adjustments like light, views, and sound can compound into major gains in performance. As one executive put it, *"It's like getting short burst energy packs while you're running a marathon. These have been highly impactful."*

Physiological Levers of Renewal

Environment influences renewal, but physiology sustains it. Sleep, nutrition, movement, and recovery are what ultimately determine how much attentional energy we have to give—and how long we can give it. While environment shapes the conditions, physiology provides the fuel. The body's systems don't just support focus; they set its upper limits. Sleep, nutrition, movement, and even temperature shifts all play a direct role in how much energy we can access and how long we can sustain it. Managing physiology is one of the most effective ways to extend focus, sharpen performance, and build resilience against fatigue.

Sleep

During deep sleep, the glymphatic system clears waste products from the brain (Xie et al., 2013). Without this nightly "neural housekeeping," focus erodes quickly. Research shows that just one night of restricted sleep can impair reaction times at a level comparable to legal intoxication (Williamson & Feyer, 2000).

One young NBA guard experienced this firsthand. He had been staying up until 3 a.m. playing video games to "wind down," averaging only four to six hours of sleep. After weeks of this routine, his body began to break down, and his performance grew inconsistent. By the time he was referred to sport psychology, he was frustrated and stuck. Together, we unpacked the role of sleep in brain function—from sharper decision-making to improved shooting accuracy to reduced injury risk—and he committed to increasing his nightly sleep to between seven and eight hours. The results were immediate. Within a month, his turnover rate dropped noticeably, and he reflected: "I didn't change my workouts—just my sleep. It didn't feel like I was running uphill every night. Everything slowed down for me."

Nutrition

If sleep lays the foundation for attentional energy, nutrition stabilizes it. Stable glucose supports concentration, while omega-3s aid neuronal efficiency. When blood sugar fluctuates, attention wavers.

A CEO we worked with had been running on caffeine and pastries every morning. By 11 a.m., she felt jittery and unfocused, and by mid-afternoon she was crashing. After shifting to a protein-and-slow-carb breakfast—eggs, oats, and fruit—she described her meetings and presentations as "less jittery, more steady." Her staff also noticed her attention was more consistent throughout the day. Nutrition didn't just fuel her body—it stabilized her focus.

Exercise

If nutrition provides stability, movement acts as an active reset button. Both aerobic and strength training enhance attentional systems, though through different mechanisms. Aerobic activity boosts executive function and primes attentional networks (Hillman et al., 2008). Even 10 minutes of movement reduces amygdala activity, lowering background anxiety and freeing attentional bandwidth. Strength training, on the other hand, improves working memory, increases BDNF (brain-derived neurotrophic factor), and has been shown to sharpen attentional control (Liu-Ambrose et al., 2010).

An MLB pitcher we supported discovered this through his pregame ritual. On nights he was scheduled to pitch, he began walking laps around the stadium corridors before the gates opened. It wasn't about "getting loose"—it was about quieting the noise in his head. He reported that his first-inning command sharpened, and he felt more present on the mound.

Research suggests that combining aerobic and strength training provides the most robust benefits, supporting both immediate attentional resets and long-term cognitive resilience (Best, 2010). For performers,

Intentional Attention

the lesson is simple: Movement—whether through aerobic bursts, strength sessions, or ideally both—is another reliable way to optimize attentional energy.

Cold Exposure

Cold exposure triggers a sharp increase in norepinephrine, a neuro-transmitter that heightens alertness, focus, and mood regulation (Krediet et al., 2020). This surge activates the locus coeruleus, the brain's "noradrenaline center," which is directly tied to attention and arousal. Even brief immersion—one to three minutes in cold water or a cold shower—can raise norepinephrine levels by 200–300% (Janszky & Lundberg, 2006). Unlike caffeine, which can lead to jit-teriness or sleep disruption, cold exposure provides a non-substance-based jolt that resets both body and mind.

In the NFL, many high-performing coaches have made 5 a.m. cold plunges part of their routine before diving into long film study and schematic development. They report that the natural release of neuromodulators sharpened their focus for hours, help-ing them sustain deep concentration through mentally demanding work. On the other end of the spectrum, an entrepreneur we worked with used cold plunges at night before bed. Although he felt highly alert right after, within 45 minutes he consistently fell asleep faster and reported significantly better sleep scores (from his wearable device) and less interrupted rest.

These examples highlight how timing matters. Cold exposure in the morning can prime alertness and focus, while cold exposure at night may help quiet the system and promote recovery. The larger point is that while the benefits are clear, how high perform-ers use it often depends on their schedules, rhythms, and what feels most sustainable for them. In that sense, cold exposure has become less of a one-size-fits-all prescription and more of a versatile tool—able to sharpen attention or support recovery depending on when it's used.

Circadian Rhythms

Our body's internal clock—the circadian rhythm—plays a critical role in attentional energy. Light is the primary cue that sets this rhythm, influencing the release of cortisol in the morning (to promote alertness) and melatonin at night (to promote sleep) (Czeisler, 2013; Khalsa et al., 2003). When circadian rhythms are aligned with performance demands, focus and decision-making improve. When they are misaligned, attentional energy, processing speed, and emotional regulation suffer.

One NFL quarterback we worked with admitted he struggled in prime-time night games. He shared that he felt like he wasn't as "sharp" with his reads and decision-making. His normal rhythm had him going to bed between 8–9 p.m. and waking early for film study and body prep—a routine that worked perfectly for Sunday afternoon kickoffs but left him sluggish and out of sync under the lights. His circadian rhythm was peaking hours before game time, meaning his attentional energy, processing speed, and decision-making were already on the decline by kickoff.

To prepare for a Monday night matchup, we systematically shifted his internal clock: waking later in the morning, delaying exercise, and using evening light exposure to mimic the demands of prime time. The result paid off with one of his strongest prime-time performances. He later reflected, "I felt more awake and sharper than in any night game before."

The lesson applies broadly. Morning sunlight exposure helps optimize neuromodulator release—boosting serotonin, dopamine, and cortisol at the right times for sharper focus (Czeisler, 2013; LeGates et al., 2014). Evening light cues—like watching the sunset— prepare the brain for melatonin release and restorative sleep, while excessive bright light at night disrupts this cycle. For performers, managing light exposure isn't just about sleep hygiene—it's about engineering attentional energy at the right time of day.

Breathing and HRV Training

Controlled breathing—such as slow, paced breathing at around six breaths per minute—stimulates the vagus nerve, increases heart-rate variability (HRV), and reduces sympathetic arousal. This lowers stress reactivity, steadies emotions, and stabilizes attention under pressure (Lehrer et al., 2020).

One pro baseball pitching coach we worked with believed that breath was the single most important mental skill his players could master. Every spring training, we taught diaphragmatic breathing techniques pitchers could use before taking the mound, to reset focus after giving up a hit or a walk, and to regulate themselves in the dugout between innings. He later reflected that those who embraced it were "the ones who could let go of mistakes fastest and get back to attacking the strike zone." Breath became an attentional reset they could carry anywhere.

Hydration

Even mild dehydration—just 1–2% body mass loss—impairs attention, working memory, and mood (Armstrong et al., 2012). Despite being meticulous with his mechanics, one collegiate golfer we worked with often faded mentally late in tournaments. We discovered his hydration habits were inconsistent. By integrating intentional water breaks into his pre-shot routine, he was able to sustain his focus longer into the rounds. His reflection was simple but telling: "I realized how important it was to my focus. Before understanding this, I brought everything back to my swing—in this case, it was my fuel." Sometimes the simplest lever—drinking water—makes the biggest difference for attention.

Why Phone Scrolling Doesn't Count

If exercise, sleep, and light act as energy packs for attention, scrolling on our phones is the equivalent of junk fuel. It feels like it should replenish us, but it leaves the attentional system more depleted.

Many high performers default to phone scrolling when they want to take a "break" or "turn off." It feels like a quick escape—something mindless to pass the time. But scrolling isn't mindless at all. It's engineered stimulation. Social media algorithms are specifically designed to capture and hold our attention, feeding content that provokes stronger emotional reactions and longer gazes. Every swipe, click, pause, or slowed scroll is measured and used to refine the feed, ensuring the brain stays hooked.

The cost is real. Instead of allowing attentional systems to enter broad, non-directed states that promote recovery, scrolling keeps the brain locked in cycles of micro-stimulation. Research shows that excessive social media use is linked to attentional fatigue, higher stress, disrupted sleep, and increased anxiety (Andreassen et al., 2017). Layer onto this the "compare and despair" effect—where constantly measuring our lives against curated images of others undermines mood and confidence—and it's easy to see why the experience is draining.

Neurobiologically, algorithmic feeds operate like slot machines. Every novel post delivers a small dopamine spike, followed by dips that leave the brain more depleted than before (Alter, 2017). Over time, this pattern can become addictive for attentional systems, but not in a way that serves performance or well-being.

This is why scrolling rarely leaves us feeling refreshed. Physically, we may not be doing much, but cognitively, the attentional system is working overtime—processing novelty, filtering stimuli, and emotionally reacting to content. Even watching a TV show or movie provides more renewal than scrolling, because stories are linear and not algorithmically designed to trigger constant micro-rewards.

By contrast, true renewal requires freeing attentional systems. Natural environments, music, movement, or even a few minutes of quiet rest allow executive control systems to step back and the brain to reset. Scrolling does the opposite: It pulls focus into tighter loops of stimulation.

One CEO we worked with admitted that her nightly routine of "winding down" with an hour of scrolling left her mind buzzing when she finally put the phone down. When she replaced that habit with 10 minutes of stretching and a warm shower before bed, she was surprised at how much faster she fell asleep and how much sharper she felt the next morning.

The takeaway is clear: While scrolling feels like rest, it appears to be more like junk food for attention. To truly recharge, we need practices that offload attention, not ones that keep it tethered.

Supplements and Substances: Pros and Cons

When it comes to renewal, many performers lean on external energy aids. These can provide short-term boosts, but they almost always carry costs. Unlike natural levers such as sleep, light, and movement—which build sustainable attentional energy—substances tend to create a cycle of spikes and crashes.

Caffeine

By far the most widely used and accepted of the substances we'll hit in this section, caffeine sharpens vigilance and alertness by blocking adenosine, the neurotransmitter that signals fatigue. Used strategically, it can be a powerful attentional tool. The key here is that timing matters. Taken too late in the day, caffeine disrupts sleep architecture and undermines recovery. Over time, tolerance builds, meaning the same dose yields less perceived benefit, and withdrawal leaves the brain sluggish (Drake et al., 2013).

One MLB pitcher we worked with shared that he was having trouble falling asleep after night games. It turned out he had been slamming multiple energy drinks before taking the mound, thinking more "juice" meant more focus. But his IA Framework awareness work revealed a pattern: The extra caffeine pushed him past his optimal zone of activation, amplifying anxiety and tightening his mechanics. Ironically, he threw harder and looser when he was a little less amped. Cutting back to a single energy drink—an hour before the game—not only improved his command but also helped him sleep better afterward.

Similarly, an executive we supported didn't reduce her overall caffeine intake but simply stopped after 2 p.m. The results were immediate: deeper sleep, better recovery, and sharper focus— allowing both to stack more optimal days upon each other.

Nicotine

Nicotine can enhance reaction time and short-term focus (Heishman et al., 2010), but the price is steeper than caffeine. It disrupts dopamine regulation, is highly addictive, and undermines long-term attentional health. A young entrepreneur put it bluntly: *"Nicotine got me through 14-hour coding days—but when I stopped, I couldn't think straight for a week."* The clarity came at the cost of a bigger crash.

Prescription Stimulants

Medications for ADHD can improve executive attention and are often highly effective for people diagnosed with the condition. Clinical use is associated with better impulse control and fewer accidents related to attentional lapses. But misuse—particularly in non-clinical populations—creates its own problems. We've seen executives "borrow" stimulants to power through deadlines. They reported immediate boosts in energy, speed of thought, and focus, but the rebound was steep: irritability during withdrawal, restless sleep, and attention crashes that lasted days. What began as a productivity hack often left them more depleted and inconsistent in the long run.

Alcohol and Depressants

For some, alcohol feels like a way to "switch off." But it impairs REM sleep, fragments recovery, and leaves the brain less restored (Ebrahim et al., 2013). One professional soccer player told us she had relied on alcohol as a "sleep aid." But when she tracked her sleep with a wearable, she saw the truth: While she was asleep longer, she wasn't actually recovering. What she gained in hours, she lost in quality.

Sleep and Sleep Aids

Sleep may be the single most important lever we can pull for mental health, performance, and attentional renewal. It is both a foundation for well-being and one of the most powerful determinants of how consistently we can sustain focus under pressure. Getting the right amount of sleep for ourselves is a critical starting point—but as we'll outline here, while quantity matters, quality is equally essential.

Today, wearable devices can track sleep patterns with remarkable detail, offering insight into duration, depth, and recovery trends. For high performers, these tools can be a valuable way to identify blind spots and experiment with small behavioral changes that lead to better sleep quality. Many pro and collegiate athletes are now being educated on the positive impacts of sleep—so much so that nearly every pitching staff member from a team we worked with was wearing a wearable device specifically to track their sleep. For those of us who are serious about building sustainable attentional energy, sleep is one of the first places we recommend starting.

In our work, natural strategies reliably deliver the biggest long-term gains: morning light, consistent bed/wake times, an intentional pre-sleep routine, smart caffeine timing, and managing evening light. Most performers will get further by dialing these basics before considering sleep aids or supplements.

That said, when sleep remains stubborn, many performers reach for aids. Here is a brief, neutral overview of the ones we encounter most often—what they may help with, and the tradeoffs to keep in mind.

The most common include:

- **Melatonin.** Melatonin is a hormone that regulates circadian rhythm, and supplements are often marketed as a "natural" sleep aid. The reality is more nuanced. Meta-analyses find that melatonin reduces sleep-onset latency by only about 6–7 minutes on average in adults, with no consistent improvements in total sleep time or sleep quality (Ferracioli-Oda et al., 2013). In older adults, controlled-release formulations (1–2 mg) show slightly greater effects, reducing latency by about 14 minutes and modestly improving efficiency (Wade et al., 2007). These gains are real but limited, and many trials have rated the overall evidence as low.

  The bigger concern is chronic use. Long-term safety data are still emerging, and nightly supplementation hasn't been studied as extensively as short-term, situational use. For that reason, many practitioners recommend treating melatonin as a targeted tool for circadian disruption rather than a default solution for stress-related insomnia. Side effects such as morning grogginess, vivid dreams, dizziness, and headaches are also fairly common (Buscemi et al., 2006). Where melatonin is most effective is in cases of circadian misalignment—such as jet lag or delayed sleep phase syndrome—where it can help shift the body's internal clock when taken at the right time (Herxheimer & Petrie, 2002). Side effects such as morning grogginess, vivid dreams, dizziness, and headaches are also fairly common (Buscemi et al., 2006). For high performers, it appears that melatonin can help recalibrate the clock, but it may not be a great replacement for the natural processes that restore attentional energy.

- **Over-the-counter antihistamines (for example, diphenhydramine, doxylamine).**

    Found in many "PM" sleep aids, these drugs can make people drowsy and help them fall asleep, but they may reduce sleep quality by suppressing REM cycles. The result is a night of quantity but may lack quality. They also carry risks of tolerance, next-day grogginess, slowed reaction times, and impaired memory—costs that could be impactful for anyone who relies on sharp decision-making the next morning.

- **Prescription sedatives (for example, benzodiazepines, Z-drugs like Ambien).**

    These can be effective in acute, clinically managed insomnia, but they can also alter sleep architecture, reducing restorative slow-wave and REM sleep. They also carry risks of dependence, rebound insomnia, and impaired memory consolidation. Several athletes we've worked with described waking up technically "rested," but still sluggish and unfocused—like they had skipped the mental renewal sleep should provide. These medications may be appropriate in tightly monitored medical contexts, but again should be thoughtfully considered as a potential short-term bridge, not as a long-term strategy.

The key with all sleep aids is this: while they may help us fall asleep, they don't always restore us in the way high-quality, natural sleep can. Our attentional systems perform best when both the *quantity* and *quality* of sleep are strong. That's why these aids are best evaluated not only for their short-term benefits but also for their long-term impact—using awareness as our guide to weigh both the positives and the trade-offs. In our experience, sleep aids can be valuable for those facing chronic insomnia, where the benefits clearly outweigh the drawbacks. Yet for many others, using them as a short-cut to fall asleep often reveals more costs than gains when extended over time. In those cases, sleep aids function best as temporary bridges—not as the foundation for lasting renewal.

Our stance is fairly straightforward: Substances can provide attentional boosts, but in most cases they don't create sustainable attentional energy. They are more like renting energy than owning it—and the interest always comes due. Our experiences have shown that lasting energy renewal is built on fundamentals: high-quality sleep, time in nature, moments of non-directed attention, sunlight, nutrition, movement, healthy environments, and structured reflection. Substances may have a place, but they should always be reviewed carefully before use, with a clear understanding of both benefits and costs.

Renewal and the IA Framework

Renewal is the element that keeps the IA Framework alive. Awareness shows us what shapes our attention. Assessment helps us observe where it goes. Reflection captures lessons and builds forward plans. But it's renewal that powers them all. Without renewal, even the strongest attentional system runs dry. With it, energy, clarity, and resilience can be sustained across the long run of performance.

We've seen how the brain has its own recovery systems and how practices like movement, light, and quality sleep allow them to work as designed. We've also seen how certain habits, like phone scrolling or poorly timed substances, can masquerade as recovery but leave us more depleted. And we've looked at the practical levers—environmental, physiological, and behavioral—that high-level performers can use, even while navigating the grind, to restore focus and build stamina for the pressures they face.

For many of the leaders, athletes, and professionals we work with, renewal has become the difference between *surviving* and *sustaining*. The ones who integrate short, intentional resets into their days often describe feeling clearer, steadier, and more present—not because they're working less, but because they're recovering smarter. These practices don't eliminate pressure or stress, but they give people the attentional energy to meet it more consistently.

This concludes Part II, where we've built the architecture of Intentional Attention: the roots that shape focus, the patterns that guide it, and the renewal that sustains it. The work here is foundational—because attention is not fixed. It is trainable. In Part III, we move from understanding to application, turning this architecture into protocols for performing when it matters most.

Exercise: Putting Renewal into Practice

By this point, we've seen that renewal isn't passive—it's active biology and intentional practice. But knowledge alone doesn't create change. Reflection helps us translate the science of renewal into habits that fit our own environments, physiology, and rhythms.

Here are a few guiding prompts and real-world examples that illustrate how performers can weave renewal into their lives:

1. **What small resets already exist in my day—and how can I use them with more intention?**

   - A pro soccer midfielder realized that instead of scrolling through his phone after training, he could step outside for a 15-minute walk around the complex. That short "green break" became his reset before team meetings, and he described feeling less mentally foggy and more engaged in tactical sessions.

- A CEO started parking on the far side of the office lot and used the walk in and out as her "no-phone green break." She said it helped her arrive sharper in the morning and leave with a clearer mind at night.

- A graduate student blocked 10 minutes between study sessions to sit by a campus pond. At first, it felt like lost time—but she found her recall and focus during the next session improved noticeably.

2. **Am I giving my physiology the same attention I give my schedule?**

- An NBA guard came to realize that his inconsistency wasn't just about mechanics—it was about sleep. After weeks of averaging four to six hours a night, his focus was drained. Committing to seven to eight hours became his most important "renewal rep," and his performance followed.

- A collegiate golfer didn't need a swing change; what he needed was consistent hydration. Building water breaks into his pre-shot routine helped him sustain focus deep into tournaments.

3. **What signals tell me I need to shut off—and how do I respond?**

- A tech entrepreneur described how his mind replayed mistakes at night like "a highlight reel I couldn't turn off." His breakthrough came when he paired structured reflection (see Chapter 12) with a nightly cue: *"Lessons captured—time to recover."* Within weeks, he was falling asleep faster and waking with more energy.

- An NFL coach started using music to manage his "off switch"—calm instrumentals on his drive home told his body it was time to transition out of performance mode.

Reflection Prompts

Take 5–10 minutes to pause and consider:

1. Which renewal levers do I already use? (nature, movement, music, breath, sleep, etc.)

2. Which one could I add in short bursts? (for example, a 10-minute walk, sunlight in the morning, a cold shower, a breathing reset)

3. What's my "permission to shut off" cue? (self-talk, music, stepping away from screens)

Transforming Attention: Applying Intentional Attention to Pressure, Purpose, and Life

Chapter 14

Daily Reps: Building Attentional Fitness

"We are what we repeatedly do. Excellence, then, is not an act but a habit."

—Aristotle

Not long ago, strength training was considered optional in sport. Athletes might lift weights in the offseason, but physical strength wasn't always seen as central to performance. Then came a revolution. Organizations recognized that daily physical training wasn't supplementary—it was essential. Athletes who were stronger, faster, and capable of greater endurance began to dominate their competitive arenas. Weight rooms became as indispensable as practice fields. Recovery protocols became as critical as game plans. Over time, what was once extra credit became the baseline for competing at the highest level.

That shift didn't stay contained to elite sport. It trickled into the mainstream, sparking the health and fitness boom that now touches nearly every aspect of daily life. Wearable health devices track movement, heart rates, stress levels, and recovery scores in real time. Running, group fitness, personal training, and boutique gyms became part of modern culture. The idea that physical training is optional has largely been eclipsed by the view that it's a vital part of health, identity, and lifestyle.

While the dramatic changes in the fitness arena are not identical, we believe we are standing at the precipice of a similar revolution in mental performance. Advances in brain science, psychology, technology, and applied mental training have given us new tools and methods to strengthen the mind nearly as systematically as the body.

For decades, mental performance was viewed as something innate—something you either had or didn't. It's been years since a similar belief persisted about an athlete's strength or fitness. Decades ago, physical training was often limited to the preseason; conditioning was seen as a tune-up, not a year-round discipline. In much the same way, psychological training has long been treated as episodic—something we hoped would appear when needed or tried to manufacture through last-minute motivational speeches and pep talks.

But just as strength, speed, and endurance are now recognized as core to athletic success, we're seeing the same connection between mental skills and performance. And just as strength and conditioning are developed through structured, consistent reps, the mental game can be built through intentional strategies practiced with the same discipline: repetition and routine, rooted in science.

In today's arenas, nearly every top performer receives world-class strength, speed, and endurance training. Outside of sport, the equivalents may be decision-making, strategic intelligence, presence, and relationship management. That same level of commitment and effort warrants application to the mental side—directing attention, resetting after setbacks, refocusing amid distraction, and renewing when fatigue sets in—no matter the setting.

This chapter explores how Intentional Attention can serve as the foundation for that kind of mental fitness training—built through small, steady, repeatable practices that endure over time. This training isn't reactive or reserved for slumps, playoff games, or high-stakes presentations. It's proactive—built from routines, habits, and micro-reps woven into the rhythm of everyday life. Practiced consistently, they sharpen our responses to buffer against burnout, and sustain clarity in a world designed to divide our focus.

Just as physical training relies on consistent reps, attentional training depends on routines—the deliberate repetition of actions that strengthen where and how we focus.

Before diving into how to build routines, it's important to understand *why* they matter. Under pressure, the brain defaults to what is most familiar. That's why motivation alone—while powerful at the start—rarely sustains performance when pressure is highest. Research shows that under cognitive load, people revert to learned scripts rather than improvising their way through stress (Wood & Neal, 2007). In performance terms, this means that when fatigue, nerves, or chaos hit, we fall back on whatever habits we've built—good, bad, or otherwise. Routines, then, are not just mechanical behaviors; they are pre-programmed attentional maps. They give the mind a reliable route to follow when pressure tempts it toward threat or distraction. In essence, routines create attentional biases that can automate our focus. When intentionally developed, they can help us return—again and again—to what matters most.

Performance-Relevant Routines

In sport, routines have always existed. In earlier eras, however, they were often treated more like superstition than science. Athletes clung to rituals—putting on socks a certain way, eating the same pregame meal, wearing a lucky undershirt—believing these rituals somehow controlled their performance. The problem wasn't the presence of routines, but the lack of alignment between the behavior and performance-relevant data.

Take an example of a high-school hockey player we worked with who was convinced her pregame routine was the secret to her success. What she ate, when she ate, which shirt she wore—even down to the shoes she laced up for the arena—she believed every detail determined

Daily Reps: Building Attentional Fitness

how she would perform that night. Over time, her "routine" ballooned into several hours of elaborate preparation. The routine itself became a source of anxiety: If she missed a step, she felt doomed. The issue wasn't the behaviors themselves (though the length made them unsustainable), but the meaning she attached to them. She appraised the ritual as the *cause* of performance, rather than recognizing routines as tools to support healthy behaviors and direct her attention toward what mattered—arriving with energy and focus when the puck dropped.

When routines are built with intention, attention begins to funnel toward performance-relevant data. That might mean self-talk or mantras that build confidence; gratitude practices that release energizing and calming neurochemicals such as dopamine, oxytocin, and serotonin (Fredrickson, 2013; Kok et al., 2013); or breathing sequences that regulate heart rate variability (Lehrer & Gevirtz, 2014). These intentional behaviors prime both body and mind, preparing the nervous system to execute when the time to perform arrives.

Building a Routine with Intention

Superstitions often masquerade as routines, but they rarely direct attention with precision. Intentional routines, by contrast, are more surgical and designed to anchor attention on the right cues at the right moments. Within the Intentional Attention Framework, routines act as scaffolding that guide attention through the sequence of **Awareness → Intention → Execution → Reflection → Renewal**, day after day.

Consider an MLB pitcher who came to me in the clubhouse one day before a big start and asked, *"Do NFL quarterbacks feel anxious before they start?"* That question opened the door to a longer conversation about his history. As we explored his personal inventory and attentional patterns, it became clear that he was struggling with impostor syndrome (Clance & Imes, 1978). Deep down, he never felt good enough to be a starter in the major leagues. This belief created significant spikes of nerves prior to every start. He often told himself that it was better to be lucky than good. The irony, of course, was that he *was* good—really good. But his mind's natural default pulled his attention so strongly toward doubt that he struggled to "find it" (whatever *it* was) each time he took the mound.

For years, he relied on a "lucky" undershirt and an upbeat playlist to help him "find it." At the major league level, though, inconsistency followed. Through our reflections together, he realized his activation level was often higher than he wanted it to be when he threw the first pitch. He came to recognize that everyone has thoughts of doubt or impostor feelings from time to time, and those thoughts were always sitting in the Focus Window, ready to grab attention. Research suggests that—impostor syndrome is highly prevalent among high-achieving professionals, and it often contributes to heightened anxiety, self-doubt, and impaired performance if left unchecked (Bravata et al., 2020; Neureiter & Traut-Mattausch, 2016). For him, the pattern was clear: On days when he escaped the first inning unscathed, the nerves began to fade and he settled in. But if hitters reached base—whether by a walk or a hit—his default belief became, *"I don't have it today."* The spiral began there.

With newfound awareness, he began building routines designed to generate more Intentional Attention. Each morning he practiced a short meditation session to set his focus for each part of his day. During his stretches, he implemented a breathing cadence to keep his energy levels calmer hours before the game. He built a structured sequence of warm-up activities to regulate his activation levels for the moments just before the first pitch. And he developed a mantra tied to his pitching cue ("downhill and through") to center him during the game. At the end of each day, he journaled to review what went well and what could be improved, giving himself the chance to assess whether his routines were having the desired impact.

Notice that none of these practices were about his emotions, confidence, or predicting a future outcome. Instead, his new routines

Daily Reps: Building Attentional Fitness

anchored attention to behaviors that prepared his body, reinforced growth and learning, and—most importantly for him—occupied his attention with performance-relevant data rather than worries about his legitimacy. Those questions—whether he was "good enough" or how he stacked up against other pitchers—were uncontrollables. What he found ultimately mattered was whether he was continuously improving and directing his attention where he wanted it to be.

Over time, this intentional process steadied his activation levels and made it easier for him to lock onto the variables that truly mattered. The routines worked because they gave him enough flexibility to adjust his preparation to his body's needs on a given day, while still providing enough structure to consistently bring his attention back to performance-relevant cues. Instead of fighting against anxiety by attempting to conjure up confidence or focusing on "what ifs," he focused on executing one step at a time. Breathing kept him in the present. His nervous system shifted from defensive bracing to proactive readiness. What had once been superstition became a system.

That is the essence of why routines can beat motivation while feeling significant stress. Even our strongest intrinsic motivations can be fleeting, dependent on how we feel in the moment. Routines, once established, can level-out that volatility. The subconscious begins to funnel behaviors into these intentional patterns without waiting for permission from our emotions. Over time, the system runs automatically—carrying body, mind, and attention into the performance we've trained for.

Defining a Performance-Relevant Routine

So what exactly makes a routine performance-relevant? A *performance-relevant routine* is any sequence of intentional behaviors that (1) regulates and optimizes body activation, (2) regulates and optimizes cognitive activation for what's ahead, and (3) directs attention toward data that enhance execution.

Performance-relevant routine examples are in Table 14.1.

The content of the routine can vary, but the principle is the same: channel attention where it matters most and renew our systems

Table 14.1   Routines in Action

Routine	Example in Action
Morning Intention Routine	A 3–5 minute morning visualization or meditation to set the tone for the day. For example, an executive takes a few minutes during their morning shower and visualizes the day's schedule, handling meetings with composure and clarity. This primes both body and attention for what's ahead.
Pre-Performance Routine	A sequence of intentional actions just before stepping into performance. For instance, a musician takes two deep diaphragmatic breaths, rolls their shoulders, and silently repeats a performance cue word like "steady" before walking on stage. These behaviors activate the body and channel attention away from nerves and toward execution.
During-Performance Routine	Predetermined resets to recover from distractions under pressure. For example, a softball player who swings and misses on a pitch steps away, resets with a deep breath and short mantra ("next pitch, turn on anything inside"), and takes one more slow exhale before returning to the batter's box. This re-centers attention on performance-relevant cues and prevents spirals.

(continued)

Daily Reps: Building Attentional Fitness

Table 14.1 *(continued)*

Routine	Example in Action
Reflection Routine	A short process to review and release the day. For example, after work, a leader journals two wins and one area for improvement to pick up tomorrow, then closes the notebook. This creates learning, builds self-awareness, and gives the mind permission to "turn it off" until the next day.
Renewal Routine	Intentional practices that recharge mental and physical energy. For example, an executive protects 20 minutes of phone-free outdoor walking during lunch. The non-directive attention restores focus, reduces cognitive fatigue, and supports long-term resilience.

whenever possible. When these rhythms are built into daily life, they create a baseline of stability—one that performers can lean on regardless of mood, pressure, or circumstance.

The Morning Routine: Priming the Attentional System

Perhaps no routines are more influential than the ones that start the day. The first reps we take often determine the quality of all the ones that follow. Which is why we now turn to the morning—when the attentional system is malleable, and when even the smallest choices can set the trajectory for everything that comes after. Morning routines don't just "start the day"; they prime the mind.

Intentional Attention

A Morning Intention Routine: A Case Study of an Executive

Consider an executive we worked with who was struggling with the early stages of burnout. Her team was consistently missing her standards of work. Again and again, she felt like she had to pick up the slack. While she stayed late nights and worked weekends, she would scroll through social media and see pictures of her colleagues out at happy hour or enjoying vacations with their families. These were the very things she longed for herself, but her sense of responsibility to the business—and to maintaining a high level of output—kept her tethered to the office.

She also knew she had work to do in developing this younger team. She was actively building structures and processes to elevate their performance as efficiently as possible. But underneath, she feared one specific scenario: returning from a multi-day work trip only to discover that much of what she had asked for wasn't completed. In that exhausted state, she worried she might react emotionally—say something sharp she would regret—and in doing so, derail the very progress they had been making. For her, the risk wasn't just lost productivity. It was breaking trust with her team at the moment they needed her most. She was nearing a breaking point, which is when she reached out to us.

We started with her Personal Attentional Attribute Inventory (see Chapter 8). She clarified her core values, her attentional patterns, and the specific triggers that tended to shorten her fuse under stress. She knew that fatigue plus unfinished work was her biggest derailment scenario. And she recognized something important: she couldn't blame her team for not yet knowing what she knew. It was her job to develop them—not resent them.

With that clarity, we used the SERR model (Situation + Emotion + Response = Result) to map out the situations most likely to naturally trigger her and, more importantly, the response she wanted to follow in those moments. We then anchored this plan in her morning routine.

She started waking up at 5 a.m., heading down to her exercise room, and getting on her stationary bike. But instead of immediately jumping into a virtual spin class, she dedicated the first five minutes to setting her intention for the day. During this time, she followed a simple but powerful process:

1. **Open with the Breath.** She began with slow, steady breathing, scanning her body from head to toe. By releasing tension in her shoulders, jaw, and posture, she anchored herself in the present moment. This simple act helped her nervous system settle into readiness rather than reactivity and grounded her attention before the rush of the day.

2. **Visualize Someone or Something You Love.** For her, it was her children. She pictured their smiling young faces and wide, innocent eyes. She described feeling goose bumps during this step—the kind of deep, visceral warmth that reset her entire state. Physiologically, this practice likely triggered the release of oxytocin and dopamine, neurochemicals linked to connection, empathy, and motivation (Fredrickson, 2013; Kok et al., 2013). Psychologically, it tied her effort back to transcendent motivators: her children's lives and opportunities. This gave her a foundation of love and empathy, making her more open and less defensive in every interaction that followed.

3. **Review the Day's Schedule.** She mentally walked through her day—client meetings, presentations, managerial reviews—and set clear intentions for the energy, attitude, and behaviors she wanted to bring to each. Instead of approaching the day reactively, she was now proactively shaping how she would show up.

4. **Anticipate Adversity and Triggers (SERR Model).** This was her most important step. She asked herself: *What situations are most likely to trigger me today?* Then she walked through the

SERR model: Situation + Emotion + Response = Result. If she anticipated a meeting with someone she struggled to manage, or reports of missed deadlines, she visualized responding in a way that both upheld her standards and communicated belief in her team's ability to rise. By rehearsing this in a calm, intentional state, she built a playbook for moments that once derailed her.

5. **End with Gratitude and Reframing.** She closed the session by reminding herself, *"I get to do this."* Not *"I have to."* This small shift reinforced gratitude for the position she had earned and reframed leadership not as a burden but as an opportunity.

Later, she shared that this simple five-minute routine transformed how she showed up and had a profound impact on her leadership. Instead of starting the day in fatigue and frustration, she began with more openness, empathy, and perspective. She found more joy and patience with her team—and more satisfaction in their development. The extra work no longer felt like a weight; it became a privilege to shape young professionals. As her approach shifted, so did her culture. She stopped policing and started walking alongside. Her team noticed. Those who wanted to thrive suddenly had the "nutrients" to grow, and many matured into better contributors to whom she could confidently delegate.

Tailoring Routines to Specific Demands

Our experience shows that anyone can benefit from fine-tuning their morning routines to address specific needs. When we treat mental preparation like physical training, we can tailor it to the system that needs the most support that day—alertness, energy, emotion stability, focus, etc. Here are common challenges we see, and the attentional practices that can help stabilize or optimize them.

1. **Trouble with Morning Alertness**

   Goal: Activate the system without overstimulation.

   - **Get Morning Sunlight.** Exposure to natural light within the first hour after waking stimulates cortisol release, which promotes alertness, regulates metabolism, and supports circadian alignment (Cajochen et al., 2005). Morning light also suppresses melatonin, helping the body distinguish day from night and strengthening sleep–wake rhythms (Khalsa et al., 2003). Even 10–20 minutes of outdoor light can improve energy across the day.

   - **Time Caffeine Strategically.** Caffeine enhances alertness by blocking adenosine receptors, but consuming it too early can interfere with the body's natural cortisol awakening response (Clow et al., 2004; Wilhelm et al., 2007). Waiting 60–90 minutes after waking allows caffeine to complement, rather than compete with, the body's natural rhythm.

2. **Managing Low Energy or Lethargy**

   Goal: Increase activation and mental readiness.

   - **Incorporate Movement.** Even light movement—a short walk, dynamic stretch, or mobility series—increases cerebral blood flow and boosts dopamine and norepinephrine, neurochemicals linked to improved focus and cognitive flexibility (Hillman et al., 2008). Movement primes both body and attentional systems.

   - **Use Cold Exposure.** Brief cold exposure (for example, shower, plunge, or face immersion) increases norepinephrine, heightening alertness and mood while sharpening attentional control (Janský & Pospíšilová, 2000; Kox et al., 2014). For many, it's a fast reset that shifts the nervous system from lethargy to readiness.

3. Mood Regulation and Emotional Balance

Goal: Stabilize reactivity and promote openness.

- **Find a Reason to Laugh.** Laughter releases endorphins and activates the parasympathetic nervous system, reducing defensiveness and improving openness in social interactions (Dunbar et al., 2012). A few moments of humor—through conversation, media, or a shared experience—can shift emotional tone before the day begins.

- **Pair Gratitude with Intention.** A short gratitude reflection while setting intentions fosters calm and optimism by releasing serotonin and oxytocin (Fredrickson, 2013; Kok et al., 2013). Entering the day in a state of gratitude creates greater emotional flexibility when challenges arise.

4. Anxiety or Overactivation

Goal: Calm physiological arousal and re-center attention.

- **Grounding Breathwork.** A few cycles of slow, controlled breathing—such as 4-7-8 or box breathing—activate the parasympathetic nervous system and reduce cortisol, helping reorient toward deliberate focus.

- **Mindful Body Scan.** Briefly scanning the body for tension and releasing it teaches interoceptive awareness and interrupts rumination loops that often accompany performance anxiety (Farb et al., 2012).

A well-designed morning routine is like the opening tee shot in golf. When we connect cleanly off the first tee, we often find ourselves playing from the fairway—positioned to pursue our goals with clarity and confidence. When we start the day scattered or reactive, it's like playing from the rough: The rest of the round becomes a scramble. Morning practices don't guarantee perfection, but they stack the odds in our favor. By pairing Intentional Attention with proven strategies that fit our specific needs, we start from a position of strength—and carry that rhythm through the day.

Harnessing Music for Optimal Rhythm and Focus

For years, we've watched clients use playlists as part of their pregame routine to get "in the zone," yet few consider whether their music is actually helping or hindering their focus. Many do it simply because "they've always done it," or because those they view as elite performers do. When asked why, most say, "I like it," or "It hypes me up." Those answers are understandable, but they only skim the surface of performance optimization. Beneath them may lie a deeper opportunity: to use music as a deliberate way to tune the system for optimal focus and flow. Music can be a powerful tool for attuning both mind and body—when it's used with intention. Rhythm, in particular, provides a stable external structure that the brain and body can organize around. Research on adapted rhythmic training shows that rhythmic cues enhance timing accuracy, motor coordination, and movement efficiency in sport (McCrary & Gould, 2023), suggesting that rhythm can serve as a reliable anchor for attention under pressure. The goal isn't just to get hyped; it's to find the right level of activation—one that optimizes focus and, ultimately, flow.

It seems every performer has an internal rhythm. When that rhythm aligns with the demands of the moment, attention flows more easily. Too much activation—heart rate elevated, mind racing, thoughts jumping—makes it harder to direct and hold our focus. Too little activation, and energy and urgency fade; the mind wanders. The sweet spot is what psychologists and coaches refer to as the *individual zone of optimal functioning*—a state where energy, emotion, and focus align (Hanin, 2000).

The problem is that many performers unknowingly work against their own physiology. We've seen athletes who describe feeling anxious before games—hands shaking, mind spinning—then plug in a playlist of high-tempo, heavy-beat tracks. Their system, already running hot, goes into overdrive. They call it "getting pumped," but what they're really doing is overstimulating the nervous system, which makes focus harder to sustain. These athletes would often perform better by doing the opposite—choosing slower, calmer, rhythmically steady music to downshift the activation and find a more deliberate internal tempo before competition.

Research supports this idea. A scoping review by Zapata et al. (2022) found that music enhances performance, cadence, and mood—but that tempo and genre are key moderators. Faster tempos increase arousal and movement synchronization, while slower, melodic tempos promote relaxation and attentional stability. Similarly, Song et al. (2024) showed that reflective or slower-tempo music can calm overactivation and improve concentration, while higher-tempo tracks are most beneficial when energy or motivation are low. Zhang et al. (2024) found that fast-tempo music enhanced movement flow and neural engagement during physical tasks, suggesting that rhythm can entrain both body and brain. Complementing these findings, Rhythm in Sport demonstrated that rhythmic training—through metronomes or musical pacing—can optimize timing, efficiency, and focus across a range of athletic skills.

Taken together, these studies show that music isn't just a backdrop to performance—it's a regulatory cue. The right rhythm helps align the nervous and attentional systems. It can prime the brain for readiness, synchronize movement patterns, and even anchor breathing rhythms before performance. When used intentionally, music becomes another layer of attentional training—helping performers tune the system up or down until they find their personal rhythm for optimal focus.

In practice, this means matching music to your *desired* state, not your *current* one. If energy feels flat, up-tempo tracks can raise activation and engagement. If the mind is restless or overloaded, slower-tempo or acoustic tracks can cue calm and re-center attention. Music, like breath, is a tool to direct the system. When we use it with intention, it helps us find that elusive rhythm where body, brain, and attention flow as one.

Execution: Coaching Under Fire

In the NBA, pressure is a constant. A single bad call can flip momentum, a careless turnover can ignite frustration, and a missed defensive rotation can unravel even the most detailed game plan. One coach we worked with knew this all too well. He admitted that maintaining good relationships with referees was a challenge for him, and a missed call often triggered visible anger. His passion for the game was unquestionable, but under fire his frustration leaked out. When players made mistakes, sharp words often followed. Over time, he noticed his team began to mirror his state—tight, reactive, and distracted. He realized they weren't just responding to the game; they were responding to him.

This wasn't just anecdotal. Research on emotional contagion shows that leaders' emotional states are often unconsciously mimicked by their teams, influencing collective performance (Barsade, 2002). Distress will invite distress, so when the coach lost his composure, his players followed.

Through his personal awareness work, he had mapped his triggers and recognized how easily emotions could hijack his attention. Together, we applied the SERR model—**Situation + Emotion + Response = Result**—to the realities of his coaching. The "situation" might be a questionable whistle, the "emotion" a flash of frustration, but the "response" was his choice point. If he defaulted to venting, the result was predictable: a team that spiraled with him. But if he created a plan in advance, he could ground himself, redirect his attention, and shape his behaviors—including the nonverbals his players watched most closely—in the heat of the moment.

That plan became his routine. When frustration spiked, he took a single deep breath—his cue to re-anchor in the present. Why? Research shows that paced breathing activates the parasympathetic nervous system and enhances emotion regulation under pressure (Lehrer & Gevirtz, 2014). His second cue was tactile: he touched his wedding ring, a reminder of values beyond basketball. That physical gesture softened defensiveness and steadied his perspective. Finally, after calling a timeout, he quietly asked himself: *"What do they need from me to be their best next?"* That question redirected his attention away from anger and back toward leadership.

These intentional micro-routines didn't remove his frustrated emotion, but they changed its trajectory. He noticed his players operating with greater steadiness under stress—because their leader was modeling it. Over time, the routines became automatic. What had once been reaction gave way to choice. His attention was no longer dictated by bad calls or mistakes; it was guided by intentional practice, aligning awareness, intention, and execution in real time.

Reflection: Closing the Day with Intention

The executive we met earlier, the one battling frustration and fear of derailing her team, discovered that mornings weren't the only battleground for her attention. Even after strong, productive days, she often carried the weight of unfinished tasks and team frustrations home with her. Nights had been restless, her mind often replaying conversations or ruminating on missed opportunities. Without closure, attention never reset—it drifted backward, replaying everything that hadn't gone well.

That's when we introduced an evening reflection routine. It wasn't elaborate—less than 10 minutes, often closer to 5—but it became one of her most powerful tools. Each night, she opened a small notebook and answered three prompts:

1. **What went well today?**
2. **What did I learn/what's worth improving?**
3. **What's my focus/plan for tomorrow?**

The power was in its simplicity. Instead of letting her mind cycle endlessly, she gave herself a structured channel. By naming the wins, she reinforced progress. By identifying lessons, she reframed mistakes as opportunities to grow. And by defining her plan for the next day, she freed her mind from carrying the weight of unfinished business overnight.

This simple journaling practice shifted her attention from an endless internal loop—rumination without an endpoint—toward an externalized focus with a clear, definitive close. Research supports this effect: structured reflection consolidates learning and improves subsequent performance, sometimes even more effectively than additional practice (Di Stefano et al., 2014). Similarly, studies on recovery highlight that psychological detachment (i.e., the ability to "let go") at the end of the workday is strongly linked to reduced fatigue and restored attentional control (Sonnentag & Fritz, 2007). In short, journaling provided both a release valve and a reset: a way of closing one attentional loop so that energy and focus could be renewed for the next.

Over time, she noticed she was falling asleep faster and waking with more energy. The edge she once carried into family interactions softened; she was more present, and consequently more patient with her children. At work, she no longer began the day in a reactive scramble—her mornings built on the clarity she had created the night before.

The impact wasn't about the few minutes spent journaling. It was about what the routine practice signaled: a cadence of closure and renewal. Reflection gave her subconscious brain the permission to put the day to rest and provided a clean runway for tomorrow. What once felt like "slowing down" to her became a catalyst—accelerating her growth, sharpening her performance, and deepening her sense of balance both at home and at work.

Using Renewal to Reduce Burnout

It turns out that the use of attentional routines, when applied to recovery, hold powerful potential for addressing and/or preventing burnout. Burnout has become one of the defining challenges of modern work. The World Health Organization now classifies it as an occupational phenomenon—not a personal failing. Its core dimensions—exhaustion, cynicism, and reduced efficacy—stem from chronic demand combined with insufficient recovery (Maslach & Leiter, 2016). Across industries, surveys show record-high levels of stress, disengagement, and attrition. Many organizations face not just a performance problem, but a sustainability crisis.

Burnout feels especially acute in an era when many of us feel tethered to our work and "on" nearly 24/7. Our attentional reserves are chronically drained. While it's easy to blame organizations and leaders for escalating demands—and the data backs this up that chronic job demands and work intensification are strong predictors of burnout (Bakker & Demerouti, 2007; Schaufeli, 2017)—the picture is more complex. Burnout is not only organizational; it's also personal. Factors such as self-regulation capacity and recovery routines strongly predict who sustains performance under similar conditions

(Shirom, 2003; Sonnentag, 2018). In other words, the same environment can drain one performer while another endures, depending on the habits and renewal practices they bring to recovery.

From an attentional standpoint, burnout occurs when focus is continuously consumed by demands, fragmented by distractions, and eroded by constant comparison—without opportunities to restore or reconnect. Recovery experiences such as psychological detachment, relaxation, and mastery are all associated with improved well-being and renewed attentional control (Sonnentag & Fritz, 2007). Daily attentional "reps"—micro-breaks, structured reflection, and quality sleep—create rhythms that make restoration sustainable. Renewal routines offer a structured, individualized path back to clarity. And when leaders model these practices, they do more than protect themselves; they help establish cultures where composure, recovery, and focus become collective priorities.

One executive of a professional sports organization experienced this firsthand. Responsible for staff, sponsors, and game-day operations while managing every other facet of a multibillion-dollar enterprise, he came out of COVID exhausted. The decision fatigue was immense, pushing him to consider walking away from the industry altogether. Research shows that repeated high-stakes decision-making depletes cognitive resources and impairs self-regulation, leaving individuals more vulnerable to stress and distraction (Inzlicht & Schmeichel, 2012).

Using the IA Framework, we began with the Impact Timeline and 80th Birthday Exercise to reconnect him with his core values—family and staff. He realized that his steady presence had been the anchor others relied on during uncertainty, and that recognition recharged him more effectively than any time off. He paired that meaning-driven perspective with breathwork and centering practices to return to his attentional bullseye when stress pulled him into comparison or rumination. He discovered it wasn't the workload that drained him most—it was the mental spiral of imagining escape. Left unchecked, that internal drift led straight to burnout.

By grounding his attention in meaning, practicing resets, and structuring recovery cycles, he found a way to sustain high performance without sacrificing health. And he was not alone. After COVID, a wave of executives and department heads sought the same attentional training once reserved for players. Recognizing the undeniable link between attentional training, well-being, and organizational performance, a professional team expanded its work with us beyond players and coaches to include the entire staff across the organization.

When we pair intentional practices of recovery with deeper sources of meaning, and layer in executional resets, we create an attentional architecture that is not only sustainable but deeply restorative. Renewal habits, purpose, and reset routines combine to form a powerful buffer against the modern pace of life—reminding us that how we direct our attention determines not just how we perform, but how fully we live.

Putting It All Together: Daily IA Reps

Even with clear rhythms of recovery, life will test us and can wear us down. Our real attentional work will reveal itself when acute stress accumulates—when we're tasked to apply what we've practiced to a series of unpredictable moments that don't go our way. This is where daily reps and preparation come into play.

Preparing for Adversity (SERR in Action)

Adversity is not an *if*; it is a *when*. That is why we use SERR to pre-plan hot moments: define the Situation, understand and accept the Emotion, yet choose the Response that gets us closer to the Result we want. Research on implementation intentions shows that creating simple "if–then" rules ("If X happens, then I will do Y") reduces

Daily Reps: Building Attentional Fitness

the cognitive tax of surprise and supports more adaptive attentional shifts (Gollwitzer & Sheeran, 2006). The prefrontal cortex performs best when it has a clear focus cue to guide behavior under load (Miller & Cohen, 2001).

Mental Rehearsal as Attentional Training

Visualization is often misunderstood as simply "imagining the trophy." For us, the goal is different: we rehearse what the moment will look, feel, sound, taste, and smell like—and, most importantly, where we will direct our attention when pressure peaks and distractions are at their highest. Neuroimaging studies show that motor imagery activates overlapping neural networks with execution and can significantly enhance performance when used intentionally (Hétu et al., 2013; Hardwick et al., 2018).

For example, by mentally rehearsing our breathing pattern under stress, picturing ourselves narrowing focus to the bullseye focus cues amid distractions, or running through a reset routine after an error that sparks strong emotion, we train our system to respond faster and with greater precision—activating in the way we prefer to behave and giving us the best chance to succeed in high-demand situations.

We can complement our intentional efforts of attention by shaping our environments to support, rather than sabotage, our focus. As we've outlined in prior chapters, attention is susceptible to external cues and competing stimuli.

For example, the mere presence of a smartphone—even facedown and unused—can reduce available cognitive capacity, as part of our mind subconsciously monitors it for potential signals (Ward et al., 2017). Similarly, open-plan offices increase noise and interruptions, which elevate cognitive load and force more frequent task-switching, both of which are linked to lower perceived productivity

(Kim & de Dear, 2013). In short, environments either tax or conserve our limited attentional resources.

We can stack the deck in our favor by structuring spaces that lower attentional load: phones off the table, clear transitions between tasks, and pre-performance routines. High performers don't only rely on willpower; they also engineer environments that make focus easier.

Measuring Progress: Signals of Attentional Training

Training attention is like training the body—you know it's working when the signals start to shift. But unlike squats or sprints, the markers aren't as obvious as the number of reps or the amount of weight on the bar. Instead, progress shows up in more subtle but just as powerful ways: fewer attentional slips during the day, faster resets after distractions, shorter sleep latency at night, optimal heart rate variability (HRV) across the week, and less rumination before bed. Some notice fewer emotional "blow-ups" under stress, or a quicker ability to return to baseline after frustration. These are all signs that routines are taking root and the attentional system is recalibrating.

In order to track this, self-report is often enough: Did I redirect faster? Sleep more easily? Feel less consumed by noise? For those using wearables, HRV, sleep quality, and recovery scores can provide additional validation. The key is to notice—not only if performance outcomes improve, but if the process feels steadier. Measurement gives leaders and performers confidence that progress is real and sustainable, even before the scoreboard reflects it.

When we measure the signs—fewer slips, faster resets, steadier recovery—we know the system is working. Over time, attention begins to show up where it has been trained to go. And that can help us live with greater satisfaction not only *during* but also *between* the pressure moments.

Chapter 15

Performing Under Pressure: From Clutch Moments to Chronic Demands

"Pressure is a privilege—it only comes to those who earn it."

—Billie Jean King

Acute pressure moments test whether we can deliver in the spotlight. Chronic pressure, by contrast, tests whether we can sustain ourselves when the spotlight never seems to turn off. One demands execution in the instant; the other slowly erodes resilience, motivation, and confidence over time. Both are real, both can be costly—and both require Intentional Attention. By learning to recognize where our focus drifts and deliberately steering it back to performance-relevant data, we can weather not only the clutch moment but also the prolonged storms that threaten to wear us down.

The NBA Case Study Continued

If you remember back to the Introduction, we opened with the story of an NBA All-Star who was battling an invisible opponent: his own attention. On the surface, it looked like nothing more than a shooting slump. But beneath it was a different kind of pressure—not the acute, last-shot-on-the-clock variety, but a chronic, extended pressure that stretched across weeks and months. Every miss, each skeptical media question, even a teammate's hesitation didn't register as isolated basketball moments. They accumulated, snowballing into sustained threats to his identity.

What unraveled his game wasn't a lack of skill or preparation. It was the steady, prolonged pull of his attention toward fear, doubt, and judgment—an attentional steering wheel yanked toward small threats and insecurities that compounded over time and disrupted his execution. Like so many high performers under pressure, he didn't just lose rhythm in the moment; he began to lose trust in himself. He was caught in the threat spiral, his baseline stress elevated, and his focus siphoned away from the very cues that had once fueled his success. That was his real slump.

All too often, this is the trap that pressure sets. Many high-level performers don't encounter it until they reach the top of their competitive arenas. Up to that point, their talent and drive allowed them to consistently outproduce those around them. But at the highest levels, attention begins to drift toward identity threats. For the first time, fear, negative judgment, disrespect, and insecurities feel fully exposed.

For most of us, fears and insecurities tend to get exposed at earlier stages of our lives, careers, or crafts. Regardless of when it strikes, the effect is the same: Stress and negative feedback amplify the stress response, activating the body's physiology into an anxious state and narrowing focus onto fears rather than execution. Under high-pressure conditions, self-threat disrupts attentional control and pulls focus away from performance-relevant cues (Beilock & Carr, 2001; Baumeister & Showers, 1986).

For this All-Star, the cycle was relentless. One missed shot confirmed the disrespect he felt from the defenders allowing him to shoot. That belief ignited frustration and doubt. These thoughts and emotions broke his rhythm. And the spiral repeated itself, each loop reinforcing the next.

Assessing Attention and Building a Bullseye

Our work began with improving his awareness—of what was happening to his attentional system, why it was happening, and ultimately what solutions he could use to change the cycle. We started with his basketball history: what he valued, what he had been rewarded for, and what adversity he had faced in the past. That reflection helped him see how his mind had constructed the beliefs fueling this slump. Like many athletes we've worked with, he was surprised to learn how strongly the brain is wired to scan for and lock onto threats. He felt relieved to know that nothing was "wrong" with him. For weeks, he had been telling himself he might be weak or not cut out for the game at the highest levels. His mind was so wrapped around the axle that he began to seriously contemplate walking away from the very game he loved.

It should also be noted that we assessed his mindset in a broader context. During our initial intake, he admitted to sometimes feeling gloomier than those around him and that several close relatives had experienced depression from time to time. After carefully evaluating his current symptoms, we determined that he was in a generally healthy mental state off the court. Basketball, however, was the one domain where he felt truly lost. We were deliberate not to shortchange the reality that mental health challenges can profoundly shape attentional patterns. Yet in his case, it became clear that it was not clinical depression but rather his attentional patterns that were driving the spiral he experienced on the court.

That opened the door to take the next step: reviewing his attentional patterns through the Mindset Matrix that we covered in Chapter 9. When we introduced the five variables—Focus, Thoughts, Emotions, Body Sensations, and Behaviors—he immediately assumed the most controllable factor was emotions. Like many players, he had heard the phrase "emotional control" and believed confidence was something he should be able to manufacture on demand. He was surprised to learn, however, that emotions are among the strongest yet most fleeting and least controllable variables in the system. Focus and behaviors, by contrast, tend to be far more stable and trainable.

For him, mapping his best and worst games through the Matrix was eye-opening. The difference was striking—and instantly recognizable, a pattern we've seen in countless other performers across levels and disciplines.

At his best, his focus locked onto the hoop, teammates' cuts, and defensive reads. His thoughts were sharp but simple: *Attack. Find the gap.* His emotions weren't calm so much as energized—assertive and joyful. His behaviors matched: fist bumps, loud communication, all-out sprints in transition, disruptive defense, and more smiles.

In his worst games, the contrast was glaring. His focus narrowed onto identity threats—*They don't respect me*, or what his shooting percentage would be if he hit or missed the next shot. His thoughts filled with doubt. His emotions turned frustrated and anxious. His body language sagged—shoulders slumped, head down. The difference wasn't that his skill had left him; it was about where his attention and behaviors lived.

That awareness unlocked change. Now understanding both his controllables and his default pull toward threat, he built a Focus Bullseye—a visual cue targeting his attention on performance-relevant behaviors. He wrote three anchors in the center: **Hoop. Help. Hustle.**

- **Hoop:** Attack the basket. Keep aggression locked on the hoop, not the noise.
- **Help:** Communicate and lift teammates. As an All-Star, his voice carried weight. A quick compliment, a hand to pick up a fallen teammate, a loud defensive call—these actions fueled connection.

- **Hustle:** Sprint in transition, get back on defense, disrupt opponents' rhythm. His intelligence allowed him to anticipate sets, bait passes, and force opponents into low-value shots.

These cues became his bullseye. Everything else—respect, reputation, stats—was a distraction. To reset, he tapped his chest, took a breath, or glanced at his shoe, where HHH was written discreetly on his laces. In effect, he was training himself to pre-label distractions and pair them with reset cues—a strategy shown to strengthen attentional control under pressure (Miller & Cohen, 2001; Gollwitzer & Sheeran, 2006).

Execution of this plan required repetition. Every three games, we sat down and evaluated his Intentional Attention plan. He didn't grade himself on points scored or shooting percentage but on his ability to execute the plan—how consistently he kept his attention on the bullseye rather than the noise.

Noticing the Results

Over several weeks of refining his plan, the pattern became undeniable: when his focus stayed locked on Hoop, Help, and Hustle, his game elevated.

Media, coaches, and teammates began to notice the shift. His production drew attention. A lot of attention. But with the heightened exposure came a new challenge: success could pull his focus away from his bullseye just as powerfully as failure once had. He noticed how his mind wanted to again jump to the end—production and results. Yet this time he was aware of that pattern and more importantly, where he wanted to hold his attention to yield the best performances. He stayed disciplined, returning to his cues, and by season's end had raised his three-point percentage above 33%, hit his performance bonuses, and secured another major contract. The misses still came, but they no longer defined him. Opponents sagging off no longer felt like disrespect—it felt like opportunity. He wasn't performing to chase respect or even accolades; he was performing to stay in rhythm and be his best self.

That's the deeper truth of pressure: it doesn't only test us in acute moments of failure. It also shows up in the chronic stretches of tension—and even in the glow of success.

Chronic Demands: The Stress Threshold

Pressure doesn't always announce itself with a countdown clock. Sometimes it arrives silently, through the relentless pulls of daily life. Many leaders today juggle careers, children, relationships, aging parents, the rising cost of living, and the constant comparison of keeping up with peers. Stress research shows that strain emerges not only from major life events but also from the steady accumulation of daily demands that approach or exceed our adaptive capacity (Lazarus & Folkman, 1984). When we live chronically close to that threshold, even a small curveball—a missed deadline, unfavorable feedback, an unexpected mishap—can feel like the final straw.

Physiology reflects the same reality. Allostatic load—the wear and tear that builds when stress is frequent and recovery insufficient—makes us more vulnerable to injury and breakdown when new stressors arrive (McEwen & Stellar, 1993; McEwen, 1998). Psychologically, the same holds true. A growing body of organizational evidence shows that when daily job demands remain high and recovery stays low, leaders report sharper drops in energy, higher burnout risk, more mental health struggles, and reduced effectiveness in leading teams (Ten Brummelhuis et al., 2021). In practice, the small things stop being small. They become tipping points—not because of their magnitude, but because of how close so many of us already are to the edge.

That was the case for one unit leader at a technology firm we had recently begun supporting through a transition. In our first meeting, she admitted she was probably too busy to commit to consistent coaching. Her days were consumed by email and urgent tasks, and she told me she wasn't sure there was time for reflection. We didn't push. But a few weeks later, I received a text asking if we could find time to talk—soon.

When we met, she shared that her supervisor had just delivered blunt feedback: "Your team isn't delivering at the level we need. If this doesn't improve, we'll have to make changes." As she replayed the moment, she described her knees going weak, heat flooding her chest, and her vision narrowing. Her self-talk was immediate: *I'm failing. Maybe I don't belong in this seat. I'm never enough. I'm letting everyone one down.* Within minutes, it spun into a defensive protest: *This isn't fair. They keep moving the goalposts. Leadership is terrible. They haven't communicated clearly.*

Her mind raced. Her attention scattered—searching for reasons, protection, and lifelines. It was a classic and predictable cognitive-emotional spiral, the kind we see when stress breaches our thresholds and the mind shifts from constructive focus to self-protection (Baumeister et al., 2001a; Steele, 1988). The good news: She had strong self-awareness. She didn't like what she was feeling, but she could name it. That pause created a crack in the spiral—a moment to reflect and redirect. Up until then, she hadn't been convinced she had much to work on. Now, she had a starting point.

Much like the NBA All-Star, she felt uncertain, overwhelmed, and unsure what levers to pull to change the trajectory of her performance and her team's. Beneath the professional stress was something even heavier: the fear that she was letting down her kids, her husband, her team, even her extended family. The burden wasn't just professional—it was deeply personal.

Uncovering Beliefs

We started by unpacking her goals and mapping both her and her team's perceived strengths and weaknesses. Quickly, a core belief surfaced. She admitted she often took on too much of the work herself and avoided giving her team the honest feedback they needed. Why? Because she believed people performed best when they were happy. Research does support the connection between positive affect and performance (Lyubomirsky et al., 2005). But in her case, that belief had tipped into distortion. Protecting her team from discomfort meant protecting them from growth and hitting performance standards.

Layered beneath was a second insight: Her personality profile revealed she was deeply motivated by being liked. Subconsciously, this mattered more than hitting the organizational standard. These two forces—her belief about happiness and her drive for approval—combined to drain her attention. She internalized frustrations, took on unsustainable amounts of work, and quietly resented her team for not stepping up. The cycle of overwork, frustration, and passive-aggressive communication deepened her sense of being overwhelmed.

And there was yet another layer: her beliefs about stress itself. She carried the conviction that stress was inherently harmful—that the workload was unsustainable, that imbalance would break her, that doing too much would eventually kill her. Evidence shows that how we appraise stress dramatically alters its impact. People who view stress as purely harmful experience more negative physical and psychological symptoms, while those who see it as a challenge to be harnessed show better health and performance outcomes (Crum et al., 2013). In other words, her perspective on stress was lowering her threshold. Instead of accessing resources that could help her, her belief that "stress is bad" amplified the physiological and psychological toll. And because attention and appraisal are closely linked, her lens became another hidden drain—filtering every demand as danger and making it harder to stay locked onto constructive cues. When her supervisor's feedback landed, it became the catalyst that pushed her beyond her adaptive capacity—the moment her stress crossed the threshold.

But that breaking point became the opening for change. Her insights reframed the conversation. We all have a *stress threshold*— our personal capacity for juggling demands before the system tips into overload. Her threshold wasn't just being tested by the sheer volume of responsibilities; it was also being eroded by how she perceived stress—as purely dangerous rather than as a natural response that, when channeled effectively, can provide the energy and focus we need to navigate demanding events (Crum et al., 2013).

The supervisor's feedback forced a reckoning. Her Personal Attentional Attribute Inventory (see Chapter 8) revealed that her attentional patterns under pressure were not only unsustainable but also misaligned with the organization's needs. Using the Mindset Matrix (see Chapter 9), we mapped the contrast.

During the feedback moment, her focus column read: *results, status, judgment*. Her thoughts: *They don't get it. This is on me. I'm not enough*. Her emotions: tight, resentful, exposed. Her body: shoulders high, jaw set. Her behaviors: take on more work, fire off clipped Slack messages, ruminate in cycles of self-criticism and blame.

Then we compared this to moments when she felt like she was thriving as a leader. The contrast was unmistakable. At her best, her focus was outward and task-relevant. She was constantly looking for ways to solve problems, asking sharper questions—and actually listening for answers. Her thoughts were open and collaborative: *What's the best path forward? Who else can weigh in?* Her emotions: engaged, confident, energized. Her body: open posture, leaning forward.

Her behaviors: her office door nearly always open, looking people in the eye rather than staring at her screen.

The trail of her attention was visible in every interaction. When it drifted inward, her team stalled. When it moved outward, they advanced.

Two insights surfaced. First, the supervisor's feedback landed as identity threat, not performance data—so her Focus Window locked-in on self-protection (Gross, 2015). Second, her own feedback to the team had drifted toward cheerleading—high warmth, low edge—because she didn't want them to feel what she'd just felt. That avoidance bought short-term harmony but created long-term stagnation. The science is clear: Poorly framed critical feedback undermines motivation and triggers defensiveness (Kluger & DeNisi, 1996), while feedback that is only supportive risks complacency and unclear standards (Hattie & Timperley, 2007).

The effective middle is "high standards + high belief"—what the literature calls *wise feedback* ("I'm holding you to a high bar because I believe you can meet it"), which improves acceptance and effort, especially under stress (Cohen et al., 1999; Yeager et al., 2014).

With that awareness, we used the SERR Model (see Chapter 10) to script the next high-heat moments:

- **Situation:** Supervisor pushes on misses; sprint review reveals slippage; cross-functional partner escalates.
- **Emotion:** First wave = defensiveness/embarrassment.
- **Response (her choice):** One breath + silent cue ("Data, not drama"), then two moves: (1) clarify the task-relevant facts; (2) restate standards with belief.
- **Result:** Return attention to plans, owners, and timelines; model steadiness and raise the bar without shame.

She also wrote down one sentence she would use in every tough staff one-on-one: "I'm holding us to a high standard because I believe you can get there—and we're not there yet." That "yet" matters. It signals growth trajectory rather than fixed ability (Mueller & Dweck, 1998; Yeager & Dweck, 2012).

Seeing the Shift

Then came execution. Before her next meeting with the supervisor, she ran a 60-second pre-brief: one paced breath (inhale 4, exhale 6), a glance at her notes to keep the focus window on deliverables, and a written intention: *Lead with owners and dates.* In the room, when the first critical question landed, she felt the old surge—and used the plan. Breath. Data. She summarized the gap, named who owned responsibility, and asked for constraints she might be missing. No defending. No spinning.

With her team, she shifted cadence. Sprint reviews started with two questions: *What's the user story we're solving this week? What are the obstacles I can help remove?* She delivered feedback using the wise feedback frame—high bar, high belief—and asked each direct report to commit to a next action before the meeting ended. She also began seeking feedback proactively—short, specific asks, like: "What's one thing I could do differently to make your work easier next sprint?" Feedback-seeking is strongly associated with higher performance and stronger leader–member exchange (Anseel et al., 2015).

The shift was tangible. Status meetings got shorter and clearer. People started volunteering ownership instead of waiting to be assigned. She still felt the sting of criticism—most of us do—but it no longer hijacked her attention. Feedback became information, not indictment. And her supervisor noticed: "There's a different feel to your team—tighter, more accountable."

That was the point. We hadn't made pressure disappear; she had simply learned where to place her attention when pressure arrived.

Expanding the Threshold

Pressure rarely looks the same, but it always works the same way. For the NBA All-Star, the threat came from a prolonged shooting slump that made every miss feel like an indictment of his identity. For the unit leader, it arrived as the daily grind stretched her system so close to capacity that one piece of critical feedback nearly tipped her over the edge. Different arenas, same reality: Pressure hijacks attention. With training, though, attention can be steered back toward performance-relevant data, constructive behaviors, and sustainable rhythms.

The common thread was awareness paired with structure. The Mindset Matrix gave both performers a way to see where their attention lived in their best and worst moments. The Focus Bullseye helped the All-Star anchor on controllables. Wise feedback reframed the leader's conversations with her team. And the SERR Model gave them both a sequence to follow when emotions surged. These tools didn't make pressure disappear; they taught attention where to go when pressure arrived.

But tools alone aren't enough if the system itself is depleted. Just as athletes rely on recovery to handle the demands of competition, leaders and performers can expand their *stress thresholds* through foundational routines: consistent sleep, hydration, movement, and deliberate recovery. A growing body of evidence links physical health behaviors to psychological resilience and attentional control (Kühnel et al., 2012; Sonnentag & Fritz, 2007). Add to that the reappraisal of stress itself—when our reflections interpret stress as something required for growth rather than a threat, our bodies mobilize more effectively and recover faster (Crum et al., 2013). These habits expand the baseline capacity that determines whether tomorrow's challenge becomes fuel or fatigue.

And that brings us back to a core tenet of *Intentional Attention*: the higher we climb, the deeper our roots must go. Just as taller trees need stronger roots to stay upright against a relentless storm, high performers need a deeper internal foundation as stressors mount. Those roots are built through awareness—understanding how the brain reacts under stress (see Part I), identifying our personal attentional attributes, and recognizing our patterns in high-stakes environments.

This tenet is one of the reasons we've used so many NFL Quarterbacks as example throughout this book. Few roles compress more cognitive, physical, and leadership demands into split-second decisions that are repeated for months on end. Every throw is analyzed, every decision magnified, and every mistake tied directly to the team's outcome. The constant pressure is unbelievable—and the response is visible.

The real shift of *Intentional Attention* comes when we stop asking, *"Will I be calm when the moment comes?"* and start asking, *"Have I trained my attention to return to a clear plan, purpose, and people?"* The former leaves us hoping. The latter leaves us ready.

Performers' Stress Threshold Checklist: Expanding Capacity, Directing Attention

What separates leaders who thrive under pressure from those who burn out isn't fewer demands—it's a wider capacity to absorb them. Recovery, mindset, and intentional routines act as buffers that protect performance and sustain health (McEwen & Stellar, 1993; Crum et al., 2013; Ten Brummelhuis et al., 2021).

Five important evidence-based levers that can expand our *stress threshold*:

1. Sleep

- One of the most important levers for attentional energy. Deep sleep clears metabolic waste and restores prefrontal cortex functioning—critical for attentional control (Diekelmann & Born, 2010).
- Ideally aim for 7–9 hours.
- Protect consistency of bed and wake times.

2. Hydration and Nutrition

- Even mild dehydration impairs focus and decision-making.
- Balanced nutrition stabilizes glucose levels, preventing crashes that mimic stress responses.
- Manage substances and supplements deliberately, weighing their benefits against their longer-term costs.
- Treat fueling as cognitive performance prep, not just physical health.

3. Movement

- Exercise increases neuroplasticity and stress resilience.
- Short bursts of physical activity during the day regulate cortisol and reset attentional stamina (Ratey, 2008).

4. Stress Appraisal

- Shift the lens: stress doesn't equal harm, stress equals energy to be harnessed.
- Research confirms that embracing and reframing stress can improve performance and reduces health costs (Crum et al., 2013).

- A simple reappraisal: replace "I hate this feeling" or "This will break me" with "This activation will prepare me."

5. Attentional Management

- Use IA tools like the **Mindset Matrix**, **Focus Bullseye**, or **SERR** to redirect focus when the system wavers.
- Pre-label common distractors. Pair them with reset cues.
- Build micro-routines: one breath, one phrase, one behavior that signals "reset."

Bottom line: Stress will always find us—sometimes as an acute surge, other times as the slow accumulation of demands. Performers and leaders who intentionally expand their thresholds carry it more effectively, sustaining both performance and longevity.

Chapter 16

Stacking Wins: Sustaining Attention over Time

"Small disciplines repeated with consistency every day lead to great achievements gained slowly over time."

—John C. Maxwell

There's a story—half legend, half history—that captures the essence of mastery. Pablo Picasso was once sitting in a Paris café when a woman approached and asked if he would sketch her a dog. He agreed, pulled a napkin from the table, and with a few strokes of his pen captured the form in seconds. When she reached for it, he said, "That will be 10,000 francs."

Startled, she protested, "But it only took you a minute!"

Picasso replied, "No, it took me a lifetime."

What looked effortless was anything but. Behind those few strokes were decades of practice, failures, adjustments, and countless unseen repetitions. The sketch wasn't the product of speed; it was the product of sustained attention—time layered, choices compounded.

In today's age of instant gratification, we celebrate the breakthrough story more than ever—the rookie phenom, the start-up entrepreneur who seems to hit it big overnight. Maybe it's because we want to believe it could happen for us if luck tilts our way. Perhaps it's a defense, a way of protecting our identities by dismissing others' success as fortune rather than work. Either way, our culture loves to tell these stories as if greatness arrives fully formed the moment the lights are turned on.

But in nearly two decades of working with the best of the best, we've seen a different reality. Even those who appear to have climbed the mountain quickly have usually been stacking unseen wins for years. Beneath every "overnight success" is an extreme amount of time, repetition, *and* Intentional Attention devoted to the craft. The spotlight moment is the reveal, not the origin.

Sustained success—whether in sport, leadership, or life—isn't built on one heroic burst. It's forged through the steady accumulation of consistent wins. Behind the buzzer-beater lies the unglamorous sustained effort of daily reps, invisible to everyone but the performer.

This is where Intentional Attention shows its real power. It offers a framework not only to survive high-pressure moments but to build the daily rituals that let attention strengthen over time. By grounding in core motivators, values, and even fears, we can aim attention in a constructive direction, fuel persistence, and protect it from drifting off course.

In Chapter 15, we explored how attention helps us manage acute and chronic pressure. Here, the lens widens: How do we sustain attention to thrive across seasons, careers, and lifetimes? Because high performance isn't only about clutch moments—it's about optimizing the thousands of ordinary ones that quietly add up to a legacy.

What Stacking Wins Can Look Like

Those who thrive don't just rise in big moments; they commit to systems that let small wins stack. They focus on meaningful, sustainable data. They stack performance-relevant choices that make it easier to sustain deliberate attention. They prioritize sleep, recovery, health, presence—and they often rediscover joy in the process. Above all, they embrace a central principle: consistency beats intensity.

The science of performance converges on a clear conclusion: mastery is rarely built through rare bursts of brilliance. Classic work on deliberate practice showed that excellence emerges from sustained, focused effort over time (Ericsson et al., 1993). More recent findings echo the same principle—small, marginal gains, repeated consistently, produce exponential returns (Macnamara et al., 2014). This pattern extends beyond skill acquisition. Behaviors anchored in stable routines compound more reliably than those driven by short-lived motivation (Lally et al., 2010), and long-term achievement is predicted more by perseverance and consistency than by talent or intensity alone (Duckworth et al., 2007).

For athletes, that might mean stacking practices where attention stays locked on task-relevant cues rather than drifting toward outcomes. For leaders, it might mean stacking meetings where focus remains on owners, efficient processes, and clarity, rather than on defensiveness or distraction. For any of us, it might mean stacking days where we train our attention—one breath, one reset, one reflection at a time.

We don't build a season, a career, or a legacy overnight. We build it through the disciplined stacking of days. By directing attention with intention, we can turn daily choices into lasting impact—and over time, those small instances become something extraordinary.

The NFL Quarterback

What athletes often discover is that stacking wins isn't glamorous—it's mundane. For one NFL QB we worked with, the challenge wasn't hitting the game-winning throw. He'd done that. The challenge for him was maintaining his attention across the grind of multiple NFL seasons: off-season training, Wednesday practices in November, film study on short weeks, recovery sessions when his body was bruised and aching.

His temptation—like many high performers—was to measure himself against outcomes. Every touchdown or interception, every

Stacking Wins: Sustaining Attention over Time

quarterback rating, every headline became a referendum on his worth. But those metrics swung wildly—from MVP talk one week to calls for the backup the next. The pendulum moved so quickly it could give anyone whiplash.

When we started working together, we shifted the metric: measure attention, not production. After all, production required too many external factors—coaching calls, protection up front, receivers running routes, the level of competition. Those variables changed week to week. What stayed within his control was his attention. And most importantly, if he got his attention right, he was giving himself the best opportunity to produce at a high level more consistently.

To keep his attention steady, he grounded himself in deeper motivators: honoring his parents' sacrifices that had given him the chance to play in the NFL, being a role model for his children, leading his teammates with steadiness, and making those around him better. These became his daily anchors. Each morning, he set his intentions through that lens; each evening, he reflected on whether he had lived them. When he had, he felt gratitude and pride—not from stats or rankings, but from honoring the things that he truly valued. That feeling fueled him through the monotony of the grind.

On the field, he distilled performance-relevant data into four controllables, inside his Focus Bullseye:

- Definitive pre-snap plan
- Footwork tempo
- Read progression with his eyes
- Clear communication

He knew when he did these four things, he usually played very well. So, after every practice, he didn't grade himself on completion percentage but on how consistently he tethered his attention to those four anchors. The stack wasn't always perfect—some days wavered. Growth, we reminded him, looked less like a straight line and more like a stock market graph: peaks and troughs, but trending upward over time.

By December, when fatigue and injury usually fray mechanics and decision-making, his rhythm held. Film showed fewer wasted movements, more decisive throws, faster release times, and steadier leadership in the huddle. He hadn't magically raised his talent; he had systematically stacked attentional wins until they amassed into sustained performance.

That's the hidden math of mastery: pressure moments don't build us—they reveal what's been built.

The Professional Golfer

For a professional golfer, the challenge looked different but lived in the same neighborhood of attention. His initial fixation was on the leaderboard. Each round became an emotional rollercoaster: When he was up, his attention drifted to scanning who might be chasing him. When he was down, it derailed into calculating how far he needed to climb to contend. None of it helped him hit the next shot.

He came to us aware of this trend, his presenting question simple: *Should I look at the leaderboard, or should I not?* When asked how looking served him, he said it helped him decide whether to attack or play more conservatively. When he tried avoiding it altogether, he found himself distracted anyway—guessing from crowd reactions or opponents' body language. Head up, confident stride meant they were charging. Head down, tentative walk meant they were faltering. Either way, his attention was fraying.

We ran him through the IA framework to map his attentional patterns. The leaderboard was one drain, but we uncovered another: ball flight. When shots drifted left or right, he dove inward—tinkering with mechanics mid-round, chasing fixes. What he learned was that his brain was simply doing what human brains do: scanning for problems and grabbing at quick solutions. The problem wasn't his ability—it was his attentional steering.

So he built a new plan. Range time was for mechanics. Competition time was for targets. If a shot pattern emerged, he would re-calibrate his aim—adjust the target, not his swing. He paired his external cue (the target) with a simple internal cue—a swing thought: *sweep through to the target.* Over time, he noticed something striking: by holding his attention externally on the target, his body often self-corrected. Confidence returned, tension eased, and ball flight normalized.

With the leaderboard, he realized the issue wasn't whether he looked—it was what he did after. Instead of letting the numbers dictate his confidence, he built three scripts: one for when he was ahead, one for when he was behind, and one for when he was in the heat of a close battle. Each script dictated where his attention and behaviors would go next. In short, the leaderboard became information, not identity.

The shift was profound. Errors still came, of course, but he began to see them less as failures of technique and more as lapses of attention. The best golfers he spoke with confirmed it: their real edge wasn't a perfect swing but the ability to reappraise setbacks, stay anchored on performance-relevant cues, and keep stacking reps of focus. He started to join that group.

He may not yet sit atop the leaderboard in majors, but his trajectory is clear. By stacking wins of attention—target over technique, plan over panic, controllables over outcomes—his consistency has grown, his confidence steadied, and his results climbed.

The lesson mirrored Picasso's napkin sketch: sustained success isn't about chasing outcomes. It's about stacking attention on controllables. Outcomes follow.

The NCAA National Champion Gymnast

For a gymnast preparing for the NCAA Championships, the pressure wasn't about a contract or endorsement—it was about the weight of leading her team. She had spent a lifetime training for this stage. As captain and anchor of a national championship program, she carried the respect of her teammates—including several Olympians. She wasn't the most decorated gymnast, but she was the one everyone trusted. Years of disciplined training and a deep sense of self-awareness gave her the ability not just to *hope* she could deliver, but to *know* she could.

That conviction was tested in her final year. The championship meet was close heading into the final event with the tied opponent heading to beam and her team on floor. Her team needed to "hit" 5 of the 6 routines by scoring near perfect 10's to secure the NCAA Championship team title. Momentum was on their side with floor as the last rotation and their opponent team competing on the nerve-wracking, easily shakable balance beam.

The gymnast's team was doing great with their first 4 floor routines made near to perfection. The team on beam was hitting every routine and scoring high. The battle was on, back and forth, each routine was stuck by both teams—until the unthinkable happened. The gymnast just before her, a former Olympian, fell on the final tumbling pass of her floor routine. The crowd gasped as if knowing what this meant—the mistake cost critical points and very likely a National Championship. Suddenly, the anchor's task became close to impossible: to clinch the championship, she would have to deliver near perfection—under the weight of an arena that fully understood what was at stake.

The pressure was palpable. And as if the moment needed more weight, the opposing team's final beam competitor nailed her routine.

Momentum shifted. The tension in the building was electric. Everyone was thinking the same thing: *Could this final gymnast steady herself enough, under the most dramatic conditions imaginable, to bring home the national championship?* In moments like this, most performers shift to survival thoughts: "Oh no, this is all on me now. Don't blow it. Don't let the team down. Now, I can't make a mistake!" But the captain was different. She turned to her wide-eyed teammates standing next to her and cut through the tension with a calm, humorous, almost eerily defiant tone:

"Well, it looks like we're going to do this the hard way."

In that moment, she smiled with a small chuckle and very matter-of-factly walked out on to the mat with a swagger of sass. She wasn't clinging to outcomes or consumed by "what ifs." Her attention locked onto the task at hand—one skill at a time, one pass at a time, "let's do this." She had trained herself to focus on performance-relevant cues, and now she trusted that training.

And she delivered. One skill after another executed cleanly, sealing yet another National Championship for her team.

Her performance that day wasn't just about talent or work ethic. It was the compounded outcome of years of stacking small wins in the hardest reps, grueling practices, and in the most mundane moments. That consistency and mindset toward adversity underpinned her ability to meet the moment when the pressure peaked.

This is why she carried the team's "Captain" title and responsibility. Not because of one heroic routine, but because she had demonstrated time after time that her attention could be trusted. Her teammates and coaches knew—if anyone could bring it home when it was all on the line, it was her.

The Olympian

He was nearly out of the running, a back-against-the-wall type moment with his team. Few would have blamed him for folding under the weight. Three previous Olympic Games told the same story—win Nationals, be the best in your country, and then mentally hit a wall under the pressure and expectations when on the Olympic stage. Every Olympic Games wrote the same disappointing narrative of "failure." Now, at his 4th Olympics, the morning of the make or break game, where the team wins and stays alive in the round-robin or loses and is out of the Olympics, he came across the anniversary of a powerful story—an Olympic speed skater who had fallen short over and over again before finally breaking through to win gold in the months after losing a loved one. The skater had shared racing for their loved one, rather than skating to win. The story stuck with him that morning. *If that athlete could write a new narrative on the world's biggest stage—endure setback after setback and still perform with purpose—then so could I,* he thought.

That moment reframed everything. His attention shifted from internal spirals of self-doubt and identity threat . . . to external, task-relevant cues along with his transcendent motivators: showing his kids how to enjoy playing, smiling, expressing gratitude for the opportunity, the target, the competition, the communication with his teammates. Nothing magical changed about his skill. What changed was his lens. He stopped fixating on what failure said about him and the fear of making mistakes and started locking back onto the performance cues he had rehearsed thousands of times that included being present with his teammates and reconnecting with his WHY.

That shift in perspective didn't erase the pressure, but it cleared a path through it. The noise around him receded, and what remained was the task in front of him. With each frame of his game, he trusted the reps. With each rep, he relied on his process. With each call, he was making his kids proud regardless of outcome. And they won that game, and the next one, and the next five in a row to eventually win gold. To this day, it's one of the most impressive mental shifts, in such a short amount of time, on a stage of that nature.

Studies in precision sports show that directing attention externally—to the movement effect or the target—leads to more consistent, accurate performance than focusing internally on mechanics or on self-evaluation. (Wulf, 2013; Wulf & Lewthwaite, 2016). In other words, once his focus went back to the target rather than to his identity or even his internal mechanics, his execution sharpened.

That gold-medal moment was not about a sudden surge of brilliance—it was the visible payoff of thousands of stacked, ordinary reps finally converging when his attention returned to the task. This is the essence of stacking wins. It wasn't one breakthrough moment that carried him to the podium; it was the accumulation of thousands of deliberate choices that allowed him to execute on the world's ultimate competitive stage. Once he reframed his perspective, his attention returned to the process he had already stacked day after day, silencing the threat of being a failure and a more positive outcome followed.

The Senior Executive Under Scrutiny

He wasn't chasing a medal or a trophy—he was fighting for trust. A senior executive at a Fortune 1,000 company came to us in the middle of what he described as "a year-long performance review." His division had missed targets two quarters in a row, and investor calls were starting to get testy. Every presentation to the board felt like a referendum on his leadership.

Like the golfer watching the scoreboard, he couldn't stop measuring himself against outcomes. Stock performance, revenue charts, analyst ratings—metrics that mattered, yes, but that lived outside his direct control. His days became an endless cycle of scanning dashboards, bracing for critical emails, and over-preparing decks to defend against questions that might not even come. By his own admission, his attention wasn't stacking—it was swinging wildly with each new external input.

We started with a basic reframing. "What do you actually control?" I asked. After a pause, he listed: his presence, the clarity of direction he provided to his team, the speed of decision-making, and developing his next line of leaders. Those four variables became his focus bullseye.

Just as the quarterback shifted from production to process anchors, this executive shifted from scanning outcomes to measuring attention. After every leadership meeting, he asked himself:

- Did I show up with composure?
- Did I give clarity on direction?
- Did I make timely, crisp decisions?
- Did I invest in my leaders, not just the metrics?

At first, the answers were inconsistent. He still drifted into defensiveness or micromanagement. But slowly, he noticed that when he stayed tethered to those anchors, trust began to return. His team moved faster. Meetings ended with clear owners and deadlines, not vague commitments.

The deeper shift came as he examined what fueled him. He admitted that much of his drive was fear—fear of being exposed, of losing his reputation, of disappointing the family whose sacrifices made his career possible. That fear pushed him to work harder, but it drained him. Together, we explored more sustainable motivators: modeling steadiness for his team, creating a culture where his directors

Stacking Wins: Sustaining Attention over Time

could grow into executives, and honoring the values of hard work and integrity that was instilled in him growing up.

Those anchors gave him a daily lens. Each morning, he reviewed his schedule and wrote down how he wanted to *be* in the day's key moments: walk in with a smile, check in with staff on priorities, set clear expectations in meetings, carve out time to mentor one leader. Each evening, he reflected: "Did I follow through on the intentions I set this morning?"

Within a year, things had stabilized and he was back to delivering on targets.

When asked what changed, he said: "Honestly, it wasn't the numbers. It was where I put my attention every day. I stopped chasing outcomes and started stacking wins."

His story isn't unique to the boardroom. In many ways, it reflects a broader challenge we all face today: attention isn't just drifting, it's being hunted.

The Age of Distraction: Protecting Our Wins

Sustaining attention isn't just about training through practices or shifting perspective before the gold-medal shot. Today, one of the greatest challenges to stacking wins comes from the world around us. We live in what scholars call the "attention economy," where our focus isn't just wandering—it's being actively pursued. Phones, notifications, media cycles, and endless streams of noise compete for our focus. Where earlier generations might have battled boredom and isolation, today's are battling overstimulation.

This makes consistency harder than intensity. Anyone can lock in for a burst of hours or even days. The real test is sustaining focus over weeks, months, and years when the pull of distraction is constant. Research backs this up: The mere presence of a smartphone—even turned off and face-down—reduces available cognitive capacity, as part of the mind automatically allocates resources to monitor it for potential signals (Ward et al., 2017). Related work shows that most office workers switch tasks, on average, every three minutes, often not because of necessity but because of digital interruptions (Mark et al., 2008). And recovery isn't immediate—after a single interruption, it can take over 20 minutes to return to the same level of focus (Altmann & Trafton, 2004).

In this environment, "stacking wins" becomes harder than ever. Consistency depends not only on our internal discipline but also on how well we manage external demands on our attention. Without awareness and intentional design, our daily reps of focus get diluted by distractions we don't even notice.

Why Distraction Hits So Hard

In addition to being wired for survival, the brain is also wired for novelty—a mechanism that once helped us adapt to changing environments but now leaves us vulnerable to constant digital stimulation. Each ping, buzz, or notification activates dopamine pathways, delivering a burst of reward and reinforcing the habit of checking. Over time, these micro-rewards not only condition us to crave interruption but also magnify our cognitive biases, pulling us toward more extreme content and making it harder to sustain the kind of deliberate focus required for mastery (Firth et al., 2019).

This isn't just about fractured attention in the moment; novelty bias primes us to chase whatever is new, even when it isn't useful. That wiring once served survival—helping us notice changes in the environment—but today it keeps us scrolling, clicking, and clinging to every update. Sustained focus feels harder than ever not because we're weak-willed, but because our biology is constantly being hijacked.

The cost isn't only lost minutes—it's lost depth. Our ability to settle into high-quality, deliberate attention erodes when novelty upends our focus. And the consequences reach beyond productivity. By chasing headlines and consuming clickbait, our opinions are increasingly formed with less critical thought. Critical thinking simply can't compete with novelty's instant rewards. We scroll, we consume, and we react—often without much to anchor us.

The effects are not just cognitive but emotional. Constant digital stimulation elevates baseline stress and narrows our cognitive bandwidth. Studies show that heavy media multitasking correlates with higher perceived stress and reduced working memory capacity (Uncapher et al., 2016). Frequent task-switching predicts greater burnout and emotional exhaustion among employees (Panisoara & Serban, 2013). Taken together, these trends may help explain why society feels less connected, less empathetic, and more mentally strained than at any point in recent memory.

Distraction culture exploits our wiring for novelty, taxes our cognitive resources, and drains the very capacity required to stack wins over time That's why protecting attention is critical and may require a system of habits, cues, and resets that defend our attention to allow us to live a more intentional life.

Intentional Attention as an Antidote

Holding our attention has never been harder. But improving this single skill can exponentially elevate how we live, lead, and pursue our goals. Those who thrive don't avoid distraction—they build systems that help them return to something purposeful. They refine their targets, reset quickly, and deliberately re-align their attention—again and again—until returning to focus becomes their default.

We are not naive enough to think the world will slow down. The noise will only grow—more alerts, more opinions, sharper emotions, and more demands competing for the same limited bandwidth. However, left unmanaged, this overstimulation can erode our capacity to sustain focus across careers, seasons, and life stages. But, through deliberate guardrails, rhythms, and routines, we can train our focus to strengthen amid these distractions rather than succumb to them.

That's where Intentional Attention reaches its full power—not just helping us perform in moments of pressure but allowing us to sustain purposeful momentum in a world designed to scatter it.

Attentional Maintenance: Holding the Line

Attention is remarkably slippery. Even when we know our bullseye—the focus point that best supports execution—it drifts. Failure pulls on fear; success inflates expectation. Both distort focus and redirect attention away from the performance-relevant data that drive results.

Our focus doesn't just compete with internal noise—nerves, future implications, personal beliefs, past experiences—it also collides daily with a flood of external distractions. Notifications, meetings, social feedback, and constant information each tug at the edges of concentration. In this climate, sustaining focus isn't natural; it's an act of design.

So, what do we do when we recognize that our attention is slipping off the bullseye? When clarity fades, the inner critic gets loud, and our thoughts scatter across past mistakes or future consequences?

Step 1: Name the Drift

When our mind wanders, it's rarely obvious in real time. We often realize we've lost focus only after the mistake, the pause, or the missed cue. Naming what's happening—"I'm thinking about the outcome," "I'm stuck on that last play," "I'm distracted by the noise"—interrupts that automatic cycle.

This act of metacognition—recognizing and labeling our current mental state—engages the brain's prefrontal cortex, which restores a measure of cognitive control. Awareness doesn't guarantee immediate focus, but it reopens the door to choice. And in high-pressure moments, the ability to choose is everything.

Step 2: Reset to the Bullseye

Once we name the drift, we can begin to redirect. That starts by returning attention to *performance-relevant data*—the controllable information that moves us closer to our goals.

The Mindset Matrix and Focus Bullseye models introduced in Chapter 9 serve as maps for this reset. They help us identify:

- What cues deserve our focus.
- Which behaviors reinforce execution.
- Which distractions predictably pull us away.

When those anchors are defined, we stop leaving focus to chance. The reset becomes both mechanical and mental: exhale, re-center, and reconnect to performance relevant data in this moment.

Step 3: Design for Maintenance

Motivation by itself is rarely enough. The difference maker for sustained excellence isn't heroic bursts of deep focus—it's the ability to build routines that hold attention steady against daily distraction.

Research on deliberate practice shows that mastery isn't born from endless hours of intensity but from structured, focused repetition (Ericsson et al., 1993). More recent work echoes the same principle: marginal gains, stacked consistently, create exponential returns (Macnamara et al., 2014).

In modern terms, sustaining attention requires environmental design. High performers shape the spaces around them to make focus easier and distraction harder: phones out of reach, notifications silenced, clear transitions between tasks, defined start and stop points, and brief "micro-resets" throughout the day.

The goal isn't to grind harder—it's to remove friction and build guardrails so that attention has fewer exits.

Step 4: Build the Muscle

Attention is not a fixed trait; it's a trainable system. The more often we catch drift and return to the bullseye, the faster and smoother that recovery becomes.

Each rep strengthens the neural pathways that support sustained focus. Over time, this repetition creates what we call *attentional fitness*—the ability to hold attention steady without tension, to reset without judgment, and to perform with clarity even when chaos rises.

Step 5: Lean on the Support Network

No one sustains attention alone. Even the most self-disciplined performers draw strength from structure and community. It takes a village to stay on target.

Stacking Wins: Sustaining Attention over Time

In every high-performance environment we've studied—sport, medicine, the military, business—those who sustain focus longest rarely do so through willpower alone. They surround themselves with people who help them *protect* attention—coaches, mentors, teammates, friends and family members who understand the bullseye and respect the commitment required to maintain it.

Having a shared bullseye—a collective understanding of goals, performance-relevant data, and supporting behaviors—creates alignment and accountability. It shifts the focus from *individual discipline* to *collective precision*. When others know what you're working toward and what pulls you off track, they can help you recalibrate before drift becomes derailment.

Trusted circles matter because attention is contagious. We absorb the energy, pace, and emotional tone of those around us. When the environment models calm, clarity, and intention, our nervous system follows suit. When it models urgency, chaos, or constant reactivity, focus erodes faster than we realize.

Building a support network for attentional maintenance isn't about dependence—it's about design. It means:

- **Communicate your focus cues.** Share your bullseye, key triggers, and reset routines with those closest to you. Let them know how to help you return when you drift.

- **Build feedback loops.** Trusted partners can spot attention lapses that you can't. A short check-in after critical events— "Where was your focus?"—keeps awareness sharp.

- **Normalize reflection.** In teams, families, and organizations, reflection rituals anchor collective attention: film reviews, debriefs, or simple "reset huddles" at the end of the day.

- **Curate the circle.** Protect your attentional bandwidth by choosing who and what gets access to it. A few supportive voices are often more powerful than a crowd of well-meaning platitudes.

When we integrate others into our attentional system, we create structual redundancy—like stabilizers on a tightrope. When our own balance wobbles, the system catches us.

Sustained attention isn't just a solo pursuit; it's a shared system. The athletes who endure, the leaders who remain composed, and the teams that thrive all rely on alignment—people who understand their bullseye and help them protect it. Thus, focus begins internally but is preserved collectively. The most powerful attentional systems aren't built in isolation; they're engineered through shared language, structure, and trust.

Exercise: A Stacking Wins Toolkit for Defining Focus and Building Momentum

The previous stories illustrate the principle, and the evidence reinforces it: Sustained success is built on deliberate attention repeated over time. But *knowing it* and *doing it* are different things. To defend your focus and let small wins compound, here are five evidence-based levers you can start using today:

1. **Design the Environment**
   - Create distraction-free zones when you want intentional work. For example, put phones out of sight. Even unused, their presence reduces cognitive capacity (Ward et al., 2017).
   - Protect focus blocks (45–60 minutes) with silenced notifications and cleared workspaces.

2. **Reduce Switching Costs**
   - Task-switching leaves attentional residue. On average, it takes more than 20 minutes to recover deep focus after a switch (Altmann & Trafton, 2004; Mark et al., 2008).
   - Batch similar tasks—emails, planning, creative work—into clusters to keep attention anchored.

3. Make Intentional Resets

- A single breath, a brief walk outside, a grounding phrase ("back to the bullseye"), or a movement shift can reset attention.

- Small resets regulate arousal and restore focus under stress (Lehrer & Gevirtz, 2014; Mesagno & Beckmann, 2017).

4. Prioritize Depth over Duration

- Mastery is built through quality reps of attention, not just hours logged (Ericsson et al., 1993).

- Ten minutes of full engagement beats thirty minutes half-distracted.

5. Redefine Daily Wins

- End the day by asking: Did I hit my intentions? Did I return to the bullseye when I drifted? Did I give attention to one meaningful task?

- This reframes success as the mastery of attention itself, stacking the kind of wins that compound over seasons and careers.

Chapter 17

Train It Forward: Attention as the New Leadership Skill

"A wealth of information creates a poverty of attention."
—Herbert Simon, Nobel Prize-Winning
Cognitive Psychologist

In our primary work with business and athletics, we've come to recognize that Intentional Attention strategies apply across a broader swath of life settings. That recognition is based on our observance that attention is not just personal, it's contagious. Where we place it—and how we hold it—directly shapes not only our own personal outcomes but can influence the outcomes of those around us.

Think of how a quarterback's presence ripples through a huddle; a CEO's focus sets the tone for their team. Attention cascades. It multiplies. In many ways, it may be the most underappreciated "leadership" skill of our time.

More than that, this kind of leadership skill extends far beyond boardrooms and locker rooms. Parenting, teaching, marriage, friendship—these are all leadership roles too. Think of the father's choice, recounted in Chapter 11, to be fully present with his kids on his return home; a teacher's steadiness in a classroom dictates whether 25 kids drift into chaos or settle into learning. In each, the way we handle our own attention, particularly under stressful conditions, sets the stage for what others can access in themselves. When leaders stumble, the teams or groups they lead can fall. When leaders stay grounded, others borrow that steadiness. Leadership, as it turns out, isn't always about charisma or strong personalities. It's about presence, a skill that can be trained and developed. The person who can direct, restore, and reset attention under pressure changes not just their own trajectory, but everyone else in their orbit.

From the Arena to the Everyday

We've drawn heavily from professional sports and executive leadership throughout this book, and there's a reason for that. First of course, they are the "arenas" we at Premier Sport Psychology have had the most experience with for the past two decades. Second, it's because athletes and business leaders live in crucibles where performance is measured in real time. They don't get to hide. Every missed throw, every failed quarter, every breakdown in execution shows up on video, in the numbers, and in public scrutiny.

That's what made sport and business the perfect proving grounds for Intentional Attention. The margin for error is slim, the pressure relentless, the grind unforgiving, and the results visible for everyone to see. In that environment, we could actually observe if the interventions worked. And they did. Quarterbacks held their rhythm into January. Gymnasts stuck their routines under the heaviest pressure. Executives steadied their teams through turbulence.

But because these were our primary arenas, it doesn't mean that IA is only for sports or business. Far from it.

While the spotlight moments of athletes and executives are more readily observable, it's easy to see that the same attentional dynamics play out everywhere else—just less visibly. Parents trying to stay calm through a child's meltdown. Teachers trying to hold a classroom's attention against the pull of every device. Couples trying to listen deeply while juggling many competing responsibilities.

Friends fighting to carve out moments of real connection in a world that rarely pauses.

The minds are the same. The stakes are just as real. And the opportunity is broader than any single performance domain: to train attention forward—into our families, our classrooms, our workplaces, our communities.

Reclaiming Agency in an Engineered World

There's another reason this moment matters. We don't live in a neutral environment. Our attention is under siege. The world is designed to capture it—every alert, every feed, every cycle of emotional headlines engineered on the backs of incredibly sophisticated algorithms to hook the most primitive parts of our brains. All of it designed to grab our attention—often without us realizing it.

This is where Intentional Attention can become more than a performance framework. It can become a framework for reclaiming personal agency.

We may not control the algorithmic traps around us, but we can control how we meet them. We can build systems that anchor us to what matters, even when strong forces are pulling us toward what doesn't. We can embed rituals into our teams and families that make purposeful focus easier and distraction harder.

When we train attention forward, we aren't just creating better athletes or sharper executives. We can reclaim the capacity to choose—what we notice, how we interpret, where we act. In a culture engineered to hijack our focus, that choice could be revolutionary. And if enough of us practice it, it's not just individual lives that change. Families can build homes where presence is the norm, not the exception. Classrooms can become spaces where curiosity outweighs distraction. Workplaces can shift from reactive churn to steady, intentional progress. Communities can model what it looks like to disagree without splintering and to connect without constant interruption.

We've witnessed many teams transform their cultures—shifting from fractured and distrusting to unified and aligned—through attention, one step at a time. Sustainable culture shifts, it seems, don't occur through sweeping reforms or grand initiatives. It emerges from the accumulation of daily choices made by each of us. Every reset breath, every values-based decision, every intentional act of focus casts a vote for the kind of environment we're creating. And when attention is trained forward, it doesn't just protect individual capacity—it has the potential to ripple outward, shaping families, teams, and communities alike.

Teaching Others: The Ripple Effect

The Intentional Attention framework was built in high-pressure environments, but its strength is its simplicity. Anyone can set it up and use it.

For business leaders the IA Framework offers a way to strengthen both performance and culture. By embedding a shared attentional framework, leaders can train their teams to align their collective focus on a bullseye of performance-relevant data—creating greater clarity, community, efficiency, and trust in how decisions are made, energy is managed, and attention is applied to important initiatives.

The application here isn't about asking people to complete "one more work-specific training." It's about giving them highly practical tools to strengthen presence, align controllable behaviors, and support both productivity and personal well-being.

Practical starting points often include:

- **Attentional inventories in leadership programs:** Equip employees with tools like the Personal Attentional Attribute Inventory (see Chapter 8) to highlight their identities, values, motivators, biases, and potential fears and insecurities. This section often gives employees the sense that the organization is truly investing in them as a person first. Many employees love going through this exercise because they see the benefit immediately to both their workplace but also their home life, and they appreciate the organization investing in them in this holistic manner. Ultimately this aspect of the framework provides a center for each individual that's unique to them but connected to the greater whole. It's something they can stand on to ground their decisions and behaviors under stress.

- **Normalize intention-setting:** At the start of quarters, projects, or even individual meetings, establish shared attentional priorities. Align not just on goals, but on *where attention should go— and where distractions are likely to occur either historically or in the current environment.* Make intentions explicit by naming the behaviors likely to drive success and the behaviors that derail it.

- **Train attentional resets:** Build short, structured pauses, breath work, or "back-to-the-bullseye" cues when meetings drift, tension spikes, or stress escalates. Pair these with explicit standards and nonnegotiables so people know what sits outside the bullseye versus what defines the center.

- **Encourage reflection rituals:** Move beyond outcome-only metrics. End weeks or projects by asking: *Did we place our* *attention where it mattered? Did we show up in the way we intended?* These questions help teams stack learning, celebrate growth, and avoid burnout.

- **Designed renewal:** Create spaces that protect the energy and sustain rhythms that encourage efficient attentional recovery—meeting-free and message-free blocks of time, walking meetings, mediation lounge, views of nature, and/or accessible quiet workspaces. Renewal can be a performance multiplier when structured well.

When leaders begin to model these practices, attention has a way of becoming contagious. The ripple effect can extend outward. Over time, this kind of attentional infrastructure can become a powerful advantage in goal alignment, turnover reduction, and more efficient decision-making; creating a workplace that feels both healthier and more sustainable.

One HR executive we worked with wondered if IA might help address the growing issues of burnout and turnover she was seeing in her leadership ranks. At first, the idea of "training attention" sounded abstract, even a little soft. So we recommended that she start small, using a few Intentional Attention-oriented meeting strategies.

Six months later she shared a number of improved metrics that she attributed to the new emphasis. "We didn't change the workload," she reflected. "We changed where we placed our attention. We were no longer wasting precious time working through half-baked agendas—we had a process that was far more intentional, efficient, and effective. It was game changing."

On the Field

For coaches, IA provides a framework to develop athletes' physical skills more efficiently, but also improve their mental performance. Furthermore, it can strengthen team culture by giving players a shared language for how to direct and reset attention.

Practical starting points include:

- **Personal attentional inventories:** Help athletes identify motivators, values, and fears that shape their attention under pressure. This insight becomes the foundation for consistent performance.

- **Intention-setting rituals:** Begin practices or games by clarifying attentional targets: *Where should our focus go today? What distractions do we need to let go of?*

- **Performance bullseye checks:** Define what sits in the center of the Focus Bullseye (controllables like effort, communication, execution) versus what sits outside (scoreboard, referees, opponents).

- **Reset cues under pressure:** Rather than instruction, facilitate small-group conversations where athletes exchange the simple reset cues that help them recover—breaths, words, gestures—that they can use to redirect attention after mistakes or momentum turns.

- **Reflection that accelerates learning:** Post-practice or post-game debriefs should include not just tactical review but attentional review: *Where did we place our focus? How did it impact performance?*

When coaches model steadiness—holding their own attention when games get tight—they teach athletes more than strategy. They teach how to thrive under pressure. Over time, this attentional consistency builds teams that are not only competitive, but deeply connected and resilient.

One high school coach piloted this approach by introducing a "team bullseye" built on three controllables: effort, communication, and presence (body language). At first, it seemed like a simple framework. But as the season unfolded, athletes began referencing it during games. After a sloppy quarter, instead of yelling about missed shots, players huddled and reminded each other: *"Let's reset—bullseye on effort and comms."* What began as a performance tool started showing up in classrooms and even at home. One athlete told him: *"Coach, I used the reset before my chemistry exam."*

In the Classroom

For teachers, IA can transform classrooms into spaces where learning deepens and stress management is modeled more effectively. Attention is a finite resource, and when students learn to direct and reset it, they build skills that serve both academic success and lifelong resilience.

More than a classroom management strategy, the IA framework can serve as an instrument to help students develop attentional skills that enhance both performance and well-being—something desperately needed today. The U.S. Surgeon General's 2021 advisory *Protecting Youth Mental Health* warned that youth mental health has reached crisis levels—one in three high school students reported persistent sadness or hopelessness in 2019, up about 40% from 2009. In parallel, recent peer-reviewed research has begun to point to one of the explanations: that social media algorithms, designed to maximize engagement, often hijack attention, expose youth to curated content loops, and amplify images or content that can harm self-esteem or increase anxiety (Chhabra et al., 2025; Costello et al., 2023).

The problem isn't only that kids are spending time online. It's the way their attention is being shaped. Algorithmic feeds train them to crave novelty, reward quick reactions over deep thinking, and compare themselves against unrealistic portrayals of peers and influencers. Over time, this rewiring makes it harder for them to sustain focus, tolerate discomfort, or engage in the kind of deliberate practice that underpins growth in school, sport, or life. Some researchers have argued that these attentional hijacks may play a role in the sharp rise in adolescent depression, anxiety, and loneliness (Abi-Jaoude et al., 2020; Twenge et al., 2018). In other words, youth aren't just distracted; their very capacity to focus and regulate is being eroded as a byproduct of platforms designed to keep them engaged.

That's why teaching attention may be especially important today. It's preventative. Just as we train physical fitness to offset sedentary lifestyles, we need to train attentional fitness to offset engineered distraction. And the classroom may be one of the most powerful places to start.

Practical starting points include:

- **Student attentional inventories:** Invite students to reflect on what helps or hinders their focus—whether it's internal (self-doubt, fatigue) or external (phones, social media platforms, etc). This helps normalize that attention is something we all manage, while bringing awareness to whether it's serving us in the ways we intend.

- **Daily intention-setting routines:** Begin class with a one-minute prompt: *"What do I want my attention on today?"* Over time, this builds agency and trains students to choose where they direct their focus.

- **Classroom bullseye checks:** Co-create with students what belongs at the center (listening, participation, kindness, curiosity) and what belongs outside (phones, side chatter, fear of being wrong). Post it in the room as a visual anchor.

- **Reset cues:** Teach quick resets—a breath, a grounding phrase, even a stretch break—that the whole class can use when energy drifts or stress rises. Shared resets make the classroom feel collaborative rather than punitive.

- **Reflection moments:** Close the day with one simple question or journal exercise: *"Where was my attention today, and how did it help or hurt?"* This reinforces awareness without judgment.

- **Protect renewal:** Encourage balance—highlight the role of sleep, hydration, and exercise in sustaining attention. Help students see these as part of well-being and performance.

Just as elite athletes have learned what routines, goals, and reset techniques work for them after mistakes or facing adversity, students can learn to direct and redirect their attention when stress or distractions arise. A breath before answering a test question, a reset cue before responding to a classmate's post, a daily reflection on where their focus went—and whether it supported them or pulled them toward unhelpful spirals—these are not just classroom tools. They are foundational skills of agency in a world that constantly competes for their attention.

We believe that when teachers and schools model these practices—through awareness, intention-setting, executional resets, and structured reflection in attentional language, not only could make the classroom calmer, but it also gives students permission to build their own attentional routines. And those routines aren't just about better grades. They're about resilience, confidence, and the ability to meet an over-stimulating and turbulent world without losing themselves to it.

A Final Word: Goals and Aspirations

In one sense, this has been a book of many stories. We've included them to hopefully illuminate the breadth and variety of ways attention links to high-level performance. But there's another "story" embodied in the text that bears repeating.

Just as an athlete's muscular strength, fitness, and physical skills vary by birth or circumstance, so do each of our mental skill sets. It's axiomatic these days for athletes to build on what's physically given to them, no matter the starting line. We need to develop that same expectation on the mental side. Performance under pressure—indeed performance improvement in general—is not a one-and-done proposition.

Our goal then is nothing less than to embed a common recognition that mental skills are trainable and should be an expected, substantive part of any ones education. Further, that preparation must be anchored by an understanding of and proficiency with attentional management. If we begin to view cognitive/mental improvement as more than just an aggregation of tools, and certainly more than a pep talk or motivational slogan, we can create a new expectation: that our mindsets can and must be trained, sharpened, and developed, no matter the starting line. If that expectation grows in athletics, its utility expands far beyond the playing field.

Our aspirations are equally ambitious, and they are related to the content in this chapter; we would love to see the concept of trainable attention management become a widespread expectation in our culture. We envision its acceptance and use in fields well beyond athletics and business. We are not promoting our specific model as the only way to train attention, though we certainly think it's a great place to start. However, we are advocating for a much broader recognition of attention as a key developable skill in our lives.

What's more, it is a controllable that doesn't belong only to athletes. Intentional Attention belongs to you—parent, teacher, student, partner, manager, friend. The same framework that steadies a quarterback under pressure can help each of us reset when we are running late and our kids are slow to get out the door, or regulate our emotions during a difficult conversation with someone we love. It's too important to go untrained. Fundamental to any shift in how we value trainable attention is seeing the bigger picture—not just the most visible fragments of performance, but the whole system beneath them. Intentional Attention, as we've defined and explored it here, offers that broader view and, just as importantly, provides tools to apply it in the smallest moments. Our hope is that this work sparks deeper conversation and helps move us toward a more deliberate, proactive relationship with our own attention.

So here is the story beneath all the stories: we can transform how we show up across every domain of life through an integrated framework for training attention—the most foundational human skill for performance, presence, and meaning itself. Because where mind goes, the body follows and what we attend to becomes not just our focus, but our lived reality.

Excellence, then, isn't found in doing more. It's found in protecting—and being intentional with—what we already possess and most easily lose: our attention.

Authors Note: I hope you've enjoyed the read. More than that, I hope it offered a few ideas, tools, and perspectives to carry into the meaningful moments of life—supporting both the pursuit of big goals and the smaller victories that shape us day to day. And if this work encourages even a subtle shift in how attention is noticed, protected, or shared, then perhaps something meaningful has already begun. If enough of us practice it, maybe we don't just reclaim attention—maybe we rediscover a different way of performing, living, and connecting in a distracted and divisive world. That is the possibility of Intentional Attention.

References

Abi-Jaoude, E., Naylor, K. T., & Pignatiello, A. (2020). "Smartphones, social media use, and youth mental health." *Canadian Medical Association Journal, 192*(6), E136–E141.

Alter, A. (2017). *Irresistible: The Rise of Addictive Technology and the Business of Keeping us Hooked.* New York, NY: Penguin Press.

Altmann, E. M., & Trafton, J. G. (2004). "Task interruption: Resumption lag and the role of cues." *Proceedings of the 26th Annual Conference of the Cognitive Science Society,* 43–48. Mahwah, NJ: Lawrence Erlbaum Associates.

American Psychological Association. (2019). "Guidelines for psychological practice in health care delivery systems." *American Psychologist, 74*(9), 1248–1262.

Andreassen, C. S., Pallesen, S., & Griffiths, M. D. (2017). "The relationship between addictive use of social media, narcissism, and self-esteem: Findings from a large national survey." *Addictive Behaviors, 64,* 287–293.

Anseel, F., Beatty, A. S., Shen, W., Lievens, F., & Sackett, P. R. (2015). "How are we doing after 30 years? A meta-analytic review of the antecedents and outcomes of feedback-seeking behavior." *Journal of Management, 41*(1), 318–348.

Armstrong, L. E., Ganio, M. S., Casa, D. J., Lee, E. C., McDermott, B. P., Klau, J. F., . . . & Maresh, C. M. (2012). "Mild dehydration affects mood in healthy young women." *Journal of Nutrition, 142*(2), 382–388.

Arnsten, A. F. T. (2009). "Stress signaling pathways that impair prefrontal cortex structure and function." *Nature Reviews Neuroscience, 10*(6), 410–422.

Arnsten, A. F. T. (2014). "Stress weakens prefrontal networks: Molecular insults to higher cognition." *Nature Neuroscience, 17*(10), 1376–1385.

Arnsten, A. F. T., Wang, M., & Paspalas, C. D. (2012). "Neuromodulation of thought: Flexibilities and vulnerabilities in prefrontal cortical network dynamics." *Neuron, 76*(1), 223–239.

Baddeley, A. D., & Hitch, G. J. (1993). "The recency effect: Implicit learning with explicit retrieval?" *Memory & Cognition, 21*(2), 146–155.

Bakker, A. B., & Demerouti, E. (2007). "The job demands–resources model: State of the art." *Journal of Managerial Psychology, 22*(3), 309–328.

Banich, M. T., Mackiewicz, K. L., Depue, B. E., Whitmer, A. J., Miller, G. A., & Heller, W. (2009). "Cognitive control mechanisms, emotion and memory: A neural perspective with implications for psychopathology." *Neuroscience and Biobehavioral Reviews, 33*(5), 613–630.

Bargh, J. A., & Chartrand, T. L. (1999). "The unbearable automaticity of being." *American Psychologist, 54*(7), 462–479.

Barker, J. E., Semenov, A. D., Michaelson, L., Provan, L. S., Snyder, H. R., & Munakata, Y. (2014). "Less-structured time in children's daily lives predicts self-directed executive functioning." *Frontiers in Psychology, 5*, 593.

Baron-Cohen, S., Knickmeyer, R. C., & Belmonte, M. K. (2005). "Sex differences in the brain: Implications for explaining autism." *Science, 310*(5749), 819–823.

Barsade, S. G. (2002). "The ripple effect: Emotional contagion and its influence on group behavior." *Administrative Science Quarterly, 47*(4), 644–675.

Baumeister, R. F., Bratslavsky, E., Finkenauer, C., & Vohs, K. D. (2001a). "Bad is stronger than good." *Review of General Psychology, 5*(4), 323–370.

Baumeister, R. F., & Showers, C. J. (1986). "A review of paradoxical performance effects: Choking under pressure in sports and other performance situations." *Journal of Personality and Social Psychology, 50*(5), 1083–1099.

Baumeister, R. F., Smart, L., & Boden, J. M. (2001b). "Relation of threatened egotism to violence and aggression: The dark side of high self-esteem." *Psychological Review, 103*(1), 5–33.

Beauchamp, M. R., Jackson, B., & Morton, K. L. (2021). "Self-determination in sport and exercise: Translating theory to practice." *International Review of Sport and Exercise Psychology, 14*(1), 1–27.

Bechara, A., Damasio, H., & Damasio, A. R. (2000). "Emotion, decision making and the orbitofrontal cortex." *Cerebral Cortex, 10*(3), 295–307.

Beilock, S. L., & Carr, T. H. (2001). "On the fragility of skilled performance: What governs choking under pressure?" *Journal of Experimental Psychology: General, 130*(4), 701–725.

Berman, M. G., Jonides, J., & Kaplan, S. (2008). "The cognitive benefits of interacting with nature." *Psychological Science, 19*(12), 1207–1212.

Best, J. R. (2010). "Effects of physical activity on children's executive function: Contributions of experimental research on aerobic exercise." *Developmental Review, 30*(4), 331–551.

Blakemore, S.-J., & Choudhury, S. (2006). "Development of the adolescent brain: Implications for executive function and social cognition." *Journal of Child Psychology and Psychiatry, 47*(3–4), 296–312.

Blakemore, S.-J., & Mills, K. L. (2014). "Is adolescence a sensitive period for sociocultural processing?" *Annual Review of Psychology, 65*, 187–207.

Botvinick, M. M., Braver, T. S., Barch, D. M., Carter, C. S., & Cohen, J. D. (2001). "Conflict monitoring and cognitive control." *Psychological Review, 108*(3), 624–652.

Bratman, G. N., Hamilton, J. P., Hahn, K. S., Daily, G. C., & Gross, J. J. (2015). "Nature experience reduces rumination and subgenual prefrontal cortex activation." *Proceedings of the National Academy of Sciences, 112*(28), 8567–8572.

Bravata, D. M., Watts, S. A., Keefer, A. L., Madhusudhan, D. K., Taylor, K. T., Clark, D. M., . . . & Hagg, H. K. (2020). "Prevalence, predictors, and treatment of impostor syndrome: A systematic review." *Journal of General Internal Medicine, 35*(4), 1252–1277.

Braver, T. S. (2012). "The variable nature of cognitive control: A dual mechanisms framework." *Trends in Cognitive Sciences, 16*(2), 106–113.

Brewer, B. W., Van Raalte, J. L., & Linder, D. E. (1993). Athletic identity: Hercules' muscles or Achilles heel? *International Journal of Sport Psychology, 24*(2), 237–254.

Brokaw, K., Tishler, W., Manceor, S., Hamilton, K., Gaulden, A., Parr, E., & Wamsley, E. J. (2016). "Resting state EEG correlates of memory consolidation." *Neurobiology of Learning and Memory, 140*, 41–50.

281

Brooks, A. W. (2014). "Get excited: Reappraising pre-performance anxiety as excitement." *Journal of Experimental Psychology: General, 143*(3), 1144–1158.

Buonomano, D. V., & Merzenich, M. M. (1998). "Cortical plasticity: From synapses to maps." *Annual Review of Neuroscience, 21,* 149–186.

Burriss, K. G., & Tsao, L. L. (2022). The relationship between free play and executive function in early childhood. *Early Child Development and Care, 192*(9), 1478–1489.

Buscemi, N., Vandermeer, B., Hooton, N., Pandya, R., Tjosvold, L., Hartling, L., . . . & Klassen, T. P. (2006). "The efficacy and safety of exogenous melatonin for primary sleep disorders: A systematic review." *Journal of General Internal Medicine, 21*(12), 1151–1158.

Cajochen, C., Munch, M., Kobialka, S., Krauchi, K., Steiner, R., Oelhafen, P., . . . & Wirz-Justice, A. (2005). "High sensitivity of human melatonin, alertness, thermoregulation, and heart rate to short-wavelength light." *Journal of Clinical Endocrinology and Metabolism, 90*(3), 1311–1316.

Carter, C. S. (2014). "Oxytocin pathways and the evolution of human behavior." *Annual Review of Psychology, 65,* 17–39.

Casey, B. J., Jones, R. M., & Hare, T. A. (2008). "The adolescent brain." *Annals of the New York Academy of Sciences, 1124*(1), 111–126.

Casey, B. J., Tottenham, N., Liston, C., & Durston, S. (2005). "Imaging the developing brain: What have we learned about cognitive development?" *Trends in Cognitive Sciences, 9*(3), 104–110.

Cerasoli, C. P., Nicklin, J. M., & Ford, M. T. (2014). "Intrinsic motivation and extrinsic incentives jointly predict performance: A 40-year meta-analysis." *Psychological Bulletin, 140*(4), 980–1008.

Cheng, C., Cheung, M. W., Chio, J. H., & Chan, M. P. (2013). "Cultural meaning of perceived control: A meta-analysis of locus of control and psychological symptoms across 18 cultural regions." *Psychological Bulletin, 139*(1), 152–188.

Chhabra, J., Pilkington, V., Benakovic, R., Wilson, M. J., La Sala, L., & Seidler, Z. (2025). "Social media and youth mental health: A scoping review of platform and policy recommendations." *Journal of Medical Internet Research, 27,* e72061.

Christoff, K., Gordon, A. M., Smallwood, J., Smith, R., & Schooler, J. W. (2009). "Experience sampling during fMRI reveals default network and executive system contributions to mind wandering." *Proceedings of the National Academy of Sciences, 106*(21), 8719–8724.

Christoff, K., Irving, Z. C., Fox, K. C., Spreng, R. N., & Andrews-Hanna, J. R. (2016). "Mind-wandering as spontaneous thought: A dynamic framework." *Nature Reviews Neuroscience, 17*(11), 718–731.

Clance, P. R., & Imes, S. A. (1978). "The impostor phenomenon in high achieving women: Dynamics and therapeutic intervention." *Psychotherapy: Theory, Research & Practice, 15*(3), 241–247.

Clow, A., Thorn, L., Evans, P., & Hucklebridge, F. (2004). "The awakening cortisol response: Methodological issues and significance." *Stress, 7*(1), 29–37.

Cohen, G. L., Steele, C. M., & Ross, L. D. (1999). "The mentor's dilemma: Providing critical feedback across the racial divide." *Personality and Social Psychology Bulletin, 25*(10), 1302–1318.

Corbetta, M., & Shulman, G. L. (2002). "Control of goal-directed and stimulus-driven attention in the brain." *Nature Reviews Neuroscience, 3*(3), 201–215.

Costello, N., Sutton, R., Jones, M., Almassian, M., Raffoul, A., Ojumu, O., Salvia, M., Santoso, M., Kavanaugh, J. R., & Austin, S. B. (2023). "Algorithms, addiction, and adolescent mental health: An interdisciplinary study to inform state-level policy action to protect youth from the dangers of social media." *American Journal of Law & Medicine, 49*(2–3), 257–282.

Cotterill, S. T. (2010). "Pre-performance routines in sport: Current understanding and future directions." *International Review of Sport and Exercise Psychology, 3*(2), 132–153.

Cotterill, S. T., Sanders, R., & Collins, D. (2010). "Developing effective pre-performance routines in golf: Why don't we ask the golfer?" *Journal of Applied Sport Psychology, 22*(1), 51–64.

Crum, A. J., Salovey, P., & Achor, S. (2013). "Rethinking stress: The role of mindsets in determining the stress response." *Journal of Personality and Social Psychology, 104*(4), 716–733.

Csikszentmihalyi, M. (1990). *Flow: The Psychology of Optimal Experience.* New York: Harper & Row.

Czeisler, C. A. (2013). "Perspective: Casting light on sleep deficiency." *Nature, 497*(7450), S13.

Danielmeier, C., & Ullsperger, M. (2011). "Post-error adjustments." *Frontiers in Psychology, 2,* 233.

Davenport, T. H., & Beck, J. C. (2001). *The Attention Economy: Understanding the New Currency of Business.* Harvard Business School Press.

Deci, E. L., & Ryan, R. M. (2000). The "what" and "why" of goal pursuits: Human needs and the self-determination of behavior. *Psychological Inquiry, 11*(4), 227–268.

Di Stefano, G., Gino, F., Pisano, G., & Staats, B. (2014). "Learning by thinking: How reflection aids performance." *Academy of Management Proceedings, 2014*(1), 12955.

Dickerson, S. S., & Kemeny, M. E. (2004). "Acute stressors and cortisol responses: A theoretical integration and synthesis of laboratory research." *Psychological Bulletin, 130*(3), 355–391.

Diekelmann, S., & Born, J. (2010). "The memory function of sleep." *Nature Reviews Neuroscience, 11*(2), 114–126.

Dietrich, A. (2004). "Neurocognitive mechanisms underlying the experience of flow." *Consciousness and Cognition, 13*(4), 746–761.

Drake, C., Roehrs, T., Shambroom, J., & Roth, T. (2013). "Caffeine effects on sleep taken 0, 3, or 6 hours before going to bed." *Journal of Clinical Sleep Medicine, 9*(11), 1195–1200.

Driskell, J. E., Salas, E., & Johnston, J. H. (1999). "Does stress lead to a loss of team perspective?" *Group Dynamics: Theory, Research, and Practice, 3*(4), 291–302.

Duckworth, A. L., Peterson, C., Matthews, M. D., & Kelly, D. R. (2007). "Grit: Perseverance and passion for long-term goals." *Journal of Personality and Social Psychology, 92*(6), 1087–1101.

Dunbar, R. I. M., Baron, R., Frangou, A., Pearce, E., Van Leeuwen, E. J., Stow, J., . . . & Van Vugt, M. (2012). "Social laughter is correlated with an elevated pain threshold." *Proceedings of the Royal Society B, 279* (1731), 1161–1167.

Ebbinghaus, H. (1885/1913). *Memory: A Contribution to Experimental Psychology.* New York: Teachers College, Columbia University.

Ebrahim, I. O., Shapiro, C. M., Williams, A. J., & Fenwick, P. B. (2013). "Alcohol and sleep I: Effects on normal sleep." *Alcoholism: Clinical and Experimental Research, 37*(4), 539–549.

Eisenberger, N. I., Lieberman, M. D., & Williams, K. D. (2003). "Does rejection hurt? An fMRI study of social exclusion." *Science, 302*(5643), 290–292.

Ellwood, R., & Abrams, E. (2017). "Long-term retention of skills following reflective practice." *Medical Education, 51*(12), 1239–1248.

Emmons, R. A., & McCullough, M. E. (2003). "Counting blessings versus burdens: An experimental investigation of gratitude and subjective well-being in daily life." *Journal of Personality and Social Psychology, 84*(2), 377–389.

Erickson, K. I., Voss, M. W., Prakash, R. S., Basak, C., Szabo, A., Chaddock, L., Kim, J. S., Heo, S., Alves, H., White, S. M., Wojcicki, T. R., Mailey, E., Vieira, V. J., Martin, S. A., Pence, B. D., Woods, J. A., McAuley, E., & Kramer, A. F. (2011). "Exercise training increases size of hippocampus and improves memory." *Proceedings of the National Academy of Sciences, 108*(7), 3017–3022.

Ericsson, K. A., Krampe, R. T., & Tesch-Römer, C. (1993). "The role of deliberate practice in the acquisition of expert performance." *Psychological Review, 100*(3), 363–406.

Erikson, E. H. (1968). *Identity: Youth and Crisis.* New York: W. W. Norton.

ESPN. (2024). *NFL Next Gen Stats: Time to Throw Leaders and Trends.* ESPN.

Eyre, B. & Edmunds, S. (2018). "Enhancing decision-making and accuracy in aviation: The role of reflective practice." *The International Journal of Aviation Psychology, 28*(4), 265–280.

Eysenck, M. W., Derakshan, N., Santos, R., & Calvo, M. G. (2007). "Anxiety and cognitive performance: Attentional control theory." *Emotion, 7*(2), 336–353.

Farb, N. A. S., Segal, Z. V., & Anderson, A. K. (2012). "Mindfulness meditation training alters cortical representations of interoceptive attention." *Social Cognitive and Affective Neuroscience, 7*(1), 15–26.

Feldman, R. (2017). "The neurobiology of human attachments." *Trends in Cognitive Sciences, 21*(2), 80–99.

Felisberti, F. M., & Currie, C. (2019). "The gaze as a marker of attention in visual world studies: State of the art and future directions." *Psychological Research, 83*(6), 1165–1181.

Ferracioli-Oda, E., Qawasmi, A., & Bloch, M. H. (2013). "Meta-analysis: Melatonin for the treatment of primary sleep disorders." *PLoS One, 8*(5), e63773.

Filaire, E., Alix, D., Ferrand, C., & Verger, M. (2009). "Psychophysiological stress in tennis players during the first single match of a tournament." *Psychoneuroendocrinology, 34*(1), 150–157.

Firth, J., Torous, J., Stubbs, B., Firth, J. A., Steiner, G. Z., Smith, L., Alvarez-Jimenez, M., Gleeson, J., Vancampfort, D., Armitage, C. J., & Sarris, J. (2019). "The online brain: How the Internet may be changing our cognition." *World Psychiatry, 18*(2), 119–129.

Flavell, J. H. (1979). "Metacognition and cognitive monitoring: A new area of cognitive–developmental inquiry." *American Psychologist, 34*(10), 906–911.

Fox, K. C. R., Nijeboer, S., Dixon, M. L., Floman, J. L., Ellamil, M., Rumak, S. P., . . . & Christoff, K. (2016). "Functional neuroanatomy of meditation: A review and meta-analysis of 78 functional neuroimaging investigations." *Neuroscience & Biobehavioral Reviews, 65*, 208–228.

Frankl, V. E. (2006). *Man's Search for Meaning.* Boston, MA: Beacon Press. (Original work published 1946)

Fredrickson, B. L. (2013). "Positive emotions broaden and build." *Advances in Experimental Social Psychology, 47*, 1–53.

Gazzaley, A., & Rosen, L. D. (2016). *The Distracted Mind: Ancient Brains in a High-Tech World.* MIT Press.

Giedd, J. N., Blumenthal, J., Jeffries, N. O., Castellanos, F. X., Liu, H., Zijdenbos, A., Paus, T., Evans, A. C., & Rapoport, J. L. (1999). "Brain development during childhood and adolescence: A longitudinal MRI study." *Nature Neuroscience, 2*(10), 861–863.

Gilbert, W., & Trudel, P. (2001). "Learning to coach through experience: Reflection in model youth sport coaches." *Journal of Teaching in Physical Education, 21*(1), 16–34.

Goldfarb, E. V., Fröböse, M. I., Cools, R., & Phelps, E. A. (2020). "Stress and cognitive function: A meta-analysis of effects on working memory and cognitive control." *Psychological Bulletin, 146*(6), 549–591.

Gollwitzer, P. M. (1999). "Implementation intentions: Strong effects of simple plans." *American Psychologist, 54*(7), 493–503.

Gollwitzer, P. M., & Sheeran, P. (2006). "Implementation intentions and goal achievement: A meta-analysis of effects and processes." *Advances in Experimental Social Psychology, 38,* 69–119.

Gratton, C., Sun, H., & Petersen, S. E. (2018). "Control networks and hubs." *Psychophysiology, 55*(3), e13032.

Gray, P. (2011). "The decline of play and the rise of psychopathology in children and adolescents." *American Journal of Play, 3*(4), 443–463.

Gross, J. J. (2015). "Emotion regulation: Current status and future prospects." *Psychological Inquiry, 26*(1), 1–26.

Gross, J. J., & John, O. P. (2003). "Individual differences in two emotion-regulation processes: Implications for affect, relationships, and well-being." *Journal of Personality and Social Psychology, 85*(2), 348–362.

Grossman, D. (2008). *"On Combat: The Psychology and Physiology of Deadly Conflict in War and in Peace."* Human Factor Research Group.

Haller, S. P., Kadosh, K. C., & Lau, J. Y. F. (2023). "The impact of ambiguous threat on brain circuitry and cognitive performance." *Translational Psychiatry, 13*(1), 73.

Hamilton, J. P., Furman, D. J., Chang, C., Thomason, M. E., Dennis, E., & Gotlib, I. H. (2011). "Default-mode and task-positive network activity in major depressive disorder." *Proceedings of the National Academy of Sciences, 108*(24), 10890–10895.

Hanin, Y. L. (2000). *Emotions in Sport.* Champaign, IL: Human Kinetics.

Hardwick, R. M., Caspers, S., Eickhoff, S. B., & Swinnen, S. P. (2018). "Neural correlates of action: Comparing meta-analyses of imagery, observation, and execution." *Neuroscience & Biobehavioral Reviews, 94,* 31–44.

Harvard Business Review. (2017). Why We Hold Women to Different Standards Than Men. *Harvard Business Review.*

References

Harvard Business Review. (2022). Why Leaders Micromanage Under Pressure. *Harvard Business Review.*

Harwood, C. G., Cumming, J., & Fletcher, D. (2004). "Social comparison processes in elite adolescent performers: The role of self-evaluation and motivation." *Psychology of Sport and Exercise, 5*(1), 43–58.

Hattie, J., & Timperley, H. (2007). "The power of feedback." *Review of Educational Research, 77*(1), 81–112.

Hayes, C. L. (2025). *The Sirens' Call: How Attention Became the World's Most Endangered Resource.* Penguin Press.

Heishman, S. J., Kleykamp, B. A., & Singleton, E. G. (2010). "Meta-analysis of the acute effects of nicotine and smoking on human performance." *Psychopharmacology, 210*(4), 453–469.

Henriksen, K., Dieffenbach, K., & Hvid, H. S. (2020). "Professional philosophy: Inside the mind of successful sport psychology consultants." *International Journal of Sport and Exercise Psychology, 18*(5), 565–581.

Hermans, E. J., Henckens, M. J. A. G., Joëls, M., & Fernández, G. (2014). "Dynamic adaptation of large-scale brain networks in response to acute stressors." *Trends in Neurosciences, 37*(6), 304–314.

Herxheimer, A., & Petrie, K. J. (2002). "Melatonin for the prevention and treatment of jet lag." *Cochrane Database of Systematic Reviews, 2*, CD001520.

Hétu, S., Grégoire, M., Saimpont, A., Coll, M.-P., Eugène, F., Michon, P.-E., & Jackson, P. L. (2013). "The neural network of motor imagery: An ALE meta-analysis." *Neuroscience & Biobehavioral Reviews, 37*(5), 930–949.

Hillman, C. H., Erickson, K. I., & Kramer, A. F. (2008). "Be smart, exercise your heart: Exercise effects on brain and cognition." *Nature Reviews Neuroscience, 9*(1), 58–65.

Holroyd, C. B., & Yeung, N. (2012). "Motivation of extended behaviors by anterior cingulate cortex." *Trends in Cognitive Sciences, 16*(2), 122–128.

Hölzel, B. K., Lazar, S. W., Gard, T., Schuman-Olivier, Z., Vago, D. R., & Ott, U. (2011). "How does mindfulness meditation work? Proposing mechanisms of action from a conceptual and neural perspective." *Perspectives on Psychological Science, 6*(6), 537–559.

Houtman, F., Castellar, E. N., & Notebaert, W. (2012). "Orienting to errors with and without immediate feedback." *Journal of Cognitive Psychology, 24*(3), 278–285.

Inzlicht, M., & Schmeichel, B. J. (2012). "What is ego depletion? Toward a mechanistic revision of the resource model of self-control." *Perspectives on Psychological Science, 7*(5), 450–463.

Ivarsson, A., Johnson, U., Andersen, M. B., Tranaeus, U., Stenling, A., & Lindwall, M. (2017). "Psychological predictors of injury occurrence: A prospective investigation of professional Swedish soccer players." *Journal of Sport and Exercise Psychology, 39*(1), 21–28.

Jamieson, J. P., Mendes, W. B., Blackstock, E., & Schmader, T. (2010). "Turning the knots in your stomach into bows: Reappraising arousal improves performance on the GRE." *Journal of Experimental Social Psychology, 46*(1), 208–212.

Janszky, I., & Lundberg, I. (2006). "Cold climate, mortality, and cardiovascular risk factors: The role of norepinephrine." *European Journal of Cardiovascular Prevention & Rehabilitation, 13*(1), 49–52.

Janský, L., & Pospíšilová, D. (2000). "Physiological responses to cold stress." *Journal of Thermal Biology, 25*(1–2), 23–30.

Jha, A. P., Krompinger, J., & Baime, M. J. (2007). "Mindfulness training modifies subsystems of attention." *Cognitive, Affective, & Behavioral Neuroscience, 7*(2), 109–119.

Jha, A. P., Stanley, E. A., Kiyonaga, A., Wong, L., & Gelfand, L. (2010). "Examining the protective effects of mindfulness training on working memory capacity and affective experience." *Emotion, 10*(1), 54–64.

Kabat-Zinn, J. (1990). *Full Catastrophe Living: Using the Wisdom of Your Body and Mind to Face Stress, Pain, and Illness.* New York: Delacorte.

Kamata, A., Tenenbaum, G., & Hanin, Y. L. (2002). "Individual Zone of Optimal Functioning (IZOF): A probabilistic estimation." *Journal of Sport & Exercise Psychology, 24*(2), 189–208.

Kaplan, S. (1995). "The restorative benefits of nature: Toward an integrative framework." *Journal of Environmental Psychology, 16*(3), 169–182.

Kastner, S., & Ungerleider, L. G. (2000). "Mechanisms of visual attention in the human cortex." *Annual Review of Neuroscience, 23*, 315–341.

289

References

Khalsa, S. B. S., Jewett, M. E., Cajochen, C., & Czeisler, C. A. (2003). "A phase response curve to single bright light pulses in human subjects." *Journal of Physiology, 549*(3), 945–952.

Kim, J., & de Dear, R. (2013). "Workspace satisfaction: The privacy–communication trade-off in open-plan offices." *Journal of Environmental Psychology, 36*, 18–26.

Klingberg, T. (2010). "Training and plasticity of working memory." *Trends in Cognitive Sciences, 14*(7), 317–324.

Kluger, A. N., & DeNisi, A. (1996). "The effects of feedback interventions on performance: A historical review, a meta-analysis, and a preliminary feedback intervention theory." *Psychological Bulletin, 119*(2), 254–284.

Kok, B. E., Coffey, K. A., Cohn, M. A., Catalino, L. I., Vacharkulksemsuk, T., Algoe, S. B., Brantley, M., & Fredrickson, B. L. (2013). "How positive emotions build physical health." *Psychological Science, 24*(7), 1123–1132.

Kolb, D. A. (1984). *Experiential Learning: Experience as the Source of Learning and Development.* Englewood Cliffs, NJ: Prentice Hall.

Kox, M., Van Eijk, L. T., Zwaag, J., Van Den Wildenberg, J., Sweep, F. C., Van Der Hoeven, J. G., & Pickkers, P. (2014). "Voluntary activation of the sympathetic nervous system and attenuation of the innate immune response in humans." *Proceedings of the National Academy of Sciences, 111*(20), 7379–7384.

Krediet, C. T., Bisoendial, R. J., Somsen, G. A., & de Groot, M. C. (2020). "Cold exposure and cognitive performance: A review." *Journal of Thermal Biology, 89*, 102544.

Kühnel, J., Sonnentag, S., & Westman, M. (2012). "Does work engagement increase after a short respite? The role of job involvement as a double-edged sword." *Journal of Occupational and Organizational Psychology, 85*(3), 575–594.

Lally, P., van Jaarsveld, C. H. M., Potts, H. W. W., & Wardle, J. (2010). "How are habits formed: Modelling habit formation in the real world." *European Journal of Social Psychology, 40*(6), 998–1009.

Lazarus, R. S., & Folkman, S. (1984). *Stress, Appraisal, and Coping.* Springer.

LeDoux, J. E. (1996). *The Emotional Brain.* Simon & Schuster.

Lee, K. E., Williams, K. J., Sargent, L. D., Williams, N. S., & Johnson, K. A. (2015). "40-second green roof views sustain attention: The role of micro-breaks in attention restoration." *Journal of Environmental Psychology*, *42*, 182–189.

LeGates, T. A., Fernandez, D. C., & Hattar, S. (2014). "Light as a central modulator of circadian rhythms, sleep and affect." *Nature Reviews Neuroscience*, *15*(7), 443–454.

Lehrer, P. M., & Gevirtz, R. (2014). "Heart rate variability biofeedback: How and why does it work?" *Frontiers in Psychology*, *5*, 756.

Lehrer, P. M., Gevirtz, R., & Schwartz, M. S. (2020). "Cardiorespiratory bio-feedback and health: A systems perspective." *Applied Psychophysiology and Biofeedback*, *45*(4), 207–220.

Leminen, M. M., Virkkala, J., Sauseng, P., Paavonen, E. J., & Pesonen, A. K. (2017). "Enhanced memory consolidation via slow oscillatory tDCS during non-REM sleep." *Brain Stimulation*, *10*(4), 641–651.

Leroy, S. (2009). "Why is it so hard to do my work? The challenge of attention residue when switching between work tasks." *Organizational Behavior and Human Decision Processes*, *109*(2), 168–181.

Li, J., Li, J., Liang, J., Li, L., Wang, Z., Wang, M., & Yu, J. (2019). "Physical exercise and depression in adolescents: A meta-analysis." *Frontiers in Psychiatry*, *10*, 765.

Lieberman, M. D., Eisenberger, N. I., Crockett, M. J., Tom, S. M., Pfeifer, J. H., & Way, B. M. (2007). "Putting feelings into words: Affect labeling disrupts amygdala activity in response to affective stimuli." *Psychological Science*, *18*(5), 421–428.

Liu, Y., Dolan, R. J., Kurth-Nelson, Z., & Behrens, T. E. J. (2022). "Hierarchical organization of habitual behavior and its neural basis in the human brain." *Nature Communications*, *13*, 354.

Liu-Ambrose, T., Nagamatsu, L. S., Voss, M. W., Khan, K. M., & Handy, T. C. (2010). "Resistance training and executive functions." *Archives of Internal Medicine*, *170*(2), 170–178.

Locke, E. A., & Latham, G. P. (2002). "Building a practically useful theory of goal setting and task motivation: A 35-year odyssey." *American Psychologist*, *57*(9), 705–717.

291

Locke, E. A., & Latham, G. P. (2019). "The development of goal setting theory: A half century retrospective." *Motivation Science, 5*(2), 93–105.

Lundqvist, C., & Andersen, M. B. (2021). "Psychological services in high-performance sport: Misalignments between policy and practice." *International Journal of Sport and Exercise Psychology, 19*(6), 857–875.

Lyubomirsky, S., King, L., & Diener, E. (2005). "The benefits of frequent positive affect: Does happiness lead to success?" *Psychological Bulletin, 131*(6), 803–855.

Macnamara, B. N., Hambrick, D. Z., & Oswald, F. L. (2014). "Deliberate practice and performance in music, games, sports, education, and professions: A meta-analysis." *Psychological Science, 25*(8), 1608–1618.

Mark, G., Gudith, D., & Klocke, U. (2008). "The cost of interrupted work: More speed and stress." *Proceedings of the SIGCHI Conference on Human Factors in Computing Systems (CHI '08)*, 107–110. New York, NY: ACM.

Mark, G., Gudith, D., & Klocke, U. (2016). "The cost of interrupted work: More speed and more stress." *Journal of Experimental Psychology: Applied, 22*(4), 559–570.

Martela, F., & Steger, M. F. (2016). "The three meanings of meaning in life: Distinguishing coherence, purpose, and significance." *The Journal of Positive Psychology, 11*(5), 531–545.

Maslach, C., & Leiter, M. P. (2016). "Understanding the burnout experience: Recent research and its implications for psychiatry." *World Psychiatry, 15*(2), 103–111.

Maslow, A. H. (1969). "The farther reaches of human nature." *Journal of Transpersonal Psychology, 1*(1), 1–9.

Masters, R. S. W. (1992). "Knowledge, knerves and know-how: The role of explicit versus implicit knowledge in the breakdown of a complex motor skill under pressure." *British Journal of Psychology, 83*(3), 343–358.

McCrary, J. M., & Gould, M. (2023). "Rhythm in sport: Adapted rhythmic training to optimize timing and movement efficiency." *Journal of Science and Medicine in Sport, 26*(11), 636–638.

McEwen, B. S. (1998). "Stress, adaptation, and disease: Allostasis and allostatic load." *Annals of the New York Academy of Sciences, 840*(1), 33–44.

McEwen, B. S., & Stellar, E. (1993). "Stress and the individual: Mechanisms leading to disease." *Archives of Internal Medicine, 153*(18), 2093–2101.

Mellalieu, S. D., Hanton, S., & Fletcher, D. (2006). "A competitive anxiety review: Recent directions in sport psychology research." *Journal of Sports Sciences, 24*(4), 477–507.

Mesagno, C., & Beckmann, J. (2017). "Choking under pressure: Theoretical models and interventions." *Current Opinion in Psychology, 16,* 170–175.

Miller, E. K., & Cohen, J. D. (2001). "An integrative theory of prefrontal cortex function." *Annual Review of Neuroscience, 24,* 167–202.

Moawad, T., & Staples, A. (2020). *It Takes What It Takes: How to Think Neutrally and Gain Control of Your Life.* HarperOne.

Montag, C., Lachmann, B., Herrlich, M., & Zweig, K. (2019). "Addictive features of social media/messenger platforms and freemium games against the background of psychological and economic theories." *International Journal of Environmental Research and Public Health, 16*(14), 2612.

Moore, L. J., Vine, S. J., Wilson, M. R., & Freeman, P. (2015). "Reappraising threat: How to optimize performance under pressure." *Journal of Sport and Exercise Psychology, 37*(3), 339–343.

Moore, Z. E., Bonner, B. L., & Etzel, E. F. (2019). "The ethical practice of sport psychology: Practical guidelines for professional conduct." *Journal of Clinical Sport Psychology, 13*(4), 576–593.

Moran, A. (2009). *Cognitive Psychology in Sport: Progress and Prospects.* Psychology Press.

Mrazek, M. D., Franklin, M. S., Phillips, D. T., Baird, B., & Schooler, J. W. (2013). "Mindfulness training improves working memory capacity and GRE performance while reducing mind wandering." *Psychological Science, 24*(5), 776–781.

Mueller, C. M., & Dweck, C. S. (1998). "Praise for intelligence can undermine children's motivation and performance." *Journal of Personality and Social Psychology, 75*(1), 33–52.

Murdock, B. B. (1962). "The serial position effect of free recall." *Journal of Experimental Psychology, 64*(5), 482–488.

Nesi, J., Prinstein, M. J., & Telzer, E. H. (2017). "Adolescent development in the digital media context." *Psychological Inquiry, 28*(3), 123–146.

Neureiter, M., & Traut-Mattausch, E. (2016). "Inspecting the dangers of feeling like a fake: An empirical investigation of the impostor phenomenon in the world of work." *Frontiers in Psychology, 7*, 1445.

Nickerson, R. S. (1998). "Confirmation bias: A ubiquitous phenomenon in many guises." *Psychological Bulletin, 124*(2), 175–196.

Nolen-Hoeksema, S., Wisco, B. E., & Lyubomirsky, S. (2008). "Rethinking rumination." *Perspectives on Psychological Science, 3*(5), 400–424.

Oettingen, G., & Gollwitzer, P. M. (2010). Strategies of setting and implementing goals: Mental contrasting and implementation intentions. In J. E. Maddux & J. P. Tangney (Eds.), *Social Psychological Foundations of Clinical Psychology* (pp. 114–135). New York, NY: Guilford Press.

Ohly, H., White, M. P., Wheeler, B. W., Bethel, A., Ukoumunne, O. C., Nikolaou, V., & Garside, R. (2016). "Attention restoration theory: A systematic review of the restorative benefits of exposure to natural environments." *Journal of Toxicology and Environmental Health, Part B, 19*(7), 305–343.

Ophir, E., Nass, C., & Wagner, A. D. (2009). "Cognitive control in media multitaskers." *Proceedings of the National Academy of Sciences, 106*(37), 15583–15587.

Panisoara, I. O., & Serban, M. (2013). "Relationship between time management, work stress and job satisfaction among university teachers." *Procedia - Social and Behavioral Sciences, 92*, 294–297.

Perry, J. L., Williams, J. M., & MacNamara, Á. (2021). "Reappraising stress: The role of mindset, self-efficacy, and locus of control." *Frontiers in Psychology, 12*, 684780.

Petersen, S. E., & Posner, M. I. (2012). "The attention system of the human brain: 20 years after." *Annual Review of Neuroscience, 35*, 73–89.

Piaget, J. (1952). *The Origins of Intelligence in Children* (M. Cook, Trans.). International Universities Press. (Original work published 1936)

Piedimonte, A., Lanzo, G., Campaci, F., Volpino, V., & Carlino, E. (2025). "Spreading new light on Attention Restoration Theory: An environmental Posner paradigm." *Brain Sciences, 15*(6), 578.

Posner, M. I. (1980). "Orienting of attention." *Quarterly Journal of Experimental Psychology, 32*(1), 3–25.

Posner, M. I., & Petersen, S. E. (1990). "The attention system of the human brain." *Annual Review of Neuroscience, 13,* 25–42.

Posner, M. I., & Rothbart, M. K. (2007). "Research on attention networks as a model for the integration of psychological science." *Annual Review of Psychology, 58,* 1–23.

Purcell, S. (2018, August 30). What the Aztecs can teach us about happiness and the good life. *Aeon.* https://aeon.co/essays/what-the-aztecs-can-teach-us-about-happiness-and-the-good-life

Rabbitt, P. M. (1966). "Errors and error correction in choice-response tasks." *Journal of Experimental Psychology, 71*(2), 264–272.

Rankin, L. A., Lane, D. J., Gibbons, F. X., & Gerrard, M. (2004). "Adolescent self-consciousness: Longitudinal age changes and gender differences in two cohorts." *Journal of Research on Adolescence, 14*(1), 1–21.

Ratey, J. J. (2008). *Spark: The Revolutionary New Science of Exercise and the Brain.* Little, Brown and Company.

Robbins, T. W., & Arnsten, A. F. (2009). "The neuropsychopharmacology of fronto-executive function: Monoaminergic modulation." *Annual Review of Neuroscience, 32,* 267–287.

Roediger, H. L., & Karpicke, J. D. (2006). "Test-enhanced learning: Taking memory tests improves long-term retention." *Psychological Science, 17*(3), 249–255.

Rosen, C., Lim, A. F., Carrier, L. M., & Cheever, N. A. (2020). "An empirical examination of the educational impact of text message-induced task switching in the classroom: Educational implications and strategies to enhance learning." *Educational Psychology, 40*(2), 147–164.

Rosen, L. D., Carrier, L. M., & Cheever, N. A. (2013). "Facebook and texting made me do it: Media-induced task-switching." *Computers in Human Behavior, 29*(3), 948–958.

Rotter, J. B. (1966). "Generalized expectancies for internal versus external control of reinforcement." *Psychological Monographs, 80*(1), 1–28.

Roy, M., Shohamy, D., & Wager, T. D. (2012). "Ventromedial prefrontal–subcortical systems and the generation of affective meaning." *Trends in Cognitive Sciences, 16*(3), 147–156.

Rubinstein, J. S., Meyer, D. E., & Evans, J. E. (2001). "Executive control of cognitive processes in task switching." *Journal of Experimental Psychology: Human Perception and Performance, 27*(4), 763–797.

Ryan, R. M., & Deci, E. L. (2005). "Self-determination theory and the facilitation of intrinsic motivation, social development, and well-being." *American Psychologist, 55*(1), 68–78.

Ryan, R. M., & Deci, E. L. (2000). "Self-determination theory and the facilitation of intrinsic motivation, social development, and well-being." *American Psychologist, 55*(1), 68–78.

Schacter, D. L., & Addis, D. R. (2007). "The cognitive neuroscience of constructive memory: Remembering the past and imagining the future." *Philosophical Transactions of the Royal Society, B: Biological Sciences, 362*(1481), 773–786.

Schaufeli, W. B. (2017). "Applying the job demands–resources model." *Organizational Dynamics, 46*(2), 120–132.

Shirom, A. (2003). "Job-related burnout: A review." In J. C. Quick & L. E. Tetrick (Eds.), *Handbook of Occupational Health Psychology* (pp. 245–264). Washington, DC: APA.

Silva, J. M., Gould, D., & Weinberg, R. (2020). "Ethical competence in applied sport psychology: Integrating clinical and performance boundaries." *Sport Exercise and Performance Psychology, 9*(3), 284–298.

Singer, R. N. (2002). "Preperformance state, routines, and automaticity: What does it take to realize expertise in self-paced events?" *Journal of Sport and Exercise Psychology, 24*(4), 359–375.

Song, R., Motevalli, S., & Zhou, Y. (2024). "Melodic movements: The role of music in shaping sport performance and psychological responses." *International Sports Studies, 46*(2), Article 24.

Sonnentag, S. (2018). "The recovery paradox: Portraying the complex interplay between job stressors, lack of recovery, and poor well-being." *Research in Organizational Behavior, 38*, 169–185.

Sonnentag, S., & Fritz, C. (2007). "The recovery experience questionnaire: Development and validation of a measure for assessing recuperation and unwinding from work." *Journal of Occupational Health Psychology, 12*(3), 204–221.

Steele, C. M. (1988). "The psychology of self-affirmation: Sustaining the integrity of the self." *Advances in Experimental Social Psychology, 21,* 261–302.

Steinberg, L. (2010). "A dual systems model of adolescent risk-taking." *Developmental Psychobiology, 52*(3), 216–224.

Sudimac, S., Sale, V., & Kühn, S. (2022). "How nature nurtures: Amygdala activity decreases as the result of a one-hour walk in nature." *Molecular Psychiatry, 27*(2), 646–652.

Tang, Y. Y., Hölzel, B. K., & Posner, M. I. (2015). "The neuroscience of mindfulness meditation." *Nature Reviews Neuroscience, 16*(4), 213–225.

Tang, Y. Y., Yang, L., Leve, L. D., & Posner, M. I. (2012). "Mechanisms of mindfulness meditation." *Nature Reviews Neuroscience, 13*(3), 213–222.

Ten Brummelhuis, L. L., Haar, J. M., & Roche, M. (2021). "Does recovery help people live a better life? A diary study on daily recovery experiences, well-being, and performance." *Journal of Applied Psychology, 106*(6), 894–910.

Thoma, M. V., Ryf, S., Mohiyeddini, C., Ehlert, U., & Nater, U. M. (2013). "Emotion regulation through listening to music in everyday situations." *Cognition & Emotion, 27*(3), 534–543.

Turel, O., He, Q., Xue, G., Xiao, L., & Bechara, A. (2014). "Examination of neural systems sub-serving Facebook 'addiction'." *Psychological Reports, 115*(3), 675–695.

Twenge, J. M., Joiner, T. E., Rogers, M. L., & Martin, G. N. (2018). "Increases in depressive symptoms, suicide-related outcomes, and suicide rates among U.S. adolescents after 2010 and links to increased new media screen time." *Journal of Abnormal Psychology, 127*(4), 262–269.

U.S. Surgeon General. (2021). *Protecting Youth Mental Health: The U.S. Surgeon General's Advisory.* U.S. Department of Health and Human Services.

Ulrich, R. S. (1984). "View through a window may influence recovery from surgery." *Science, 224*(4647), 420–421.

Uncapher, M. R., Thieu, M. K., & Wagner, A. D. (2016). "Media multitasking and memory: Differences in working memory and long-term memory." *Psychonomic Bulletin & Review, 23*(2), 483–490.

297

United States Air Force Reserve Command. (2024, September 26). AFRC increases realism by adding stress inoculation to training scenarios. Retrieved from https://www.afrc.af.mil/News/Features/Display/Article/3764178/afrc-increases-realism-by-adding-stress-inoculation-to-training-scenarios/

Valkenburg, P. M., Meier, A., & Beyens, I. (2022). "Social media use and its impact on adolescent mental health: An umbrella review." *Current Opinion in Psychology, 46*, 101–108.

Van der Linden, D., Frese, M., & Meijman, T. F. (2003). "Mental fatigue and the control of cognitive processes: Effects on perseveration and planning." *Acta Psychologica, 113*(1), 45–65.

Vealey, R. S., & Greenleaf, C. (2010). Seeing is believing: Understanding and using imagery in sport. In J. M. Williams (Ed.), *Applied Sport Psychology: Personal Growth to Peak Performance* (6th ed., pp. 267–304). McGraw-Hill.

Vickers, J. N. (2007). *Perception, Cognition, and Decision Training: The Quiet Eye in Action.* Champaign, IL: Human Kinetics.

Wade, A. G., Ford, I., Crawford, G., McMahon, A. D., Nir, T., Laudon, M., & Zisapel, N. (2007). "Efficacy of prolonged-release melatonin in insomnia patients aged 55–80 years: Quality of sleep and next-day alertness outcomes." *Current Medical Research and Opinion, 23*(10), 2597–2605.

Wandell, B. A., Dumoulin, S. O., & Brewer, A. A. (2007). "Visual field maps in human cortex." *Neuron, 56*(2), 366–383.

Ward, A. F., Duke, K., Gneezy, A., & Bos, M. W. (2017). "Brain drain: The mere presence of one's own smartphone reduces available cognitive capacity." *Journal of the Association for Consumer Research, 2*(2), 140–154.

Wegner, D. M. (1994). "Ironic processes of mental control." *Psychological Review, 101*(1), 34–52.

Wegner, D. M., Schneider, D. J., Carter, S. R., & White, T. L. (1987). "Paradoxical effects of thought suppression." *Journal of Personality and Social Psychology, 53*(1), 5–13.

Weinberg, R. S., & Gould, D. (2019). *Foundations of Sport and Exercise Psychology* (7th ed.). Human Kinetics.

Weisinger, H., & Pawliw-Fry, J. (2015). *Performing Under Pressure: The Science of Doing Your Best When It Matters Most.* Crown Business.

Wilhelm, I., Born, J., Kudielka, B. M., Schlotz, W., & Wüst, S. (2007). "Is the cortisol awakening rise a response to awakening?" *Psychoneuroendocrinology, 32*(4), 358–366.

Williams, J. (2018). *Stand Out of Our Light: Freedom and Resistance in the Attention Economy.* Cambridge University Press.

Williamson, A. M., & Feyer, A. M. (2000). "Moderate sleep deprivation produces impairments in cognitive and motor performance equivalent to legally prescribed levels of alcohol intoxication." *Occupational and Environmental Medicine, 57*(10), 649–655.

Wilmer, H. H., Sherman, L. E., & Chein, J. M. (2017). "Smartphones and cognition: A review of research exploring the links between mobile technology habits and cognitive functioning." *Frontiers in Psychology, 8,* 605.

Wood, W., & Neal, D. T. (2007). "A new look at habits and the habit–goal interface." *Psychological Review, 114*(4), 843–863.

Wu, T. (2016). *The Attention Merchants: The Epic Scramble to Get Inside Our Heads.* Alfred A. Knopf.

Wulf, G. (2013). "Attentional focus and motor learning: A review of 15 years." *International Review of Sport and Exercise Psychology, 6*(1), 77–104.

Wulf, G., & Lewthwaite, R. (2016). "Optimizing performance through intrinsic motivation and attention for learning: The OPTIMAL theory of motor learning." *Psychonomic Bulletin & Review, 23*(5), 1382–1414.

Xie, L., Kang, H., Xu, Q., Chen, M. J., Liao, Y., Thiyagarajan, M., O'Donnell, J., Christensen, D. J., Nicholson, C., Iliff, J. J., & Nedergaard, M. (2013). "Sleep drives metabolite clearance from the adult brain." *Science, 342*(6156), 373–377.

Yeager, D. S., & Dweck, C. S. (2012). "Mindsets that promote resilience: When students believe that personal characteristics can be developed." *Educational Psychologist, 47*(4), 302–314.

Yeager, D. S., Purdie-Vaughns, V., Garcia, J., Apfel, N., Brzustoski, P., Master, A., Hessert, W. T., Williams, M. E., & Cohen, G. L. (2014). "Breaking the cycle of mistrust: Wise interventions to provide critical feedback across the racial divide." *Journal of Experimental Psychology: General, 143*(2), 804–824.

Yiend, J. (2010). "The effects of emotion on attention: A review of attentional processing of emotional information." *Cognition and Emotion, 24*(1), 3–47.

Yogman, M., Garner, A., Hutchinson, J., Hirsh-Pasek, K., & Golinkoff, R. M. (2018). "The power of play: A pediatric role in enhancing development in young children." *Pediatrics, 142*(3), e20182058.

Zapata, J., Lewis, Z., & Kwon, M. (2022). "Let the rhythm move you: A scoping review of music and athletic performance." *International Journal of Exercise Science Abstracts, 14*(2), 96.

Zeki, S. (1993). *A Vision of the Brain.* Oxford, UK: Blackwell Scientific.

Zhang, W., Chen, L., & Liu, Y. (2025). "A systematic review of the impacts of nature exposure on the nervous system." *Journal of Environmental Psychology, 91*, 102319.

Zhang, Y., Liu, M., Wang, Z., Chen, H., Lin, Y., & Li, X. (2024). "The effect of music tempo on movement flow: EEG and behavioral evidence." *Frontiers in Psychology, 15*, 1292516.

About the Author

Dr. Justin Anderson is a high-performance psychologist trusted by elite athletes, teams, and organizations competing in the most pressure-filled arenas in the world. For more than two decades, his work has been driven by a single, consequential question: *Why do capable, well-prepared people often fall short of their potential in the very moments that matter most—and what can be deliberately trained to prevent it?*

He is the Founder and CEO of Premier Sport Psychology and Premier Performance Advising, two of the nation's leading consulting firms in applied performance psychology. Premier partners with Olympic, professional, and collegiate teams, as well as executives and leadership groups across industries. His work has supported Hall of Famers, All-Pros, gold medalists, world and national champions, and organizations across the NFL, NBA, WNBA, MLB, NHL, MLS, and NWSL.

Grounded in neuroscience, sport and organizational psychology, and thousands of hours embedded inside real performance environments—locker rooms, sidelines, boardrooms, and leadership teams—Justin's approach bridges scientific rigor with practical execution. Through years of applied work, he recognized a consistent truth: under pressure, talent is rarely the separator—attention is.

That insight became the foundation of *Intentional Attention*.

A licensed psychologist, Certified Mental Performance Consultant, former collegiate quarterback, and long-time business owner, Justin

301

brings a distinctive blend of clinical expertise, scientific depth, and lived experience leading high-performing teams of his own. In a distracted and high-stakes world, attention is the most valuable and trainable asset we possess—and those who learn to direct it intentionally gain a decisive edge when it counts.

Index

AAA (Awareness, Acceptance, and Action) Model, 158–160, 162–163
Abrams, E., 168
acceptance, 158–159, 275
acting self vs observing self, 105
action, 159
    routines in, 211–212
activation level regulation, 209
acute pressure, 229
adaptive capacity, 234, 237
adolescence, cognitive transition during, 39–40
adrenaline, 28, 95, 155
adversity anticipation, 130, 214–215
adversity plan (SERR), 144
aerobic activity, 188
agency loss, 51–52
agency, reclaiming, 267–268
alcohol and depressants, 195
algorithmic feeds, 192, 273
allostatic load, 234
amygdala, 27, 94–95, 146, 181
    emotional reactivity in adolescence, 39
    movement and regulation of, 181–182
    and threat response cycle, 28–29
anterior cingulate cortex (ACC), 30, 147
anticipating adversity (SERR model), 214–215
antihistamines, 197
Anxiety Cycle, 28
anxiety, heightened, 209

anxiety/overactivation, 217
    body scan, mindful, 217
    grounding breathwork, 217
Aristotle, 103, 205
Army Rangers, 119
Arnsten, A. F. T., 30
assessing attention and Focus Bullseye, 231–233
athletes, 12, 18, 39, 40, 47, 86, 100, 105, 106, 116, 127, 129, 152, 207, 219. *See also* elite performers
    in flow, 160
    in paradoxical space, 43
    physical skill development, 271
    professional, xii, 100, 152, 234
    reaching physical peak, 41
athletics, 134, 206, 275
attentional architecture, xvii, xix, 19, 225
attentional bias, 83–84, 131
attentional control, 7–8, 38, 44, 120, 141, 151, 168, 179, 180, 188, 222, 224, 233
attentional development, 42
attentional energy, 185–188, 190–191
Attentional Execution, 145, 149, 152
    flow state (focus bullseye), 160–161
    Focus Window (cars on freeway), 147–149
    perspective-taking and reappraisal, 154–156
    testing attention, 156–159
    training, attention, 149–154

307

Index

309

Index

311

Index